Marjorie Ray.

Burke.

Born, Dublin 1729 - 1854. (Span 125 yrs?)

Parents - Father protestant attorney mother catholic.

Education. Went to Quaker school. Later went to Oxford - took degree at Dublin. Never achieved any academic distinction. Graduated from Trinity. Member of Parliament delivered speech on American Taxation 1774. Was a Paymaster.

Contemporaries - Shakleton, Goldsmith, Henry Flood Walburton, Reynolds - Garrick, Johnson. Pitt, Clyde Hastings - Fox

Rank. As a great statesman - one of foremost orators of world.

Later Life. Devoted leisure to political subjects - Was private to Hamilton.

Appearance small & slight, reddish hair gray eyes, black when excited. One forgot small stature when he spoke, majesty & impressiveness marvellous voice. full, deep, mellow, now soft & tender & then loud & thrilling in denunciation of plea.

Character. Always an enigma to his friends occupied positions of trust. Several times the one having mind & influence in a crisis. Recognized as America's best friend in Indep. Died poor. rather in dimmed & never occupied a gov. position. In Am. Boston paid tardy tribute by naming English college for him. Burke's Hall. Harvard.

Orations and Arguments

BY

English and American Statesmen

EDITED, WITH

NOTES, EXPLANATORY AND CRITICAL,

BY

CORNELIUS BEACH BRADLEY

Professor of Rhetoric in the University
of California

ALLYN AND BACON

Boston and Chicago

DDN

Typography by C. J. Peters & Son, Boston.

Presswork by Berwick & Smith.

PREFACE.

The purpose of this book is to furnish a collection of oratorical and argumentative masterpieces, suitable for students in the schools and for general readers. In making the selection the following considerations have had determining weight: 1. That every speech included should be in itself memorable — a great utterance upon a great subject, attaining its distinction through the essential qualities of nobility and force of ideas, rather than through accidents of occasion, of feeling, or of rhetorical display; 2. That each should be in topic so related to the great thoughts, memories, or problems of our own time, as to have for us still an inherent and vital interest; 3. That the collection as a whole should include material enough to permit of a varied selection for the use of successive classes in the schools.

The speeches thus chosen have been printed from the best available texts, without change, save that the spelling has been made uniform throughout, and that three of the speeches — those of Webster, Calhoun, and Seward — have been shortened somewhat by the omission of matters of merely temporary or local interest. Yet even the omitted portions have been summarized for the reader, whenever they have seemed to bear upon the main argument.

In the preparation of the notes, it has been the aim to furnish the reader with whatever help seems necessary to the proper understanding and appreciation of the speeches; to avoid bewildering him with mere subtleties and display of erudition; and to encourage in him the habit of self-help and the familiarity with sources of information, which mark the scholar. A special feature of this part of the work is a sketch of the English Constitution and Government, intended as a general introduction to the English speeches.

It has not been thought best to propound any set scheme for instruction. To enter into the high thought of such speeches as these, to appreciate the masterly forging of argument, to realize the far-reaching force and application of ideas, to feel the uplift of noble emotions — these are the ends to be reached; and competent teachers will reach them best by their own methods.

I desire to acknowledge in general my indebtedness to earlier works in this field, particularly to Professor Goodrich's *British Eloquence*, and to E. J. Payne's *Burke: Select Works*. But wherever I have availed myself of more than mere suggestion or clew, I have endeavored to make due acknowledgment in the Notes.

First in the list of those to whom I am personally indebted for assistance rendered, I would name Mr. George A. Bacon and Mr. John Allyn, my publishers. From them came the original suggestion of the work; and to their wise counsel and untiring interest it owes far more than its excellence of outward form. To Prof. Charles Mills Gayley, my colleague in the English Department, I am indebted for valuable suggestion in selecting the speeches, and for criticism of portions of my manuscript Notes. In this last acknowledgment must be included also Prof. Carl C. Plehn and Prof. William Carey Jones, who have generously given me the benefit of their criticism on a number of historical and political points encountered in my study. Nor must I forget the kind service rendered me by my nephew, Mr. Evander B. McGilvary, in reading throughout the proof of the Notes.

C. B. BRADLEY.

UNIVERSITY OF CALIFORNIA,
November 30, 1894.

CONTENTS.

EDMUND BURKE.

ON MOVING HIS
RESOLUTIONS FOR CONCILIATION WITH THE COLONIES.
HOUSE OF COMMONS, MARCH 22, 1775.

I HOPE, Sir, that notwithstanding the austerity of the Chair, your good nature will incline you to some degree of indulgence towards human frailty. You will not think it unnatural that those who have an object depending, which strongly engages their hopes and fears, should be somewhat inclined to superstition. As I came into the House full of anxiety about the event of my motion, I found, to my infinite surprise, that the grand penal bill, by which we had passed sentence on the trade and sustenance of America, is to be returned to us from the other House. I do confess I could not help looking on this event as a fortunate omen. I look upon it as a sort of providential favor, by which we are put once more in possession of our deliberative capacity upon a business so very questionable in its nature, so very uncertain in its issue. By the return of this bill, which seemed to have taken its flight forever, we are at this very instant nearly as free to choose a plan for our American Government as we were on the first day of the session. If, Sir, we incline to the side of conciliation, we are not at all embarrassed (unless we please to make ourselves so) by any incongruous mixture of coercion and restraint.

We are therefore called upon, as it were by a superior warning voice, again to attend to America; to attend to the whole of it together; and to review the subject with an unusual degree of care and calmness.

Surely it is an awful subject, or there is none so on this side of the grave. When I first had the honor of a seat in this House, the affairs of that continent pressed themselves upon us as the most important and most delicate object of Parliamentary attention. My little share in this great deliberation oppressed me. I found myself a partaker in a very high trust; and, having no sort of reason to rely on the strength of my natural abilities for the proper execution of that trust, I was obliged to take more than common pains to instruct myself in everything which relates to our Colonies. I was not less under the necessity of forming some fixed ideas concerning the general policy of the British Empire. Something of this sort seemed to be indispensable, in order, amidst so vast a fluctuation of passions and opinions, to concentre my thoughts, to ballast my conduct, to preserve me from being blown about by every wind of fashionable doctrine. I really did not think it safe or manly to have fresh principles to seek upon every fresh mail which should arrive from America.

At that period I had the fortune to find myself in perfect concurrence with a large majority in this House. Bowing under that high authority, and penetrated with the sharpness and strength of that early impression, I have continued ever since, without the least deviation, in my original sentiments. Whether this be owing to an obstinate perseverance in error, or to a religious adherence to what appears to me truth and reason, it is in your equity to judge.

Sir, Parliament having an enlarged view of objects, made, during this interval, more frequent changes in their sentiments and their conduct than could be justified in a particular person upon the contracted scale of private information. But though I do not hazard anything approaching to a censure on the motives of former Parliaments to all those alterations, one fact is undoubted — that under them the state of America has been kept in continual agitation. Everything administered as remedy to the public complaint, if it did not produce, was at least followed by, an heightening of the distemper; until, by a variety of experiments, that important country has been brought into her present situation — a situation which I will not miscall, which I dare not name, which I scarcely know how to comprehend in the terms of any description.

In this posture, Sir, things stood at the beginning of the session. About that time, a worthy member of great Parliamentary experience, who, in the year 1766, filled the chair of the American committee with much ability, took me aside; and, lamenting the present aspect of our politics, told me things were come to such a pass that our former methods of proceeding in the House would be no longer tolerated: that the public tribunal (never too indulgent to a long and unsuccessful opposition) would now scrutinize our conduct with unusual severity: that the very vicissitudes and shiftings of Ministerial measures, instead of convicting their authors of inconstancy and want of system, would be taken as an occasion of charging us with a predetermined discontent, which nothing could satisfy; whilst we accused every measure of vigor as cruel, and every proposal of lenity as weak and irresolute. The public, he said, would not have patience to see us play the game out with our adversaries; we must produce our hand. It would be expected that those who for many years had been active in such affairs should show that they had formed some clear and decided idea of the principles of Colony government; and were capable of drawing out something like a platform of the ground which might be laid for future and permanent tranquillity.

I felt the truth of what my honorable friend represented; but I felt my situation too. His application might have been made with far greater propriety to many other gentlemen. No man was indeed ever better disposed, or worse qualified, for such an undertaking than myself. Though I gave so far in to his opinion that I immediately threw my thoughts into a sort of Parliamentary form, I was by no means equally ready to produce them. It generally argues some degree of natural impotence of mind, or some want of knowledge of the world, to hazard plans of government except from a seat of authority. Propositions are made, not only ineffectually, but somewhat disreputably, when the minds of men are not properly disposed for their reception; and, for my part, I am not ambitious of ridicule — not absolutely a candidate for disgrace.

Besides, Sir, to speak the plain truth, I have in general no very exalted opinion of the virtue of paper government; nor of any politics in which the plan is to be wholly separated from the execution. But when I saw that anger and violence prevailed every day more and more, and that things were hastening towards an incurable alienation of our Colonies, I confess my caution gave way. I felt this as one of those few moments in which decorum yields to a higher duty. Public calamity is a mighty leveller; and there are occasions when any, even the slightest, chance of doing good must be laid hold on, even by the most inconsiderable person.

To restore order and repose to an empire so great and so distracted as ours, is, merely in the attempt, an undertaking that would ennoble the flights of the highest genius, and obtain pardon for the efforts of the meanest understanding. Struggling a good while with these thoughts, by degrees I felt myself more firm. I derived, at length, some confidence from what in other circumstances usually produces timidity. I grew less anxious, even from the idea of my own insignificance. For, judging of what you are by what you ought to be, I persuaded myself that you would not reject a reasonable proposition because it had nothing but its reason to recommend it. On the other hand, being totally destitute of all shadow of influence, natural or adventitious, I was very sure that, if my proposition were futile or dangerous — if it were weakly conceived, or improperly timed — there was nothing exterior to it of power to awe, dazzle, or delude you. You will see it just as it is; and you will treat it just as it deserves.

The proposition is peace. Not peace through the medium of war; not peace to be hunted through the labyrinth of intricate and endless negotiations; not peace to arise out of universal discord fomented, from principle, in all parts of the Empire; not peace to depend on the juridical determination of perplexing questions, or the precise marking the shadowy boundaries of a complex government. It is simple peace; sought in its natural course, and in its ordinary haunts. It is peace sought in the spirit of peace, and laid in principles purely pacific. I propose, by removing the ground of the difference, and by restoring the former unsuspecting confidence of the Colonies in the Mother Country, to give permanent satisfaction to your people; and (far from a scheme of ruling by discord) to reconcile them to each other in the same act and by the bond of the very same interest which reconciles them to British government.

My idea is nothing more. Refined policy ever has been the parent of confusion; and ever will be so, as long as the world endures. Plain good intention, which is as easily discovered at the first view as fraud is surely detected at last, is, let me say, of no mean force in the government of mankind. Genuine simplicity of heart is an healing and cementing principle. My plan, therefore, being formed upon the most simple grounds imaginable, may disappoint some people when they hear it. It has nothing to recommend it to the pruriency of curious ears. There is nothing at all new and captivating in it. It has nothing of the splendor of the project which has been lately laid upon your table by the noble lord in the blue ribbon. It does not propose to fill your lobby with squabbling Colony agents, who will require the interposition of your mace, at every instant, to keep the peace amongst them. It does not institute a magnificent auction of finance, where captivated provinces come to general ransom by bidding against each other, until you knock down the hammer, and determine a proportion of payments beyond all the powers of algebra to equalize and settle.

The plan which I shall presume to suggest derives, however, one great advantage from the proposition and registry of that noble lord's project. The idea of conciliation is admissible. First, the House, in accepting the resolution moved by the noble lord, has admitted, notwithstanding the menacing front of our address, notwithstanding our heavy bills of pains and penalties — that we do not think ourselves precluded from all ideas of free grace and bounty.

The House has gone farther; it has declared conciliation admissible, previous to any submission on the part of America. It has even shot a good deal beyond that mark, and has admitted that the complaints of our former mode of exerting the right of taxation were not wholly unfounded. That right thus exerted is allowed to have something reprehensible in it, something unwise, or something grievous; since, in the midst of our heat and resentment, we, of ourselves, have proposed a capital alteration; and in order to get rid of what seemed so very exceptionable, have instituted a mode that is altogether new; one that is, indeed, wholly alien from all the ancient methods and forms of Parliament.

The principle of this proceeding is large enough for my purpose. The means proposed by the noble lord for carrying his ideas into execution, I think, indeed, are very indifferently suited to the end; and this I shall endeavor to show you before I sit down. But, for the present, I take my ground on the admitted principle. I mean to give peace. Peace implies reconciliation; and where there has been a material dispute, reconciliation does in a manner always imply concession on the one part or on the other. In this state of things I make no difficulty in affirming that the proposal ought to originate, from us. Great and acknowledged force is not impaired, either in effect or in opinion, by an unwillingness to exert itself. The superior power may offer peace with honor and with safety. Such an offer from such a power will be attributed to magnanimity. But the concessions of the weak are the concessions of fear. When such a one is disarmed, he is wholly at the mercy of his superior; and he loses forever that time and those chances, which, as they happen to all men, are the strength and resources of all inferior power.

The capital leading questions on which you must this day decide are these two: First, whether you ought to concede; and secondly, what your concession ought to be. On the first of these questions we have gained, as I have just taken the liberty of observing to you, some ground. But I am sensible that a good deal more is still to be done. Indeed, Sir, to enable us to determine both on the one and the other of these great questions with a firm and precise judgment, I think it may be necessary to consider distinctly the true nature and the peculiar circumstances of the object which we have before us; because after all our struggle, whether we will or not, we must govern America according to that nature and to those circumstances, and not according to our own imaginations, nor according to abstract ideas of right — by no means according to mere general theories of government, the resort to which appears to me, in our present situation, no better than arrant trifling. I shall therefore endeavor, with your leave, to lay before you some of the most material of these circumstances in as full and as clear a manner as I am able to state them.

The first thing that we have to consider with regard to the nature of the object is — the number of people in the Colonies. I have taken for some years a good deal of pains on that point. I can by no calculation justify myself in placing the number below two millions of inhabitants of our own European blood and color, besides at least five hundred thousand others, who form no inconsiderable part of the strength and opulence of the whole. This, Sir, is, I believe, about the true number. There is no occasion to exaggerate where plain truth is of so much weight and importance. But whether I put the present numbers too high or too low is a matter of little moment. Such is the strength with which population shoots in that part of the world, that, state the numbers as high as we will, whilst the dispute continues, the exaggeration ends. Whilst we are discussing any given magnitude, they are grown to it. Whilst we spend our time in deliberating on the mode of governing two millions, we shall find we have millions more to manage. Your children do not grow faster from infancy to manhood than they spread from families to communities, and from villages to nations.

I put this consideration of the present and the growing numbers in the front of our deliberation, because, Sir, this consideration will make it evident to a blunter discernment than yours, that no partial, narrow, contracted, pinched, occasional system will be at all suitable to such an object. It will show you that it is not to be considered as one of those *minima* which are out of the eye and consideration of the law; not a paltry excrescence of the state; not a mean dependant, who may be neglected with little damage and provoked with little danger. It will prove that some degree of care and caution is required in the handling such an object; it will show that you ought not, in reason, to trifle with so large a mass of the interests and feelings of the human race. You could at no time do so without guilt; and be assured you will not be able to do it long with impunity.

But the population of this country, the great and growing population, though a very important consideration, will lose much of its weight if not combined with other circumstances. The commerce of your Colonies is out of all proportion beyond the numbers of the people. This ground of their commerce indeed has been trod some days ago, and with great ability, by a distinguished person at your bar. This gentleman, after thirty-five years — it is so long since he first appeared at the same place to plead for the commerce of Great Britain — has come again before you to plead the same cause, without any other effect of time, than that to the fire of imagination and extent of erudition which even then marked him as one of the first literary characters of his age, he has added a consummate knowledge in the commercial interest of his country, formed by a long course of enlightened and discriminating experience.

Sir, I should be inexcusable in coming after such a person with any detail, if a great part of the members who now fill the House had not the misfortune to be absent when he appeared at your bar. Besides, Sir, I propose to take the matter at periods of time somewhat different from his. There is, if I mistake not, a point of view from whence, if you will look at the subject, it is impossible that it should not make an impression upon you.

I have in my hand two accounts; one a comparative state of the export trade of England to its Colonies, as it stood in the year 1704, and as it stood in the year 1772; the other a state of the export trade of this country to its Colonies alone, as it stood in 1772, compared with the whole trade of England to all parts of the world (the Colonies included) in the year 1704. They are from good vouchers; the latter period from the accounts on your table, the earlier from an original manuscript of Davenant, who first established the Inspector-General's office, which has been ever since his time so abundant a source of Parliamentary information.

The export trade to the Colonies consists of three great branches: the African — which, terminating almost wholly in the Colonies, must be put to the account of their commerce, — the West Indian, and the North American. All these are so interwoven that the attempt to separate them would tear to pieces the contexture of the whole; and, if not entirely destroy, would very much depreciate the value of all the parts. I therefore consider these three denominations to be, what in effect they are, one trade.

The trade to the Colonies, taken on the export side, at the beginning of this century, that is, in the year 1704, stood thus: —

Exports to North America and the West Indies .	£483,265
To Africa	86,665
	£569,930

In the year 1772, which I take as a middle year between the highest and lowest of those lately laid on your table, the account was as follows: —

To North America and the West Indies . . .	£4,791,734
To Africa	866,398
To which, if you add the export trade from Scotland, which had in 1704 no existence . .	364,000
	£6,022,132

From five hundred and odd thousand, it has grown to six millions. It has increased no less than twelve-fold. This is the state of the Colony trade as compared with itself at these two periods within this century; — and this is matter for meditation. But this is not all. Examine my second account. See how the export trade to the Colonies alone in 1772 stood in the other point of view; that is, as compared to the whole trade of England in 1704: —

The whole export trade of England, including that to the Colonies, in 1704	£6,509,000
Export to the Colonies alone, in 1772	6,024,000
Difference,	£485,000

The trade with America alone is now within less than £500,000 of being equal to what this great commercial nation, England, carried on at the beginning of this century with the whole world! If I had taken the largest year of those on your table, it would rather have exceeded. But, it will be said, is not this American trade an unnatural protuberance, that has drawn the juices from the rest of the body? The reverse. It is the very food that has nourished every other part into its present magnitude. Our general trade has been greatly augmented, and augmented more or less in almost every part to which it ever extended; but with this material difference, that of the six millions which in the beginning of the century constituted the whole mass of our export commerce, the Colony trade was but one-twelfth part; it is now (as a part of sixteen millions) considerably more than a third of the whole. This is the relative proportion of the importance of the Colonies at these two periods; and all reasoning concerning our mode of treating them must have this proportion as its basis; or it is a reasoning weak, rotten, and sophistical.

Mr. Speaker, I cannot prevail on myself to hurry over this great consideration. *It is good for us to be here.* We stand where we have an immense view of what is, and what is past. Clouds, indeed, and darkness, rest upon the future. Let us, however, before we descend from this noble eminence, reflect that this growth of our national prosperity has happened within the short period of the life of man. It has happened within sixty-eight years. There are those alive whose memory might touch the two extremities. For instance, my Lord Bathurst might remember all the stages of the progress. He was in 1704 of an age at least to be made to comprehend such things. He was then old enough *acta parentum jam legere, et quæ sit potuit cognoscere virtus.* Suppose, Sir, that the angel of this auspicious youth, foreseeing the many virtues which made him one of the most amiable, as he is one of the most fortunate, men of his age, had opened to him in vision that when in the fourth generation the third Prince of the House of Brunswick had sat twelve years on the throne of that nation which, by the happy issue of moderate and healing counsels, was to be made Great Britain, he should see his son, Lord Chancellor of England, turn back the current of hereditary dignity to its fountain, and raise him to a higher rank of peerage, whilst he enriched the family with a new one — if, amidst these bright and happy scenes of domestic honor and prosperity, that angel should have drawn up the curtain, and unfolded the rising glories of his country, and, whilst he was gazing with admiration on the then commercial grandeur of England, the genius should point out to him a little speck, scarcely visible in the mass of the national interest, a small seminal principle, rather than a formed body, and should tell him: "Young man, there is America — which at this day serves for little more than to amuse you with stories of savage men, and uncouth manners; yet shall, before you taste of death, show itself equal to the whole of that commerce which now attracts the envy of the world. Whatever England has been growing to by a progressive increase of improvement, brought in by varieties of people, by succession of civilizing conquests and civilizing settlements in a series of seventeen hundred years, you shall see as much added to her by America in the course of a single life!" If this state of his country had been foretold to him, would it not require all the sanguine credulity of youth, and all the fervid glow of enthusiasm, to make him believe it? Fortunate man, he has lived to see it! Fortunate, indeed, if he lives to see nothing that shall vary the prospect, and cloud the setting of his day!

Excuse me, Sir, if turning from such thoughts I resume this comparative view once more. You have seen it on a large scale; look at it on a small one. I will point out to your attention a particular instance of it in the single province of Pennsylvania. In the year 1704 that province called for £11,459 in value of your commodities, native and foreign. This was the whole. What did it demand in 1772? Why, nearly fifty times as much; for in that year the export to Pennsylvania was £507,909, nearly equal to the export to all the Colonies together in the first period.

I choose, Sir, to enter into these minute and particular details, because generalities, which in all other cases are apt to heighten and raise the subject, have here a tendency to sink it. When we speak of the commerce with our Colonies, fiction lags after truth, invention is unfruitful, and imagination cold and barren.

So far, Sir, as to the importance of the object, in view of its commerce, as concerned in the exports from England. If I were to detail the imports, I could show how many enjoyments they procure which deceive the burthen of life; how many materials which invigorate the springs of national industry, and extend and animate every part of our foreign and domestic commerce. This would be a curious subject indeed; but I must prescribe bounds to myself in a matter so vast and various.

I pass, therefore, to the Colonies in another point of view, their agriculture. This they have prosecuted with such a spirit, that, besides feeding plentifully their own growing multitude, their annual export of grain, comprehending rice, has some years ago exceeded a million in value. Of their last harvest I am persuaded they will export much more. At the beginning of the century some of these Colonies imported corn from the Mother Country. For some time past the Old World has been fed from the New. The scarcity which you have felt would have been a desolating famine, if this child of your old age, with a true filial piety, with a Roman charity, had not put the full breast of its youthful exuberance to the mouth of its exhausted parent.

As to the wealth which the Colonies have drawn from the sea by their fisheries, you had all that matter fully opened at your bar. You surely thought those acquisitions of value, for they seemed even to excite your envy; and yet the spirit by which that enterprising employment has been exercised ought rather, in my opinion, to have raised your esteem and admiration. And pray, Sir, what in the world is equal to it? Pass by the other parts, and look at the manner in which the people of New England have of late carried on the whale fishery. Whilst we follow them among the tumbling mountains of ice, and behold them penetrating into the deepest frozen recesses of Hudson's Bay and Davis's Straits, whilst we are looking for them beneath the arctic circle, we hear that they have pierced into the opposite region of polar cold, that they are at the antipodes, and engaged under the frozen Serpent of the south. Falkland Island, which seemed too remote and romantic an object for the grasp of national ambition, is but a stage and resting-place in the progress of their victorious industry. Nor is the equinoctial heat more discouraging to them than the accumulated winter of both the poles. We know that whilst some of them draw the line and strike the harpoon on the coast of Africa, others run the longitude and pursue their gigantic game along the coast of Brazil. No sea but what is vexed by their fisheries; no climate that is not witness to their toils. Neither the perseverance of Holland, nor the activity of France, nor the dexterous and firm sagacity of English enterprise ever carried this most perilous mode of hardy industry to the extent to which it has been pushed by this recent people; a people who are still, as it were, but in the gristle, and not yet hardened into the bone of manhood. When I contemplate these things; when I know that the Colonies in general owe little or nothing to any care of ours, and that they are not squeezed into this happy form by the constraints of watchful and suspicious government, but that, through a wise and salutary neglect, a generous nature has been suffered to take her own way to perfection; when I reflect upon these effects, when I see how profitable they have been to us, I feel all the pride of power sink, and all presumption in the wisdom of human contrivances melt and die away within me. My rigor relents. I pardon something to the spirit of liberty.

I am sensible, Sir, that all which I have asserted in my detail is admitted in the gross; but that quite a different conclusion is drawn from it. America, gentlemen say, is a noble object. It is an object well worth fighting for. Certainly it is, if fighting a people be the best way of gaining them. Gentlemen in this respect will be led to their choice of means by their complexions and their habits. Those who understand the military art will of course have some predilection for it. Those who wield the thunder of the state may have more confidence in the efficacy of arms. But I confess, possibly for want of this knowledge, my opinion is much more in favor of prudent management than of force; considering force not as an odious, but a feeble instrument for preserving a people so numerous, so active, so growing, so spirited as this, in a profitable and subordinate connection with us.

First, Sir, permit me to observe that the use of force alone is but temporary. It may subdue for a moment, but it does not remove the necessity of subduing again; and a nation is not governed which is perpetually to be conquered.

My next objection is its uncertainty. Terror is not always the effect of force, and an armament is not a victory. If you do not succeed, you are without resource; for, conciliation failing, force remains; but, force failing, no further hope of reconciliation is left. Power and authority are sometimes bought by kindness; but they can never be begged as alms by an impoverished and defeated violence.

A further objection to force is, that you impair the object by your very endeavors to preserve it. The thing you fought for is not the thing which you recover; but depreciated, sunk, wasted, and consumed in the contest. Nothing less will content me than *whole America.* I do not choose to consume its strength along with our own, because in all parts it is the British strength that I consume. I do not choose to be caught by a foreign enemy at the end of this exhausting conflict; and still less in the midst of it. I may escape; but I can make no insurance against such an event. Let me add, that I do not choose wholly to break the American spirit; because it is the spirit that has made the country.

Lastly, we have no sort of experience in favor of force as an instrument in the rule of our Colonies. Their growth and their utility has been owing to methods altogether different. Our ancient indulgence has been said to be pursued to a fault. It may be so. But we know, if feeling is evidence, that our fault was more tolerable than our attempt to mend it; and our sin far more salutary than our penitence.

These, Sir, are my reasons for not entertaining that high opinion of untried force by which many gentlemen, for whose sentiments in other particulars I have great respect, seem to be so greatly captivated. But there is still behind a third consideration concerning this object which serves to determine my opinion on the sort of policy which ought to be pursued in the management of America, even more than its population and its commerce — I mean its temper and character.

In this character of the Americans, a love of freedom is the predominating feature which marks and distinguishes the whole; and as an ardent is always a jealous affection, your Colonies become suspicious, restive, and untractable whenever they see the least attempt to wrest from them by force, or shuffle from them by chicane, what they think the only advantage worth living for. This fierce spirit of liberty is stronger in the English

Colonies probably than in any other people of the earth, and this from a great variety of powerful causes; which, to understand the true temper of their minds and the direction which this spirit takes, it will not be amiss to lay open somewhat more largely.

First, the people of the Colonies are descendants of Englishmen. England, Sir, is a nation which still, I hope, respects, and formerly adored, her freedom. The Colonists emigrated from you when this part of your character was most predominant; and they took this bias and direction the moment they parted from your hands. They are therefore not only devoted to liberty, but to liberty according to English ideas, and on English principles. Abstract liberty, like other mere abstractions, is not to be found. Liberty inheres in some sensible object; and every nation has formed to itself some favorite point, which by way of eminence becomes the criterion of their happiness. It happened, you know, Sir, that the great contests for freedom in this country were from the earliest times chiefly upon the question of taxing. Most of the contests in the ancient commonwealths turned primarily on the right of election of magistrates; or on the balance among the several orders of the state. The question of money was not with them so immediate. But in England it was otherwise. On this point of taxes the ablest pens, and most eloquent tongues, have been exercised; the greatest spirits have acted and suffered. In order to give the fullest satisfaction concerning the importance of this point, it was not only necessary for those who in argument defended the excellence of the English Constitution to insist on this privilege of granting money as a dry point of fact, and to prove that the right had been acknowledged in ancient parchments and blind usages to reside in a certain body called a House of Commons. They went much farther;

they attempted to prove, and they succeeded, that in theory it ought to be so, from the particular nature of a House of Commons as an immediate representative of the people, whether the old records had delivered this oracle or not. They took infinite pains to inculcate, as a fundamental principle, that in all monarchies the people must in effect themselves, mediately or immediately, possess the power of granting their own money, or no shadow of liberty can subsist. The Colonies draw from you, as with their life-blood, these ideas and principles. Their love of liberty, as with you, fixed and attached on this specific point of taxing. Liberty might be safe, or might be endangered, in twenty other particulars, without their being much pleased or alarmed. Here they felt its pulse; and as they found that beat, they thought themselves sick or sound. I do not say whether they were right or wrong in applying your general arguments to their own case. It is not easy, indeed, to make a monopoly of theorems and corollaries. The fact is, that they did thus apply those general arguments; and your mode of governing them, whether through lenity or indolence, through wisdom or mistake, confirmed them in the imagination that they, as well as you, had an interest in these common principles.

They were further confirmed in this pleasing error by the form of their provincial legislative assemblies. Their governments are popular in an high degree; some are merely popular; in all, the popular representative is the most weighty; and this share of the people in their ordinary government never fails to inspire them with lofty sentiments, and with a strong aversion from whatever tends to deprive them of their chief importance.

If anything were wanting to this necessary operation of the form of government, religion would have given it a complete effect. Religion, always a principle of energy, in this new people is no way worn out or impaired; and their mode of professing it is also one main cause of this free spirit. The people are Protestants; and of that kind which is the most adverse to all implicit submission of mind and opinion. This is a persuasion not only favorable to liberty, but built upon it. I do not think, Sir, that the reason of this averseness in the dissenting churches from all that looks like absolute government is so much to be sought in their religious tenets, as in their history. Every one knows that the Roman Catholic religion is at least co-eval with most of the governments where it prevails; that it has generally gone hand in hand with them, and received great favor and every kind of support from authority. The Church of England too was formed from her cradle under the nursing care of regular government. But the dissenting interests have sprung up in direct opposition to all the ordinary powers of the world, and could justify that opposition only on a strong claim to natural liberty. Their very existence depended on the powerful and unremitted assertion of that claim. All Protestantism, even the most cold and passive, is a sort of dissent. But the religion most prevalent in our Northern Colonies is a refinement on the principle of resistance; it is the dissidence of dissent, and the protestantism of the Protestant religion. This religion, under a variety of denominations agreeing in nothing but in the communion of the spirit of liberty, is predominant in most of the Northern Provinces, where the Church of England, notwithstanding its legal rights, is in reality no more than a sort of private sect, not composing most probably the tenth of the people. The Colonists left England when this spirit was high, and in the emigrants was the highest of all; and even that stream of foreigners which has been constantly flowing into these Colonies has, for the greatest part, been composed of dissenters from the establishments of their several countries, who have brought with them a temper and character far from alien to that of the people with whom they mixed.

Sir, I can perceive by their manner that some gentlemen object to the latitude of this description, because in the Southern Colonies the Church of England forms a large body, and has a regular establishment. It is certainly true. There is, however, a circumstance attending these Colonies which, in my opinion, fully counterbalances this difference, and makes the spirit of liberty still more high and haughty than in those to the northward. It is that in Virginia and the Carolinas they have a vast multitude of slaves. Where this is the case in any part of the world, those who are free are by far the most proud and jealous of their freedom. Freedom is to them not only an enjoyment, but a kind of rank and privilege. Not seeing there, that freedom, as in countries where it is a common blessing and as broad and general as the air, may be united with much abject toil, with great misery, with all the exterior of servitude; liberty looks, amongst them, like something that is more noble and liberal. I do not mean, Sir, to commend the superior morality of this sentiment, which has at least as much pride as virtue in it; but I cannot alter the nature of man. The fact is so; and these people of the Southern Colonies are much more strongly, and with an higher and more stubborn spirit, attached to liberty than those to the northward. Such were all the ancient commonwealths; such were our Gothic ancestors; such in our days were the Poles; and such will be all masters of slaves, who are not slaves themselves. In such a people the haughtiness of domination combines with the spirit of freedom, fortifies it, and renders it invincible.

Permit me, Sir, to add another circumstance in our

Colonies which contributes no mean part towards the growth and effect of this untractable spirit. I mean their education. In no country perhaps in the world is the law so general a study. The profession itself is numerous and powerful; and in most provinces it takes the lead. The greater number of the deputies sent to the Congress were lawyers. But all who read, and most do read, endeavor to obtain some smattering in that science. I have been told by an eminent bookseller, that in no branch of his business, after tracts of popular devotion, were so many books as those on the law exported to the Plantations. The Colonists have now fallen into the way of printing them for their own use. I hear that they have sold nearly as many of Blackstone's Commentaries in America as in England. General Gage marks out this disposition very particularly in a letter on your table. He states that all the people in his government are lawyers, or smatterers in law; and that in Boston they have been enabled, by successful chicane, wholly to evade many parts of one of your capital penal constitutions. The smartness of debate will say that this knowledge ought to teach them more clearly the rights of legislature, their obligations to obedience, and the penalties of rebellion. All this is mighty well. But my honorable and learned friend on the floor, who condescends to mark what I say for animadversion, will disdain that ground. He has heard, as well as I, that when great honors and great emoluments do not win over this knowledge to the service of the state, it is a formidable adversary to government. If the spirit be not tamed and broken by these happy methods, it is stubborn and litigious. *Abeunt studia in mores.* This study renders men acute, inquisitive, dexterous, prompt in attack, ready in defence, full of resources. In other countries, the people, more simple, and of a less mercurial cast, judge of an ill principle in government only by an actual grievance; here they anticipate the evil, and judge of the pressure of the grievance by the badness of the principle. They augur misgovernment at a distance, and snuff the approach of tyranny in every tainted breeze.

The last cause of this disobedient spirit in the Colonies is hardly less powerful than the rest, as it is not merely moral, but laid deep in the natural constitution of things. Three thousand miles of ocean lie between you and them. No contrivance can prevent the effect of this distance in weakening government. Seas roll, and months pass, between the order and the execution; and the want of a speedy explanation of a single point is enough to defeat a whole system. You have, indeed, winged ministers of vengeance, who carry your bolts in their pounces to the remotest verge of the sea. But there a power steps in that limits the arrogance of raging passions and furious elements, and says, *So far shalt thou go, and no farther.* Who are you, that you should fret and rage, and bite the chains of nature? Nothing worse happens to you than does to all nations who have extensive empire; and it happens in all the forms into which empire can be thrown. In large bodies the circulation of power must be less vigorous at the extremities. Nature has said it. The Turk cannot govern Egypt and Arabia and Kurdistan as he governs Thrace; nor has he the same dominion in Crimea and Algiers which he has at Brusa and Smyrna. Despotism itself is obliged to truck and huckster. The Sultan gets such obedience as he can. He governs with a loose rein, that he may govern at all; and the whole of the force and vigor of his authority in his centre is derived from a prudent relaxation in all his borders. Spain, in her provinces, is, perhaps, not so well obeyed as you are in yours. She complies, too; she submits; she watches times. This is the immutable condition, the eternal law of extensive and detached empire.

Then, Sir, from these six capital sources — of descent, of form of government, of religion in the Northern Provinces, of manners in the Southern, of education, of the remoteness of situation from the first mover of government — from all these causes a fierce spirit of liberty has grown up. It has grown with the growth of the people in your Colonies, and increased with the increase of their wealth; a spirit that unhappily meeting with an exercise of power in England which, however lawful, is not reconcilable to any ideas of liberty, much less with theirs, has kindled this flame that is ready to consume us.

I do not mean to commend either the spirit in this excess, or the moral causes which produce it. Perhaps a more smooth and accommodating spirit of freedom in them would be more acceptable to us. Perhaps ideas of liberty might be desired more reconcilable with an arbitrary and boundless authority. Perhaps we might wish the Colonists to be persuaded that their liberty is more secure when held in trust for them by us, as their guardians during a perpetual minority, than with any part of it in their own hands. The question is, not whether their spirit deserves praise or blame, but — what, in the name of God, shall we do with it? You have before you the object, such as it is, with all its glories, with all its imperfections on its head. You see the magnitude, the importance, the temper, the habits, the disorders. By all these considerations we are strongly urged to determine something concerning it. We are called upon to fix some rule and line for our future conduct which may give a little stability to our politics, and prevent the return of such unhappy deliberations as the present. Every such return will bring the matter before us in a still more untractable form. For, what astonishing and incredible things have we not seen already! What monsters have not been generated from this unnatural contention! Whilst every principle of authority and resistance has been pushed, upon both sides, as far as it would go, there is nothing so solid and certain, either in reasoning or in practice, that has not been shaken. Until very lately all authority in America seemed to be nothing but an emanation from yours. Even the popular part of the Colony Constitution derived all its activity and its first vital movement from the pleasure of the Crown. We thought, Sir, that the utmost which the discontented Colonists could do was to disturb authority; we never dreamt they could of themselves supply it—knowing in general what an operose business it is to establish a government absolutely new. But having, for our purposes in this contention, resolved that none but an obedient Assembly should sit, the humors of the people there, finding all passage through the legal channel stopped, with great violence broke out another way. Some provinces have tried their experiment, as we have tried ours; and theirs has succeeded. They have formed a government sufficient for its purposes, without the bustle of a revolution or the troublesome formality of an election. Evident necessity and tacit consent have done the business in an instant. So well they have done it, that Lord Dunmore—the account is among the fragments on your table—tells you that the new institution is infinitely better obeyed than the ancient government ever was in its most fortunate periods. Obedience is what makes government, and not the names by which it is called; not the name of Governor, as formerly, or Committee, as at present. This new government has originated directly from the people, and was not transmitted through any of the ordinary artificial media of a positive constitution. It was not a manufacture ready formed, and transmitted to them in that condition from England. The evil arising from hence is this; that the Colonists having once found the possibility of enjoying the advantages of order in the midst of a struggle for liberty, such struggles will not henceforward seem so terrible to the settled and sober part of mankind as they had appeared before the trial.

Pursuing the same plan of punishing by the denial of the exercise of government to still greater lengths, we wholly abrogated the ancient government of Massachusetts. We were confident that the first feeling, if not the very prospect, of anarchy would instantly enforce a complete submission. The experiment was tried. A new, strange, unexpected face of things appeared. Anarchy is found tolerable. A vast province has now subsisted, and subsisted in a considerable degree of health and vigor for near a twelvemonth, without Governor, without public Council, without judges, without executive magistrates. How long it will continue in this state, or what may arise out of this unheard-of situation, how can the wisest of us conjecture? Our late experience has taught us that many of those fundamental principles, formerly believed infallible, are either not of the importance they were imagined to be, or that we have not at all adverted to some other far more important and far more powerful principles, which entirely overrule those we had considered as omnipotent. I am much against any further experiments which tend to put to the proof any more of these allowed opinions which contribute so much to the public tranquillity. In effect, we suffer as much at home by this loosening of all ties, and this concussion of all established opinions, as we do abroad; for in order to prove that the Americans have no right to their liberties, we are every day endeavoring to subvert the maxims which preserve the whole spirit of our own.

To prove that the Americans ought not to be free, we are obliged to depreciate the value of freedom itself; and we never seem to gain a paltry advantage over them in debate without attacking some of those principles, or deriding some of those feelings, for which our ancestors have shed their blood.

But, Sir, in wishing to put an end to pernicious experiments, I do not mean to preclude the fullest inquiry. Far from it. Far from deciding on a sudden or partial view, I would patiently go round and round the subject, and survey it minutely in every possible aspect. Sir, if I were capable of engaging you to an equal attention, I would state that, as far as I am capable of discerning, there are but three ways of proceeding relative to this stubborn spirit which prevails in your Colonies, and disturbs your government. These are — to change that spirit, as inconvenient, by removing the causes; to prosecute it as criminal; or to comply with it as necessary. I would not be guilty of an imperfect enumeration; I can think of but these three. Another has indeed been started, — that of giving up the Colonies; but it met so slight a reception that I do not think myself obliged to dwell a great while upon it. It is nothing but a little sally of anger, like the frowardness of peevish children, who, when they cannot get all they would have, are resolved to take nothing.

The first of these plans — to change the spirit, as inconvenient, by removing the causes — I think is the most like a systematic proceeding. It is radical in its principle; but it is attended with great difficulties, some of them little short, as I conceive, of impossibilities. This will appear by examining into the plans which have been proposed.

As the growing population in the Colonies is evidently one cause of their resistance, it was last session mentioned in both Houses, by men of weight, and received not without applause, that in order to check this evil it would be proper for the Crown to make no further grants of land. But to this scheme there are two objections. The first, that there is already so much unsettled land in private hands as to afford room for an immense future population, although the Crown not only withheld its grants, but annihilated its soil. If this be the case, then the only effect of this avarice of desolation, this hoarding of a royal wilderness, would be to raise the value of the possessions in the hands of the great private monopolists, without any adequate check to the growing and alarming mischief of population.

But if you stopped your grants, what would be the consequence? The people would occupy without grants. They have already so occupied in many places. You cannot station garrisons in every part of these deserts. If you drive the people from one place, they will carry on their annual tillage, and remove with their flocks and herds to another. Many of the people in the back settlements are already little attached to particular situations. Already they have topped the Appalachian Mountains. From thence they behold before them an immense plain, one vast, rich, level meadow; a square of five hundred miles. Over this they would wander without a possibility of restraint; they would change their manners with the habits of their life; would soon forget a government by which they were disowned; would become hordes of English Tartars; and, pouring down upon your unfortified frontiers a fierce and irresistible cavalry, become masters of your governors and your counsellors, your collectors and comptrollers, and of all the slaves that adhered to them. Such would, and in no long time must be, the effect of attempting to forbid as a crime and to suppress as an evil the command and blessing of providence, *Increase and multiply.* Such would be the happy result of the endeavor to keep as a lair of wild beasts that earth which God, by an express charter, has given to the children of men. Far different, and surely much wiser, has been our policy hitherto. Hitherto we have invited our people, by every kind of bounty, to fixed establishments. We have invited the husbandman to look to authority for his title. We have taught him piously to believe in the mysterious virtue of wax and parchment. We have thrown each tract of land, as it was peopled, into districts, that the ruling power should never be wholly out of sight We have settled all we could; and we have carefully attended every settlement with government.

Adhering, Sir, as I do, to this policy, as well as for the reasons I have just given, I think this new project of hedging-in population to be neither prudent nor practicable.

To impoverish the Colonies in general, and in particular to arrest the noble course of their marine enterprises, would be a more easy task. I freely confess it. We have shown a disposition to a system of this kind, a disposition even to continue the restraint after the offence, looking on ourselves as rivals to our Colonies, and persuaded that of course we must gain all that they shall lose. Much mischief we may certainly do. The power inadequate to all other things is often more than sufficient for this. I do not look on the direct and immediate power of the Colonies to resist our violence as very formidable. In this, however, I may be mistaken. But when I consider that we have Colonies for no purpose but to be serviceable to us, it seems to my poor understanding a little preposterous to make them unserviceable in order to keep them obedient. It is, in truth, nothing more than the old and, as I thought, exploded problem of tyranny, which proposes to beggar its subjects into submission. But remember, when you have completed your system of impoverishment, that nature still proceeds in her ordinary course; that discontent will increase with misery; and that there are critical moments in the fortune of all states when they who are too weak to contribute to your prosperity may be strong enough to complete your ruin. *Spoliatis arma supersunt.*

The temper and character which prevail in our Colonies are, I am afraid, unalterable by any human art. We cannot, I fear, falsify the pedigree of this fierce people, and persuade them that they are not sprung from a nation in whose veins the blood of freedom circulates. The language in which they would hear you tell them this tale would detect the imposition; your speech would betray you. An Englishman is the unfittest person on earth to argue another Englishman into slavery.

I think it is nearly as little in our power to change their republican religion as their free descent; or to substitute the Roman Catholic as a penalty, or the Church of England as an improvement. The mode of inquisition and dragooning is going out of fashion in the Old World, and I should not confide much to their efficacy in the New. The education of the Americans is also on the same unalterable bottom with their religion. You cannot persuade them to burn their books of curious science; to banish their lawyers from their courts of laws; or to quench the lights of their assemblies by refusing to choose those persons who are best read in their privileges. It would be no less impracticable to think of wholly annihilating the popular assemblies in which these lawyers sit. The army, by which we must govern in their place, would be far more chargeable to us, not quite so effectual, and perhaps in the end full as difficult to be kept in obedience.

With regard to the high aristocratic spirit of Virginia and the Southern Colonies, it has been proposed, I know, to reduce it by declaring a general enfranchisement of their slaves. This object has had its advocates and panegyrists; yet I never could argue myself into any opinion of it. Slaves are often much attached to their masters. A general wild offer of liberty would not always be accepted. History furnishes few instances of it. It is sometimes as hard to persuade slaves to be free, as it is to compel freemen to be slaves; and in this auspicious scheme we should have both these pleasing tasks on our hands at once. But when we talk of enfranchisement, do we not perceive that the American master may enfranchise too, and arm servile hands in defence of freedom? — a measure to which other people have had recourse more than once, and not without success, in a desperate situation of their affairs.

Slaves as these unfortunate black people are, and dull as all men are from slavery, must they not a little suspect the offer of freedom from that very nation which has sold them to their present masters? — from that nation, one of whose causes of quarrel with those masters is their refusal to deal any more in that inhuman traffic? An offer of freedom from England would come rather oddly, shipped to them in an African vessel which is refused an entry into the ports of Virginia or Carolina with a cargo of three hundred Angola negroes. It would be curious to see the Guinea captain attempting at the same instant to publish his proclamation of liberty, and to advertise his sale of slaves.

But let us suppose all these moral difficulties got over. The ocean remains. You cannot pump this dry; and as long as it continues in its present bed, so long all the causes which weaken authority by distance will continue.

> "Ye gods, annihilate but space and time,
> And make two lovers happy!"

was a pious and passionate prayer; but just as reasonable as many of the serious wishes of grave and solemn politicians.

If then, Sir, it seems almost desperate to think of any alterative course for changing the moral causes, and not quite easy to remove the natural, which produce prejudices irreconcilable to the late exercise of our authority — but that the spirit infallibly will continue, and, continuing, will produce such effects as now embarrass us — the second mode under consideration is to prosecute that spirit in its overt acts as criminal.

At this proposition I must pause a moment. The thing seems a great deal too big for my ideas of jurisprudence. It should seem to my way of conceiving such matters that there is a very wide difference, in reason and policy, between the mode of proceeding on the irregular conduct of scattered individuals, or even of bands of men who disturb order within the state, and the civil dissensions which may, from time to time, on great questions, agitate the several communities which compose a great empire. It looks to me to be narrow and pedantic to apply the ordinary ideas of criminal justice to this great public contest. I do not know the method of drawing up an indictment against a whole people. I cannot insult and ridicule the feelings of millions of my fellow-creatures as Sir Edward Coke insulted one excellent individual (Sir Walter Raleigh) at the bar. I hope I am not ripe to pass sentence on the gravest public bodies, intrusted with magistracies of great authority and dignity, and charged with the safety of their fellow-citizens, upon the very same title that I am. I really think that, for wise men, this is not judicious; for sober men, not decent; for minds tinctured with humanity, not mild and merciful.

Perhaps, Sir, I am mistaken in my idea of an empire,

as distinguished from a single state or kingdom. But my idea of it is this; that an empire is the aggregate of many states under one common head, whether this head be a monarch or a presiding republic. It does, in such constitutions, frequently happen — and nothing but the dismal, cold, dead uniformity of servitude can prevent its happening — that the subordinate parts have many local privileges and immunities. Between these privileges and the supreme common authority the line may be extremely nice. Of course disputes, often, too, very bitter disputes, and much ill blood, will arise. But though every privilege is an exemption, in the case, from the ordinary exercise of the supreme authority, it is no denial of it. The claim of a privilege seems rather, *ex vi termini*, to imply a superior power; for to talk of the privileges of a state or of a person who has no superior is hardly any better than speaking nonsense. Now, in such unfortunate quarrels among the component parts of a great political union of communities, I can scarcely conceive anything more completely imprudent than for the head of the empire to insist that, if any privilege is pleaded against his will or his acts, his whole authority is denied; instantly to proclaim rebellion, to beat to arms, and to put the offending provinces under the ban. Will not this, Sir, very soon teach the provinces to make no distinctions on their part? Will it not teach them that the government, against which a claim of liberty is tantamount to high treason, is a government to which submission is equivalent to slavery? It may not always be quite convenient to impress dependent communities with such an idea.

We are, indeed, in all disputes with the Colonies, by the necessity of things, the judge. It is true, Sir. But I confess that the character of judge in my own cause is a thing that frightens me. Instead of filling me with pride, I am exceedingly humbled by it. I cannot proceed with a stern, assured, judicial confidence, until I find myself in something more like a judicial character. I must have these hesitations as long as I am compelled to recollect that, in my little reading upon such contests as these, the sense of mankind has at least as often decided against the superior as the subordinate power. Sir, let me add, too, that the opinion of my having some abstract right in my favor would not put me much at my ease in passing sentence, unless I could be sure that there were no rights which, in their exercise under certain circumstances, were not the most odious of all wrongs and the most vexatious of all injustice. Sir, these considerations have great weight with me when I find things so circumstanced, that I see the same party at once a civil litigant against me in point of right and a culprit before me, while I sit as a criminal judge on acts of his whose moral quality is to be decided upon the merits of that very litigation. Men are every now and then put, by the complexity of human affairs, into strange situations; but justice is the same, let the judge be in what situation he will.

There is, Sir, also a circumstance which convinces me that this mode of criminal proceeding is not, at least in the present stage of our contest, altogether expedient; which is nothing less than the conduct of those very persons who have seemed to adopt that mode by lately declaring a rebellion in Massachusetts Bay, as they had formerly addressed to have traitors brought hither, under an Act of Henry the Eighth, for trial. For though rebellion is declared, it is not proceeded against as such, nor have any steps been taken towards the apprehension or conviction of any individual offender, either on our late or our former Address; but modes of public coercion have been adopted, and such as have much more resemblance to a sort of qualified hostility towards an independent power than the punishment of rebellious subjects. All this seems rather inconsistent; but it shows how difficult it is to apply these juridical ideas to our present case.

In this situation, let us seriously and coolly ponder. What is it we have got by all our menaces, which have been many and ferocious? What advantage have we derived from the penal laws we have passed, and which, for the time, have been severe and numerous? What advances have we made towards our object by the sending of a force which, by land and sea, is no contemptible strength? Has the disorder abated? Nothing less. When I see things in this situation after such confident hopes, bold promises, and active exertions, I cannot, for my life, avoid a suspicion that the plan itself is not correctly right.

If, then, the removal of the causes of this spirit of American liberty be for the greater part, or rather entirely, impracticable; if the ideas of criminal process be inapplicable — or, if applicable, are in the highest degree inexpedient; what way yet remains? No way is open but the third and last, — to comply with the American spirit as necessary; or, if you please, to submit to it as a necessary evil.

If we adopt this mode, — if we mean to conciliate and concede, — let us see of what nature the concession ought to be. To ascertain the nature of our concession, we must look at their complaint. The Colonies complain that they have not the characteristic mark and seal of British freedom. They complain that they are taxed in a Parliament in which they are not represented. If you mean to satisfy them at all, you must satisfy them with regard to this complaint. If you mean to please any people you must give them the boon which they ask;

not what you may think better for them, but of a kind totally different. Such an act may be a wise regulation, but it is no concession; whereas our present theme is the mode of giving satisfaction.

Sir, I think you must perceive that I am resolved this day to have nothing at all to do with the question of the right of taxation. Some gentlemen startle — but it is true; I put it totally out of the question. It is less than nothing in my consideration. I do not indeed wonder, nor will you, Sir, that gentlemen of profound learning are fond of displaying it on this profound subject. But my consideration is narrow, confined, and wholly limited to the policy of the question. I do not examine whether the giving away a man's money be a power excepted and reserved out of the general trust of government, and how far all mankind, in all forms of polity, are entitled to an exercise of that right by the charter of nature; or whether, on the contrary, a right of taxation is necessarily involved in the general principle of legislation, and inseparable from the ordinary supreme power. These are deep questions, where great names militate against each other, where reason is perplexed, and an appeal to authorities only thickens the confusion; for high and reverend authorities lift up their heads on both sides, and there is no sure footing in the middle. This point is the great

> "Serbonian bog,
> Betwixt Damiata and Mount Casius old,
> Where armies whole have sunk."

I do not intend to be overwhelmed in that bog, though in such respectable company. The question with me is, not whether you have a right to render your people miserable, but whether it is not your interest to make them happy. It is not what a lawyer tells me I *may* do, but what humanity, reason, and justice tell me I *ought* to do. Is a politic act the worse for being a generous one? Is no concession proper but that which is made from your want of right to keep what you grant? Or does it lessen the grace or dignity of relaxing in the exercise of an odious claim because you have your evidence-room full of titles, and your magazines stuffed with arms to enforce them? What signify all those titles, and all those arms? Of what avail are they, when the reason of the thing tells me that the assertion of my title is the loss of my suit, and that I could do nothing but wound myself by the use of my own weapons?

Such is steadfastly my opinion of the absolute necessity of keeping up the concord of this Empire by an unity of spirit, though in a diversity of operations, that, if I were sure the Colonists had, at their leaving this country, sealed a regular compact of servitude; that they had solemnly abjured all the rights of citizens; that they had made a vow to renounce all ideas of liberty for them and their posterity to all generations; yet I should hold myself obliged to conform to the temper I found universally prevalent in my own day, and to govern two million of men, impatient of servitude, on the principles of freedom. I am not determining a point of law, I am restoring tranquillity; and the general character and situation of a people must determine what sort of government is fitted for them. That point nothing else can or ought to determine.

My idea, therefore, without considering whether we yield as matter of right, or grant as matter of favor, is to admit the people of our Colonies into an interest in the Constitution; and, by recording that admission in the journals of Parliament, to give them as strong an assurance as the nature of the thing will admit, that we mean forever to adhere to that solemn declaration of systematic indulgence.

Some years ago the repeal of a revenue Act, upon its understood principle, might have served to show that we intended an unconditional abatement of the exercise of a taxing power. Such a measure was then sufficient to remove all suspicion, and to give perfect content. But unfortunate events since that time may make something further necessary; and not more necessary for the satisfaction of the Colonies than for the dignity and consistency of our own future proceedings.

I have taken a very incorrect measure of the disposition of the House if this proposal in itself would be received with dislike. I think, Sir, we have few American financiers. But our misfortune is, we are too acute, we are too exquisite in our conjectures of the future, for men oppressed with such great and present evils. The more moderate among the opposers of Parliamentary concession freely confess that they hope no good from taxation, but they apprehend the Colonists have further views; and if this point were conceded, they would instantly attack the trade laws. These gentlemen are convinced that this was the intention from the beginning, and the quarrel of the Americans with taxation was no more than a cloak and cover to this design. Such has been the language even of a gentleman of real moderation, and of a natural temper well adjusted to fair and equal government. I am, however, Sir, not a little surprised at this kind of discourse, whenever I hear it; and I am the more surprised on account of the arguments which I constantly find in company with it, and which are often urged from the same mouths and on the same day.

For instance, when we allege that it is against reason to tax a people under so many restraints in trade as the Americans, the noble lord in the blue ribbon shall tell you that the restraints on trade are futile and useless —

of no advantage to us, and of no burthen to those on whom they are imposed; that the trade to America is not secured by the Acts of Navigation, but by the natural and irresistible advantage of a commercial preference.

Such is the merit of the trade laws in this posture of the debate. But when strong internal circumstances are urged against the taxes; when the scheme is dissected; when experience and the nature of things are brought to prove, and do prove, the utter impossibility of obtaining an effective revenue from the Colonies; when these things are pressed, or rather press themselves, so as to drive the advocates of Colony taxes to a clear admission of the futility of the scheme; then, Sir, the sleeping trade laws revive from their trance, and this useless taxation is to be kept sacred, not for its own sake, but as a counter-guard and security of the laws of trade.

Then, Sir, you keep up revenue laws which are mischievous, in order to preserve trade laws that are useless. Such is the wisdom of our plan in both its members. They are separately given up as of no value, and yet one is always to be defended for the sake of the other; but I cannot agree with the noble lord, nor with the pamphlet from whence he seems to have borrowed these ideas concerning the inutility of the trade laws. For, without idolizing them, I am sure they are still, in many ways, of great use to us; and in former times they have been of the greatest. They do confine, and they do greatly narrow, the market for the Americans; but my perfect conviction of this does not help me in the least to discern how the revenue laws form any security whatsoever to the commercial regulations, or that these commercial regulations are the true ground of the quarrel, or that the giving way, in any one instance of authority, is to lose all that may remain unconceded.

One fact is clear and indisputable. The public and

avowed origin of this quarrel was on taxation. This quarrel has indeed brought on new disputes on new questions; but certainly the least bitter, and the fewest of all, on the trade laws. To judge which of the two be the real radical cause of quarrel, we have to see whether the commercial dispute did, in order of time, precede the dispute on taxation? There is not a shadow of evidence for it. Next, to enable us to judge whether at this moment a dislike to the trade laws be the real cause of quarrel, it is absolutely necessary to put the taxes out of the question by a repeal. See how the Americans act in this position, and then you will be able to discern correctly what is the true object of the controversy, or whether any controversy at all will remain. Unless you consent to remove this cause of difference, it is impossible, with decency, to assert that the dispute is not upon what it is avowed to be. And I would, Sir, recommend to your serious consideration whether it be prudent to form a rule for punishing people, not on their own acts, but on your conjectures? Surely it is preposterous at the very best. It is not justifying your anger by their misconduct, but it is converting your ill-will into their delinquency.

But the Colonies will go further. Alas! alas! when will this speculation against fact and reason end? What will quiet these panic fears which we entertain of the hostile effect of a conciliatory conduct? Is it true that no case can exist in which it is proper for the sovereign to accede to the desires of his discontented subjects? Is there anything peculiar in this case to make a rule for itself? Is all authority of course lost when it is not pushed to the extreme? Is it a certain maxim that the fewer causes of dissatisfaction are left by government, the more the subject will be inclined to resist and rebel?

All these objections being in fact no more than suspicions, conjectures, divinations, formed in defiance of fact and experience, they did not, Sir, discourage me from entertaining the idea of a conciliatory concession founded on the principles which I have just stated.

In forming a plan for this purpose, I endeavored to put myself in that frame of mind which was the most natural and the most reasonable, and which was certainly the most probable means of securing me from all error. I set out with a perfect distrust of my own abilities, a total renunciation of every speculation of my own, and with a profound reverence for the wisdom of our ancestors who have left us the inheritance of so happy a constitution and so flourishing an empire, and, what is a thousand times more valuable, the treasury of the maxims and principles which formed the one and obtained the other.

During the reigns of the kings of Spain of the Austrian family, whenever they were at a loss in the Spanish councils, it was common for their statesmen to say that they ought to consult the genius of Philip the Second. The genius of Philip the Second might mislead them, and the issue of their affairs showed that they had not chosen the most perfect standard; but, Sir, I am sure that I shall not be misled when, in a case of constitutional difficulty, I consult the genius of the English Constitution. Consulting at that oracle — it was with all due humility and piety — I found four capital examples in a similar case before me; those of Ireland, Wales, Chester, and Durham.

Ireland, before the English conquest, though never governed by a despotic power, had no Parliament. How far the English Parliament itself was at that time modelled according to the present form is disputed among antiquaries; but we have all the reason in the world to be assured that a form of Parliament such as England then enjoyed she instantly communicated to Ireland, and we are equally sure that almost every successive improvement in constitutional liberty, as fast as it was made here, was transmitted thither. The feudal baronage and the feudal knighthood, the roots of our primitive Constitution, were early transplanted into that soil, and grew and flourished there. Magna Charta, if it did not give us originally the House of Commons, gave us at least a House of Commons of weight and consequence. But your ancestors did not churlishly sit down alone to the feast of Magna Charta. Ireland was made immediately a partaker. This benefit of English laws and liberties, I confess, was not at first extended to all Ireland. Mark the consequence. English authority and English liberties had exactly the same boundaries. Your standard could never be advanced an inch before your privileges. Sir John Davis shows beyond a doubt that the refusal of a general communication of these rights was the true cause why Ireland was five hundred years in subduing; and after the vain projects of a military government, attempted in the reign of Queen Elizabeth, it was soon discovered that nothing could make that country English, in civility and allegiance, but your laws and your forms of legislature. It was not English arms, but the English Constitution, that conquered Ireland. From that time Ireland has ever had a general Parliament, as she had before a partial Parliament. You changed the people; you altered the religion; but you never touched the form or the vital substance of free government in that Kingdom. You deposed kings; you restored them; you altered the succession to theirs, as well as to your own Crown; but you never altered their Constitution, the principle of which was respected by usurpation, restored with the restoration of monarchy, and established, I trust, forever, by the glorious Revolution. This has made Ireland the great and flourishing kingdom that it is, and, from a disgrace and a burthen intolerable to this nation, has rendered her a principal part of our strength and ornament. This country cannot be said to have ever formally taxed her. The irregular things done in the confusion of mighty troubles and on the hinge of great revolutions, even if all were done that is said to have been done, form no example. If they have any effect in argument, they make an exception to prove the rule. None of your own liberties could stand a moment, if the casual deviations from them at such times were suffered to be used as proofs of their nullity. By the lucrative amount of such casual breaches in the constitution, judge what the stated and fixed rule of supply has been in that kingdom. Your Irish pensioners would starve, if they had no other fund to live on than taxes granted by English authority. Turn your eyes to those popular grants from whence all your great supplies are come, and learn to respect that only source of public wealth in the British Empire.

My next example is Wales. This country was said to be reduced by Henry the Third. It was said more truly to be so by Edward the First. But though then conquered, it was not looked upon as any part of the realm of England. Its old Constitution, whatever that might have been, was destroyed, and no good one was substituted in its place. The care of that tract was put into the hands of Lords Marchers — a form of government of a very singular kind; a strange heterogeneous monster, something between hostility and government; perhaps it has a sort of resemblance, according to the modes of those terms, to that of Commander-in-chief at present, to whom all civil power is granted as secondary. The manners of the Welsh nation followed the genius of the government. The people were ferocious, restive, savage, and uncultivated; sometimes composed, never pacified. Wales, within itself, was in perpetual disorder, and it kept the frontier of England in perpetual alarm. Benefits from it to the state there were none. Wales was only known to England by incursion and invasion.

Sir, during that state of things, Parliament was not idle. They attempted to subdue the fierce spirit of the Welsh by all sorts of rigorous laws. They prohibited by statute the sending all sorts of arms into Wales, as you prohibit by proclamation (with something more of doubt on the legality) the sending arms to America. They disarmed the Welsh by statute, as you attempted (but still with more question on the legality) to disarm New England by an instruction. They made an Act to drag offenders from Wales into England for trial, as you have done (but with more hardship) with regard to America. By another Act, where one of the parties was an Englishman, they ordained that his trial should be always by English. They made Acts to restrain trade, as you do; and they prevented the Welsh from the use of fairs and markets, as you do the Americans from fisheries and foreign ports. In short, when the Statute Book was not quite so much swelled as it is now, you find no less than fifteen acts of penal regulation on the subject of Wales. Here we rub our hands. — A fine body of precedents for the authority of Parliament and the use of it! — I admit it fully; and pray add likewise to these precedents that all the while Wales rid this Kingdom like an incubus, that it was an unprofitable and oppressive burthen, and that an Englishman travelling in that country could not go six yards from the high road without being murdered.

The march of the human mind is slow. Sir, it was not until after two hundred years discovered that, by an eternal law, providence had decreed vexation to violence, and poverty to rapine. Your ancestors did however at length open their eyes to the ill-husbandry of injustice. They found that the tyranny of a free people could of all tyrannies the least be endured, and that laws made against a whole nation were not the most effectual methods of securing its obedience. Accordingly, in the twenty-seventh year of Henry the Eighth the course was entirely altered. With a preamble stating the entire and perfect rights of the Crown of England, it gave to the Welsh all the rights and privileges of English subjects. A political order was established; the military power gave way to the civil; the Marches were turned into Counties. But that a nation should have a right to English liberties, and yet no share at all in the fundamental security of these liberties — the grant of their own property — seemed a thing so incongruous, that, eight years after, that is, in the thirty-fifth of that reign, a complete and not ill proportioned representation by counties and boroughs was bestowed upon Wales by Act of Parliament. From that moment, as by a charm, the tumults subsided; obedience was restored; peace, order, and civilization followed in the train of liberty. When the day-star of the English Constitution had arisen in their hearts, all was harmony within and without —

> "— simul alba nautis
>   Stella refulsit,
> Defluit saxis agitatus humor;
> Concidunt venti, fugiuntque nubes,
> Et minax (quod sic voluere) ponto
>   Unda recumbit."

The very same year the County Palatine of Chester received the same relief from its oppressions and the same remedy to its disorders. Before this time Chester was little less distempered than Wales. The inhabitants, without rights themselves, were the fittest to destroy the rights of others; and from thence Richard the Second drew the standing army of archers with which for a time he oppressed England. The people of Chester applied to Parliament in a petition penned as I shall read to you:

"To the King, our Sovereign Lord, in most humble wise shewen unto your excellent Majesty the inhabitants of your Grace's County Palatine of Chester: (1) That where the said County Palatine of Chester is and hath been always hitherto exempt, excluded, and separated out and from your High Court of Parliament, to have any Knights and Burgesses within the said Court; by reason whereof the said inhabitants have hitherto sustained manifold disherisons, losses, and damages, as well in their lands, goods, and bodies, as in the good, civil, and politic governance and maintenance of the commonwealth of their said county; (2) And forasmuch as the said inhabitants have always hitherto been bound by the Acts and Statutes made and ordained by your said Highness and your most noble progenitors, by authority of the said Court, as far forth as other counties, cities, and boroughs have been, that have had their Knights and Burgesses within your said Court of Parliament, and yet have had neither Knight ne Burgess there for the said County Palatine; the said inhabitants, for lack thereof, have been oftentimes touched and grieved with Acts and Statutes made within the said Court, as well derogatory unto the most ancient jurisdictions, liberties, and privileges of your said County Palatine, as prejudicial unto the commonwealth, quietness, rest, and peace of your Grace's most bounden subjects inhabiting within the same."

What did Parliament with this audacious address? — Reject it as a libel? Treat it as an affront to Government? Spurn it as a derogation from the rights of legislature? Did they toss it over the table? Did they burn it by the hands of the common hangman? — They took the petition of grievance, all rugged as it was, without softening or temperament, unpurged of the original bitterness and indignation of complaint — they made it the very preamble to their Act of redress, and consecrated its principle to all ages in the sanctuary of legislation.

Here is my third example. It was attended with the success of the two former. Chester, civilized as well as Wales, has demonstrated that freedom, and not servitude, is the cure of anarchy; as religion, and not atheism, is the true remedy for superstition. Sir, this pattern of Chester was followed in the reign of Charles the Second with regard to the County Palatine of Durham, which is my fourth example. This county had long lain out of the pale of free legislation. So scrupulously was the example of Chester followed that the style of the preamble is nearly the same with that of the Chester Act; and, without affecting the abstract extent of the authority of Parliament, it recognizes the equity of not suffering any considerable district in which the British subjects may act as a body, to be taxed without their own voice in the grant.

Now if the doctrines of policy contained in these preambles, and the force of these examples in the Acts of Parliaments, avail anything, what can be said against applying them with regard to America? Are not the people of America as much Englishmen as the Welsh? The preamble of the Act of Henry the Eighth says the Welsh speak a language no way resembling that of his Majesty's English subjects. Are the Americans not as numerous? If we may trust the learned and accurate Judge Barrington's account of North Wales, and take that as a standard to measure the rest, there is no comparison. The people cannot amount to above 200,000; not a tenth part of the number in the Colonies. Is America in rebellion? Wales was hardly ever free from it. Have you attempted to govern America by penal statutes? You made fifteen for Wales. But your legislative authority is perfect with regard to America. Was it less perfect in Wales, Chester, and Durham? But America is virtually represented. What! does the electric force of virtual representation more easily pass over the Atlantic than pervade Wales, which lies in your neighborhood — or than Chester and Durham, surrounded by abundance of representation that is actual and palpable? But, Sir, your ancestors thought this sort of virtual representation, however ample, to be totally insufficient for the freedom of the inhabitants of territories that are so near, and comparatively so inconsiderable. How then can I think it sufficient for those which are infinitely greater, and infinitely more remote?

You will now, Sir, perhaps imagine that I am on the point of proposing to you a scheme for a representation of the Colonies in Parliament. Perhaps I might be inclined to entertain some such thought; but a great flood stops me in my course. *Opposuit natura.* — I cannot remove the eternal barriers of the creation. The thing, in that mode, I do not know to be possible. As I meddle with no theory, I do not absolutely assert the impracticability of such a representation; but I do not see my way to it, and those who have been more confident have not been more successful. However, the arm of public benevolence is not shortened, and there are often several means to the same end. What nature has disjoined in one way, wisdom may unite in another. When we cannot give the benefit as we would wish, let us not refuse it altogether. If we cannot give the principal, let us find a substitute. But how? Where? What substitute?

Fortunately I am not obliged, for the ways and means of this substitute, to tax my own unproductive invention. I am not even obliged to go to the rich treasury of the fertile framers of imaginary commonwealths — not to the Republic of Plato, not to the Utopia of More, not to the Oceana of Harrington. It is before me — it is at my feet,

> "And the rude swain
> Treads daily on it with his clouted shoon."

I only wish you to recognize, for the theory, the ancient constitutional policy of this kingdom with regard to representation, as that policy has been declared in Acts of Parliament; and as to the practice, to return to that mode which a uniform experience has marked out to you as best, and in which you walked with security, advantage, and honor, until the year 1763.

My Resolutions therefore mean to establish the equity and justice of a taxation of America by *grant*, and not by *imposition;* to mark the *legal competency* of the Colony Assemblies for the support of their government in peace, and for public aids in time of war; to acknowledge that this legal competency has had a *dutiful and beneficial exercise;* and that experience has shown the *benefit of their grants*, and the *futility of Parliamentary taxation* as a method of supply.

These solid truths compose six fundamental propositions. There are three more Resolutions corollary to these. If you admit the first set, you can hardly reject the others. But if you admit the first, I shall be far from solicitous whether you accept or refuse the last. I think these six massive pillars will be of strength sufficient to support the temple of British concord. I have no more doubt than I entertain of my existence that, if you admitted these, you would command an immediate peace, and, with but tolerable future management, a lasting obedience in America. I am not arrogant in this confident assurance. The propositions are all mere matters of fact, and if they are such facts as draw irresistible conclusions even in the stating, this is the power of truth, and not any management of mine.

Sir, I shall open the whole plan to you, together with such observations on the motions as may tend to illustrate them where they may want explanation. The first is a Resolution —

> "That the Colonies and Plantations of Great Britain in North America, consisting of fourteen separate Governments, and containing two millions and upwards of free inhabitants, have not had the liberty and privilege of electing and sending any Knights and Burgesses, or others, to represent them in the High Court of Parliament."

This is a plain matter of fact, necessary to be laid down, and, excepting the description, it is laid down in the language of the Constitution; it is taken nearly *verbatim* from acts of Parliament.

The second is like unto the first —

> "That the said Colonies and Plantations have been liable to, and bounden by, several subsidies, payments, rates, and taxes given and granted by Parliament, though the said Colonies and Plantations have not their Knights and Burgesses in the said High Court of Parliament, of their own election, to represent the condition of their country; by lack whereof they have been oftentimes touched and grieved by subsidies given, granted, and assented to, in the said Court, in a manner prejudicial to the commonwealth, quietness, rest, and peace of the subjects inhabiting within the same."

Is this description too hot, or too cold; too strong, or too weak? Does it arrogate too much to the supreme legislature? Does it lean too much to the claims of the people? If it runs into any of these errors, the fault is not mine. It is the language of your own ancient Acts of Parliament.

> "Non meus hic sermo, sed quæ præcepit Ofellus,
> Rusticus, abnormis sapiens."

It is the genuine produce of the ancient, rustic, manly, homebred sense of this country. — I did not dare to rub off a particle of the venerable rust that rather adorns and preserves, than destroys, the metal. It would be a profanation to touch with a tool the stones which constuct the sacred altar of peace. I would not violate with modern polish the ingenuous and noble roughness of these truly Constitutional materials. Above all things, I was resolved not to be guilty of tampering, the odious vice of restless and unstable minds. I put my foot in the tracks of our forefathers, where I can neither wander nor stumble. Determining to fix articles of peace, I was resolved not to be wise beyond what was written; I was resolved to use nothing else than the form of sound words, to let others abound in their own sense, and carefully to abstain from all expressions of my own. What the law has said, I say. In all things else I am silent. I have no organ but for her words. This, if it be not ingenious, I am sure is safe.

There are indeed words expressive of grievance in this second Resolution, which those who are resolved always to be in the right will deny to contain matter of fact, as applied to the present case, although Parliament thought them true with regard to the counties of Chester and Durham. They will deny that the Americans were ever "touched and grieved" with the taxes. If they consider nothing in taxes but their weight as pecuniary impositions, there might be some pretence for this denial; but men may be sorely touched and deeply grieved in their privileges, as well as in their purses. Men may lose little in property by the act which takes away all their freedom. When a man is robbed of a trifle on the highway, it is not the two-pence lost that constitutes the capital outrage. This is not confined to privileges. Even ancient indulgences, withdrawn without offence on the part of those who enjoyed such favors, operate as grievances. But were the Americans then not touched and grieved by the taxes, in some measure, merely as taxes? If so, why were they almost all either wholly repealed, or exceedingly reduced? Were they not touched and grieved even by the regulating duties of the sixth of George the Second? Else, why were the duties first reduced to one third in 1764, and afterwards to a third of that third in the year 1766? Were they not touched and grieved by the Stamp Act? I shall say they were, until that tax is revived. Were they not touched and grieved by the duties of 1767, which were likewise repealed, and which Lord Hillsborough tells you, for the Ministry, were laid contrary to the true principle of commerce? Is not the assurance given by that noble person to the Colonies of a resolution to lay no more taxes on them an admission that taxes would touch and grieve them? Is not the Resolution of the noble lord in the blue ribbon, now standing on your Journals, the strongest of all proofs that Parliamentary subsidies really touched and grieved them? Else why all these changes, modifications, repeals, assurances, and resolutions?

The next proposition is —

"That, from the distance of the said Colonies, and from other circumstances, no method hath hitherto been devised for procuring a representation in Parliament for the said Colonies."

This is an assertion of a fact. I go no further on the paper, though, in my private judgment, a useful representation is impossible — I am sure it is not desired by them, nor ought it perhaps by us — but I abstain from opinions.

The fourth Resolution is —

"That each of the said Colonies hath within itself a body, chosen in part, or in the whole, by the freemen, freeholders, or other free inhabitants thereof, commonly called the General Assembly, or General Court, with powers legally to raise, levy, and assess, according to the several usage of such Colonies, duties and taxes towards defraying all sorts of public services."

This competence in the Colony Assemblies is certain. It is proved by the whole tenor of their Acts of Supply in all the Assemblies, in which the constant style of granting is, "an aid to his Majesty;" and Acts granting to the Crown have regularly for near a century passed the public offices without dispute. Those who have been pleased paradoxically to deny this right, holding that none but the British Parliament can grant to the Crown, are wished to look to what is done, not only in the Colonies, but in Ireland, in one uniform unbroken tenor every session. Sir, I am surprised that this doctrine should come from some of the law servants of the Crown. I say that if the Crown could be responsible, His Majesty — but certainly the Ministers, — and even these law officers themselves through whose hands the Acts passed, biennially in Ireland, or annually in the Colonies — are in an habitual course of committing impeachable offences. What habitual offenders have been all Presidents of the Council, all Secretaries of State, all First Lords of Trade, all Attorneys and all Solicitors-General! However, they are safe, as no one impeaches them; and there is no ground of charge against them except in their own unfounded theories.

The fifth resolution is also a resolution of fact —

"That the said General Assemblies, General Courts, or other bodies legally qualified as aforesaid, have at sundry times freely granted several large subsidies and public aids for his Majesty's service, according to their abilities, when required thereto by letter from one of his Majesty's principal Secretaries of State; and that their right to grant the same, and their cheerfulness and sufficiency in the said grants, have been at sundry times acknowledged by Parliament."

To say nothing of their great expenses in the Indian wars, and not to take their exertion in foreign ones so high as the supplies in the year 1695 — not to go back to their public contributions in the year 1710 — I shall begin to travel only where the journals give me light, resolving to deal in nothing but fact, authenticated by Parliamentary record, and to build myself wholly on that solid basis.

On the 4th of April, 1748, a Committee of this House came to the following resolution:

> "Resolved: That it is the opinion of this Committee that it is just and reasonable that the several Provinces and Colonies of Massachusetts Bay, New Hampshire, Connecticut, and Rhode Island, be reimbursed the expenses they have been at in taking and securing to the Crown of Great Britain the Island of Cape Breton and its dependencies."

The expenses were immense for such Colonies. They were above £200,000 sterling; money first raised and advanced on their public credit.

On the 28th of January, 1756, a message from the King came to us, to this effect:

> "His Majesty, being sensible of the zeal and vigor with which his faithful subjects of certain Colonies in North America have exerted themselves in defence of his Majesty's just rights and possessions, recommends it to this House to take the same into their consideration, and to enable his Majesty to give them such assistance as may be a proper reward and encouragement."

On the 3d of February, 1756, the House came to a suitable Resolution, expressed in words nearly the same as those of the message, but with the further addition, that the money then voted was as an encouragement to the Colonies to exert themselves with vigor. It will not be necessary to go through all the testimonies which your own records have given to the truth of my Resolutions. I will only refer you to the places in the Journals:

Vol. xxvii. — 16th and 19th May, 1757.
Vol. xxviii. — June 1st, 1758; April 26th and 30th, 1759; March 26th and 31st, and April 28th, 1760; Jan. 9th and 20th, 1761.
Vol. xxix. — Jan. 22d and 26th, 1762; March 14th and 17th, 1763.

Sir, here is the repeated acknowledgment of Parliament that the Colonies not only gave, but gave to satiety. This nation has formally acknowledged two things: first, that the Colonies had gone beyond their abilities, Parliament having thought it necessary to reimburse them; secondly, that they had acted legally and laudably in their grants of money, and their maintenance of troops, since the compensation is expressly given as reward and encouragement. Reward is not bestowed for acts that are unlawful; and encouragement is not held out to things that deserve reprehension. My Resolution therefore does nothing more than collect into one proposition what is scattered through your Journals. I give you nothing but your own; and you cannot refuse in the gross what you have so often acknowledged in detail. The admission of this, which will be so honorable to them and to you, will, indeed, be mortal to all the miserable stories by which the passions of the misguided people have been engaged in an unhappy system. The people heard, indeed, from the beginning of these disputes, one thing continually dinned in their ears, that reason and justice demanded that the Americans, who paid no taxes, should be compelled to contribute. How did that fact of their paying nothing stand when the taxing system began? When Mr. Grenville began to form his system of American revenue, he stated in this

House that the Colonies were then in debt two millions six hundred thousand pounds sterling money, and was of opinion they would discharge that debt in four years. On this state, those untaxed people were actually subject to the payment of taxes to the amount of six hundred and fifty thousand a year. In fact, however, Mr. Grenville was mistaken. The funds given for sinking the debt did not prove quite so ample as both the Colonies and he expected. The calculation was too sanguine; the reduction was not completed till some years after, and at different times in different Colonies. However, the taxes after the war continued too great to bear any addition, with prudence or propriety; and when the burthens imposed in consequence of former requisitions were discharged, our tone became too high to resort again to requisition. No Colony, since that time, ever has had any requisition whatsoever made to it.

We see the sense of the Crown, and the sense of Parliament, on the productive nature of a *revenue by grant.* Now search the same Journals for the produce of the *revenue by imposition.* Where is it? Let us know the volume and the page. What is the gross, what is the net produce? To what service is it applied? How have you appropriated its surplus? What! Can none of the many skilful index-makers that we are now employing find any trace of it? — Well, let them and that rest together. But are the Journals, which say nothing of the revenue, as silent on the discontent? Oh no! a child may find it. It is the melancholy burthen and blot of every page.

I think, then, I am, from those Journals, justified in the sixth and last Resolution, which is —

"That it hath been found by experience that the manner of granting the said supplies and aids, by the said General Assemblies, hath been more agreeable to the said Colonies, and more beneficial and conducive to the public service, than the mode of giving and granting aids in Parliament, to be raised and paid in the said Colonies."

This makes the whole of the fundamental part of the plan. The conclusion is irresistible. You cannot say that you were driven by any necessity to an exercise of the utmost rights of legislature. You cannot assert that you took on yourselves the task of imposing Colony taxes from the want of another legal body that is competent to the purpose of supplying the exigencies of the state without wounding the prejudices of the people. Neither is it true that the body so qualified, and having that competence, had neglected the duty.

The question now, on all this accumulated matter, is: whether you will choose to abide by a profitable experience, or a mischievous theory; whether you choose to build on imagination, or fact; whether you prefer enjoyment, or hope; satisfaction in your subjects, or discontent?

If these propositions are accepted, everything which has been made to enforce a contrary system must, I take it for granted, fall along with it. On that ground, I have drawn the following Resolution, which, when it comes to be moved, will naturally be divided in a proper manner:

"That it may be proper to repeal an Act made in the seventh year of the reign of his present Majesty, entitled, An Act for granting certain duties in the British Colonies and Plantations in America; for allowing a drawback of the duties of customs upon the exportation from this Kingdom of coffee and cocoa-nuts of the produce of the said Colonies or Plantations; for discontinuing the drawbacks payable on china earthenware exported to America; and for more effectually preventing the clandestine running of goods in the said Colonies and Plantations. And that it may be proper to repeal an Act made in the fourteenth year of the reign of his present Majesty, entitled, An Act to discontinue, in such manner and for such time as are therein mentioned, the landing and discharging, lading or shipping of goods, wares, and merchandise at the town and within the harbor of Boston, in the Province of Massachusetts Bay, in North America. And that it may be proper to repeal an Act made in the fourteenth year of the reign of his present Majesty, intitled, An Act for the impartial administration of justice in the cases of persons questioned for any acts done by them in the execution of the law, or for the suppression of riots and tumults, in the Province of Massachusetts Bay, in New England. And that it may be proper to repeal an Act made in the fourteenth year of the reign of his present Majesty, intitled, An Act for the better regulating of the Government of the Province of the Massachusetts Bay, in New England. And also that it may be proper to explain and amend an Act made in the thirty-fifth year of the reign of King Henry the Eighth, intitled, An Act for the Trial of Treasons committed out of the King's Dominions."

I wish, Sir, to repeal the Boston Port Bill, because — independently of the dangerous precedent of suspending the rights of the subject during the King's pleasure — it was passed, as I apprehend, with less regularity and on more partial principles than it ought. The corporation of Boston was not heard before it was condemned. Other towns, full as guilty as she was, have not had their ports blocked up. Even the Restraining Bill of the present session does not go to the length of the Boston Port Act. The same ideas of prudence which induced you not to extend equal punishment to equal guilt, even when you were punishing, induced me, who mean not to chastise, but to reconcile, to be satisfied with the punishment already partially inflicted.

Ideas of prudence and accommodation to circumstances prevent you from taking away the charters of Connecticut and Rhode Island, as you have taken away that of Massachusetts Bay, though the Crown has far less power in the two former provinces than it enjoyed in the latter, and though the abuses have been full as great, and as flagrant, in the exempted as in the punished. The same reasons of prudence and accommodation have weight with me in restoring the Charter of Massachusetts Bay. Besides, Sir, the Act which changes the charter of Massachusetts is in many particulars so exceptionable that if I did not wish absolutely to repeal, I would by all means desire to alter it, as several of its provisions tend to the subversion of all public and private justice. Such, among others, is the power in the Governor to change the sheriff at his pleasure, and to make a new returning officer for every special cause. It is shameful to behold such a regulation standing among English laws.

The Act for bringing persons accused of committing murder, under the orders of Government to England for trial, is but temporary. That Act has calculated the probable duration of our quarrel with the Colonies, and is accommodated to that supposed duration. I would hasten the happy moment of reconciliation, and therefore must, on my principle, get rid of that most justly obnoxious Act.

The Act of Henry the Eighth, for the Trial of Treasons, I do not mean to take away, but to confine it to its proper bounds and original intention; to make it expressly for trial of treasons — and the greatest treasons may be committed — in places where the jurisdiction of the Crown does not extend.

Having guarded the privileges of local legislature, I would next secure to the Colonies a fair and unbiassed judicature, for which purpose, Sir, I propose the following Resolution:

"That, from the time when the General Assembly or General Court of any Colony or Plantation in North America shall have appointed by Act of Assembly, duly confirmed, a settled salary to the offices of the Chief Justice and other

Judges of the Superior Court, it may be proper that the said Chief Justice and other Judges of the Superior Courts of such Colony shall hold his and their office and offices during their good behavior, and shall not be removed therefrom but when the said removal shall be adjudged by his Majesty in Council, upon a hearing on complaint from the General Assembly, or on a complaint from the Governor, or Council, or the House of Representatives severally, or of the Colony in which the said Chief Justice and other Judges have exercised the said offices."

The next Resolution relates to the Courts of Admiralty. It is this:

"That it may be proper to regulate the Courts of Admiralty or Vice-Admiralty authorized by the fifteenth Chapter of the Fourth of George the Third, in such a manner as to make the same more commodious to those who sue, or are sued, in the said Courts, and to provide for the more decent maintenance of the Judges in the same."

These courts I do not wish to take away; they are in themselves proper establishments. This court is one of the capital securities of the Act of Navigation. The extent of its jurisdiction, indeed, has been increased, but this is altogether as proper, and is indeed on many accounts more eligible, where new powers were wanted, than a court absolutely new. But courts incommodiously situated, in effect, deny justice; and a court partaking in the fruits of its own condemnation is a robber. The Congress complain, and complain justly, of this grievance.

These are the three consequential propositions. I have thought of two or three more, but they come rather too near detail, and to the province of executive government, which I wish Parliament always to superintend, never to assume. If the first six are granted, congruity will carry the latter three. If not, the things that remain unrepealed will be, I hope, rather unseemly incumbrances on the building, than very materially detrimental to its strength and stability.

Here, Sir, I should close; but I plainly perceive some objections remain which I ought, if possible, to remove. The first will be that, in resorting to the doctrine of our ancestors, as contained in the preamble to the Chester Act, I prove too much; that the grievance from a want of representation, stated in that preamble, goes to the whole of legislation as well as to taxation; and that the Colonies, grounding themselves upon that doctrine, will apply it to all parts of legislative authority.

To this objection, with all possible deference and humility, and wishing as little as any man living to impair the smallest particle of our supreme authority, I answer, that the words are the words of Parliament, and not mine, and that all false and inconclusive inferences drawn from them are not mine, for I heartily disclaim any such inference. I have chosen the words of an Act of Parliament which Mr. Grenville, surely a tolerably zealous and very judicious advocate for the sovereignty of Parliament, formerly moved to have read at your table in confirmation of his tenets. It is true that Lord Chatham considered these preambles as declaring strongly in favor of his opinions. He was a no less powerful advocate for the privileges of the Americans. Ought I not from hence to presume that these preambles are as favorable as possible to both, when properly understood; favorable both to the rights of Parliament, and to the privilege of the dependencies of this Crown? But, Sir, the object of grievance in my Resolution I have not taken from the Chester, but from the Durham Act, which confines the hardship of want of representation to the case of subsidies, and which therefore falls in exactly with the case of the Colonies. But whether the unrepresented counties were *de jure* or *de facto* bound, the preambles do not accurately distinguish, nor indeed was it necessary; for, whether *de jure* or *de facto*, the Legislature thought the exercise of the power of taxing as of right, or as of fact without right, equally a grievance, and equally oppressive.

I do not know that the Colonies have, in any general way, or in any cool hour, gone much beyond the demand of humanity in relation to taxes. It is not fair to judge of the temper or dispositions of any man, or any set of men, when they are composed and at rest, from their conduct or their expressions in a state of disturbance and irritation. It is besides a very great mistake to imagine that mankind follow up practically any speculative principle, either of government or of freedom, as far as it will go in argument and logical illation. We Englishmen stop very short of the principles upon which we support any given part of our Constitution, or even the whole of it together. I could easily, if I had not already tired you, give you very striking and convincing instances of it. This is nothing but what is natural and proper. All government, indeed every human benefit and enjoyment, every virtue, and every prudent act, is founded on compromise and barter. We balance inconveniences; we give and take; we remit some rights, that we may enjoy others; and we choose rather to be happy citizens than subtle disputants. As we must give away some natural liberty to enjoy civil advantages, so we must sacrifice some civil liberties for the advantages to be derived from the communion and fellowship of a great empire. But, in all fair dealings, the thing bought must bear some proportion to the purchase paid. None will barter away the immediate jewel of his soul. Though a great house is apt to make slaves haughty, yet it is purchasing a part of the artificial importance of a great empire too dear to pay for it all essential rights and all the intrinsic dignity of human nature. None of us who would not risk his life rather than fall under a government purely arbitrary. But although there are some amongst us who think our Constitution wants many improvements to make it a complete system of liberty, perhaps none who are of that opinion would think it right to aim at such improvement by disturbing his country, and risking everything that is dear to him. In every arduous enterprise we consider what we are to lose, as well as what we are to gain; and the more and better stake of liberty every people possess, the less they will hazard in a vain attempt to make it more. These are the cords of man. Man acts from adequate motives relative to his interest, and not on metaphysical speculations. Aristotle, the great master of reasoning, cautions us, and with great weight and propriety, against this species of delusive geometrical accuracy in moral arguments as the most fallacious of all sophistry.

The Americans will have no interest contrary to the grandeur and glory of England, when they are not oppressed by the weight of it; and they will rather be inclined to respect the acts of a superintending legislature when they see them the acts of that power which is itself the security, not the rival, of their secondary importance. In this assurance my mind most perfectly acquiesces, and I confess I feel not the least alarm from the discontents which are to arise from putting people at their ease, nor do I apprehend the destruction of this Empire from giving, by an act of free grace and indulgence, to two millions of my fellow-citizens some share of those rights upon which I have always been taught to value myself.

It is said, indeed, that this power of granting, vested in American Assemblies, would dissolve the unity of the

Empire, which was preserved entire, although Wales, and Chester, and Durham were added to it. Truly, Mr. Speaker, I do not know what this unity means, nor has it ever been heard of, that I know, in the constitutional policy of this country. The very idea of subordination of parts excludes this notion of simple and undivided unity. England is the head; but she is not the head and the members too. Ireland has ever had from the beginning a separate, but not an independent, legislature, which, far from distracting, promoted the union of the whole. Everything was sweetly and harmoniously disposed through both islands for the conservation of English dominion, and the communication of English liberties. I do not see that the same principles might not be carried into twenty islands and with the same good effect. This is my model with regard to America, as far as the internal circumstances of the two countries are the same. I know no other unity of this Empire than I can draw from its example during these periods, when it seemed to my poor understanding more united than it is now, or than it is likely to be by the present methods.

But since I speak of these methods, I recollect, Mr. Speaker, almost too late, that I promised, before I finished, to say something of the proposition of the noble lord on the floor, which has been so lately received and stands on your Journals. I must be deeply concerned whenever it is my misfortune to continue a difference with the majority of this House; but as the reasons for that difference are my apology for thus troubling you, suffer me to state them in a very few words. I shall compress them into as small a body as I possibly can, having already debated that matter at large when the question was before the Committee.

First, then, I cannot admit that proposition of a ransom by auction; because it is a mere project. It is a thing new, unheard of; supported by no experience; justified by no analogy; without example of our ancestors, or root in the Constitution. It is neither regular Parliamentary taxation, nor Colony grant. *Experimentum in corpore vili* is a good rule, which will ever make me adverse to any trial of experiments on what is certainly the most valuable of all subjects, the peace of this Empire.

Secondly, it is an experiment which must be fatal in the end to our Constitution. For what is it but a scheme for taxing the Colonies in the ante-chamber of the noble lord and his successors? To settle the quotas and proportions in this House is clearly impossible. You, Sir, may flatter yourself you shall sit a state auctioneer, with your hammer in your hand, and knock down to each Colony as it bids. But to settle, on the plan laid down by the noble lord, the true proportional payment for four or five and twenty governments according to the absolute and the relative wealth of each, and according to the British proportion of wealth and burthen, is a wild and chimerical notion. This new taxation must therefore come in by the back door of the Constitution. Each quota must be brought to this House ready formed; you can neither add nor alter. You must register it. You can do nothing further; for on what grounds can you deliberate either before or after the proposition? You cannot hear the counsel for all these provinces, quarrelling each on its own quantity of payment, and its proportion to others. If you should attempt it, the Committee of Provincial Ways and Means, or by whatever other name it will delight to be called, must swallow up all the time of Parliament.

Thirdly, it does not give satisfaction to the complaint of the Colonies. They complain that they are taxed without their consent; you answer, that you will fix the sum at which they shall be taxed. That is, you give them the very grievance for the remedy. You tell them, indeed, that you will leave the mode to themselves. I really beg pardon — it gives me pain to mention it — but you must be sensible that you will not perform this part of the compact. For, suppose the Colonies were to lay the duties, which furnished their contingent, upon the importation of your manufactures, you know you would never suffer such a tax to be laid. You know, too, that you would not suffer many other modes of taxation; so that, when you come to explain yourself, it will be found that you will neither leave to themselves the quantum nor the mode, nor indeed anything. The whole is delusion from one end to the other.

Fourthly, this method of ransom by auction, unless it be universally accepted, will plunge you into great and inextricable difficulties. In what year of our Lord are the proportions of payments to be settled? To say nothing of the impossibility that Colony agents should have general powers of taxing the Colonies at their discretion, consider, I implore you, that the communication by special messages and orders between these agents and their constituents, on each variation of the case, when the parties come to contend together and to dispute on their relative proportions, will be a matter of delay, perplexity, and confusion that never can have an end.

If all the Colonies do not appear at the outcry, what is the condition of those assemblies who offer, by themselves or their agents, to tax themselves up to your ideas of their proportion? The refractory Colonies who refuse all composition will remain taxed only to your old impositions, which, however grievous in principle, are trifling as to production. The obedient Colonies in this scheme are heavily taxed; the refractory remain unburdened. What will you do? Will you lay new and heavier taxes by Parliament on the disobedient? Pray consider in what way you can do it. You are perfectly convinced that, in the way of taxing, you can do nothing but at the ports. Now suppose it is Virginia that refuses to appear at your auction, while Maryland and North Carolina bid handsomely for their ransom, and are taxed to your quota, how will you put these Colonies on a par? Will you tax the tobacco of Virginia? If you do, you give its death-wound to your English revenue at home, and to one of the very greatest articles of your own foreign trade. If you tax the import of that rebellious Colony, what do you tax but your own manufactures, or the goods of some other obedient and already well-taxed Colony? Who has said one word on this labyrinth of detail, which bewilders you more and more as you enter into it? Who has presented, who can present you with a clue to lead you out of it? I think, Sir, it is impossible that you should not recollect that the Colony bounds are so implicated in one another — you know it by your other experiments in the bill for prohibiting the New England fishery,—that you can lay no possible restraints on almost any of them which may not be presently eluded, if you do not confound the innocent with the guilty, and burthen those whom, upon every principle, you ought to exonerate. He must be grossly ignorant of America who thinks that, without falling into this confusion of all rules of equity and policy, you can restrain any single Colony, especially Virginia and Maryland, the central and most important of them all.

Let it also be considered that, either in the present confusion you settle a permanent contingent, which will and must be trifling, and then you have no effectual revenue; or you change the quota at every exigency, and then on every new repartition you will have a new quarrel.

Reflect, besides, that when you have fixed a quota for every Colony, you have not provided for prompt and punctual payment. Suppose one, two, five, ten years' arrears. You cannot issue a Treasury Extent against the failing Colony. You must make new Boston Port Bills, new restraining laws, new acts for dragging men to England for trial. You must send out new fleets, new armies. All is to begin again. From this day forward the Empire is never to know an hour's tranquillity. An intestine fire will be kept alive in the bowels of the Colonies, which one time or other must consume this whole Empire. I allow indeed that the empire of Germany raises her revenue and her troops by quotas and contingents; but the revenue of the empire, and the army of the empire, is the worst revenue and the worst army in the world.

Instead of a standing revenue, you will therefore have a perpetual quarrel. Indeed, the noble lord who proposed this project of a ransom by auction seems himself to be of that opinion. His project was rather designed for breaking the union of the Colonies than for establishing a revenue. He confessed he apprehended that his proposal would not be to their taste. I say this scheme of disunion seems to be at the bottom of the project; for I will not suspect that the noble lord meant nothing but merely to delude the nation by an airy phantom which he never intended to realize. But whatever his views may be, as I propose the peace and union of the Colonies as the very foundation of my plan, it cannot accord with one whose foundation is perpetual discord.

Compare the two. This I offer to give you is plain and simple. The other full of perplexed and intricate mazes. This is mild; that harsh. This is found by experience effectual for its purposes; the other is a new project. This is universal; the other calculated for certain Colonies only. This is immediate in its conciliatory operation; the other remote, contingent, full of hazard. Mine is what becomes the dignity of a ruling people — gratuitous, unconditional, and not held out as a matter of bargain and sale. I have done my duty in proposing it to you. I have indeed tired you by a long discourse; but this is the misfortune of those to whose influence nothing will be conceded, and who must win every inch of their ground by argument. You have heard me with goodness. May you decide with wisdom! For my part, I feel my mind greatly disburthened by what I have done to-day. I have been the less fearful of trying your patience, because on this subject I mean to spare it altogether in future. I have this comfort, that in every stage of the American affairs I have steadily opposed the measures that have produced the confusion, and may bring on the destruction, of this Empire. I now go so far as to risk a proposal of my own. If I cannot give peace to my country, I give it to my conscience.

But what, says the financier, is peace to us without money? Your plan gives us no revenue. No! But it does; for it secures to the subject the power of refusal, the first of all revenues. Experience is a cheat, and fact a liar, if this power in the subject of proportioning his grant, or of not granting at all, has not been found the richest mine of revenue ever discovered by the skill or by the fortune of man. It does not indeed vote you 152,750*l.* 11*s.* 2$\frac{3}{4}$*d.*, nor any other paltry limited sum; but it gives the strong box itself, the fund, the bank — from whence only revenues can arise amongst a people sensible of freedom. *Posita luditur arca.* Cannot you, in England — cannot you, at this time of day — cannot you, a House of Commons, trust to the principle which has raised so mighty a revenue, and accumulated a debt of near 140,000,000 in this country? Is this principle to be true in England, and false everywhere else? Is it not true in Ireland? Has it not hitherto been true in the Colonies? Why should you presume that, in any country, a body duly constituted for any function will neglect to perform its duty and abdicate its trust? Such a presumption would go against all governments in all modes. But, in truth, this dread of penury of supply from a free assembly has no foundation in nature; for first, observe that, besides the desire which all men have naturally of supporting the honor of their own government, that sense of dignity and that security to property which ever attends freedom has a tendency to increase the stock of the free community. Most may be taken where most is accumulated. And what is the soil or climate where experience has not uniformly proved that the voluntary flow of heaped-up plenty, bursting from the weight of its own rich luxuriance, has ever run with a more copious stream of revenue than could be squeezed from the dry husks of oppressed indigence by the straining of all the politic machinery in the world?

Next, we know that parties must ever exist in a free country. We know, too, that the emulations of such parties — their contradictions, their reciprocal necessities, their hopes, and their fears — must send them all in their turns to him that holds the balance of the State. The parties are the gamesters; but Government keeps the table, and is sure to be the winner in the end. When this game is played, I really think it is more to be feared that the people will be exhausted, than that government will not be supplied; whereas, whatever is got by acts of absolute power ill obeyed, because odious, or by contracts ill kept, because constrained, will be narrow, feeble, uncertain, and precarious.

> "Ease would retract
> Vows made in pain, as violent and void."

I, for one, protest against compounding our demands. I declare against compounding, for a poor limited sum, the immense, ever-growing, eternal debt which is due to generous government from protected freedom. And so may I speed in the great object I propose to you, as I think it would not only be an act of injustice, but would be the worst economy in the world, to compel the Colonies to a sum certain, either in the way of ransom or in the way of compulsory compact.

But to clear up my ideas on this subject: a revenue from America transmitted hither — do not delude yourselves — you never can receive it; no, not a shilling. We have experience that from remote countries it is not to be expected. If, when you attempted to extract revenue from Bengal, you were obliged to return in loan what you had taken in imposition, what can you expect from North America? For certainly, if ever there was a country qualified to produce wealth, it is India; or an institution fit for the transmission, it is the East India Company. America has none of these aptitudes. If America gives you taxable objects on which you lay your duties here, and gives you, at the same time, a surplus by a foreign sale of her commodities to pay the duties on these objects which you tax at home, she has performed her part to the British revenue. But with regard to her own internal establishments, she may, I doubt not she will, contribute in moderation. I say in moderation, for she ought not to be permitted to exhaust herself. She ought to be reserved to a war, the weight of which, with the enemies that we are most likely to have, must be considerable in her quarter of the globe. There she may serve you, and serve you essentially.

For that service — for all service, whether of revenue, trade, or empire — my trust is in her interest in the British Constitution. My hold of the Colonies is in the close affection which grows from common names, from kindred blood, from similar privileges, and equal protection. These are ties which, though light as air, are as strong as links of iron. Let the Colonists always keep the idea of their civil rights associated with your government, — they will cling and grapple to you, and no force under heaven will be of power to tear them from their allegiance. But let it be once understood that your government may be one thing, and their privileges another, that these two things may exist without any mutual relation, the cement is gone — the cohesion is loosened — and everything hastens to decay and dissolution. As long as you have the wisdom to keep the sovereign authority of this country as the sanctuary of liberty, the sacred temple consecrated to our common faith, wherever the chosen race and sons of England worship freedom, they will turn their faces towards you. The more they multiply, the more friends you will have; the more ardently they love liberty, the more perfect will be their obedience. Slavery they can have anywhere — it is a weed that grows in every soil. They may have it from Spain; they may have it from Prussia. But, until you become lost to all feeling of your true interest and your natural dignity, freedom they can have from none but you. This is the commodity of price of which you have the monopoly. This is the true Act of Navigation which binds to you the commerce of the Colonies, and through them secures to you the wealth of the world. Deny them this participation of freedom, and you break that sole bond which originally made, and must still preserve, the unity of the Empire. Do not entertain so weak an imagination as that your registers and your bonds, your affidavits and your sufferances, your cockets and your clearances, are what form the great securities of your commerce. Do not dream that your letters of office, and your instructions, and your suspending clauses, are the things that hold together the great contexture of the mysterious whole. These things do not make your government. Dead instruments, passive tools as they are, it is the spirit of the English communion that gives all their life and efficacy to them. It is the spirit of the English Constitution which, infused through the mighty mass, pervades, feeds, unites, invigorates, vivifies every part of the Empire, even down to the minutest member.

Is it not the same virtue which does everything for us here in England? Do you imagine, then, that it is the Land Tax Act which raises your revenue? that it is the annual vote in the Committee of Supply which gives you your army? or that it is the Mutiny Bill which inspires it with bravery and discipline? No! surely no! It is the love of the people; it is their attachment to their government, from the sense of the deep stake they have in such a glorious institution, which gives you your army and your navy, and infuses into both that liberal obedience without which your army would be a base rabble, and your navy nothing but rotten timber.

All this, I know well enough, will sound wild and chimerical to the profane herd of those vulgar and mechanical politicians who have no place among us; a sort of people who think that nothing exists but what is gross and material, and who, therefore, far from being qualified to be directors of the great movement of empire, are not fit to turn a wheel in the machine. But to men truly initiated and rightly taught, these ruling and master principles which, in the opinion of such men as I have mentioned, have no substantial existence, are in truth everything, and all in all. Magnanimity in politics is not seldom the truest wisdom; and a great empire and little minds go ill together. If we are conscious of our station, and glow with zeal to fill our places as becomes our situation and ourselves, we ought to auspicate all our public proceedings on America with the old warning of the church, *Sursum corda!* We ought to elevate our minds to the greatness of that trust to which the order of providence has called us. By adverting to the dignity of this high calling our ancestors have turned a savage wilderness into a glorious empire, and have made the most extensive and the only honorable conquests — not by destroying, but by promoting the wealth, the number, the happiness, of the human race. Let us get an American revenue as we have got an American empire. English privileges have made it all that it is; English privileges alone will make it all it can be.

In full confidence of this unalterable truth, I now, *quod felix faustumque sit*, lay the first stone of the Temple of Peace; and I move you —

> "That the Colonies and Plantations of Great Britain in North America, consisting of fourteen separate governments, and containing two millions and upwards of free inhabitants, have not had the liberty and privilege of electing and sending any Knights and Burgesses, or others, to represent them in the High Court of Parliament."

LORD CHATHAM.

ON AN ADDRESS TO THE THRONE CONCERNING AFFAIRS IN AMERICA. HOUSE OF LORDS, NOVEMBER 18, 1777.

I RISE, my Lords, to declare my sentiments on this most solemn and serious subject. It has imposed a load upon my mind which I fear nothing can remove, but which impels me to endeavor its alleviation by a free and unreserved communication of my sentiments.

In the first part of the Address I have the honor of heartily concurring with the noble Earl who moved it. No man feels sincerer joy than I do — none can offer more genuine congratulations — on every accession of strength to the Protestant succession. I therefore join in every congratulation on the birth of another Princess, and the happy recovery of her Majesty.

But I must stop here. My courtly complaisance will carry me no farther. I will not join in congratulation on misfortune and disgrace. I cannot concur in a blind and servile Address which approves, and endeavors to sanctify, the monstrous measures which have heaped disgrace and misfortune upon us. This, my Lords, is a perilous and tremendous moment! It is not a time for adulation. The smoothness of flattery cannot now avail — cannot save us in this rugged and awful crisis. It is now necessary to instruct the Throne in the language of truth. We must dispel the illusion and the darkness which envelop it, and display, in its full danger and true colors, the ruin that is brought to our doors.

This, my Lords, is our duty. It is the proper function of this noble assembly, sitting, as we do, upon our honors in this House, the hereditary council of the Crown. *Who* is the Minister — *where* is the Minister, that has dared to suggest to the Throne the contrary, unconstitutional language this day delivered from it? The accustomed language from the Throne has been application to Parliament for advice, and a reliance on its constitutional advice and assistance. As it is the right of Parliament to give, so it is the duty of the Crown to ask it. But on this day, and in this extreme momentous exigency, no reliance is reposed on our constitutional counsels! no advice is asked from the sober and enlightened care of Parliament! but the Crown, from itself and by itself, declares an unalterable determination to pursue measures — and what measures, my Lords? The measures that have produced the imminent perils that threaten us; the measures that have brought ruin to our doors.

Can the Minister of the day now presume to expect a continuance of support in this ruinous infatuation? Can Parliament be so dead to its dignity and its duty as to be thus deluded into the loss of the one and the violation of the other? To give an unlimited credit and support for the steady perseverance in measures not proposed for our parliamentary advice, but dictated and forced upon us — in measures, I say, my Lords, which have reduced this late flourishing empire to ruin and contempt? "But yesterday, and England might have stood against the world: now none so poor to do her reverence." I use the words of a poet; but though it be poetry, it is no fiction. It is a shameful truth that not only the power and strength of this country are wasting away and expiring, but her well-earned glories, her true honor and substantial dignity, are sacrificed.

France, my Lords, has insulted you; she has encouraged and sustained America; and, whether America be wrong or right, the dignity of this country ought to spurn at the officious insult of French interference. The ministers and embassadors of those who are called rebels and enemies are in Paris; in Paris they transact the reciprocal interests of America and France. Can there be a more mortifying insult? Can even our Ministers sustain a more humiliating disgrace? Do they dare to resent it? Do they presume even to hint a vindication of their honor and the dignity of the state, by requiring the dismission of the plenipotentiaries of America? Such is the degradation to which they have reduced the glories of England! The people whom they affect to call contemptible rebels, but whose growing power has at last obtained the name of enemies; the people with whom they have engaged this country in war, and against whom they now command our implicit support in every measure of desperate hostility — this people, despised as rebels, or acknowledged as enemies, are abetted against you, supplied with every military store, their interests consulted, and their embassadors entertained, by your inveterate enemy! and our Ministers dare not interpose with dignity or effect. Is this the honor of a great kingdom? Is this the indignant spirit of England, who "but yesterday" gave law to the house of Bourbon? My Lords, the dignity of nations demands a decisive conduct in a situation like this. Even when the greatest prince that perhaps this country ever saw filled our throne, the requisition of a Spanish general, on a similar subject, was attended to, and complied with; for, on the spirited remonstrance of the Duke of Alva, Elizabeth found herself obliged to deny the Flemish exiles all countenance, support, or even entrance into her dominions, and the Count Le Marque, with his few desperate followers, were expelled the kingdom. Happening to arrive at the Brille, and finding it weak in defence, they made themselves masters of the place; and this was the foundation of the United Provinces.

My Lords, this ruinous and ignominious situation, where we cannot act with success, nor suffer with honor, calls upon us to remonstrate in the strongest and loudest language of truth, to rescue the ear of Majesty from the delusions which surround it. The desperate state of our arms abroad is in part known. No man thinks more highly of them than I do. I love and honor the English troops. I know their virtues and their valor. I know they can achieve anything except impossibilities; and I know that the conquest of English America is an impossibility. You cannot, I venture to say it, you cannot conquer America. Your armies last war effected everything that could be effected; and what was it? It cost a numerous army, under the command of a most able general, now a noble lord in this House, a long and laborious campaign to expel five thousand Frenchmen from French America. My Lords, *you cannot conquer America.*

What is your present situation there? We do not know the worst; but we know that in three campaigns we have done nothing and suffered much. Besides the sufferings, perhaps total loss, of the northern force, the best appointed army that ever took the field, commanded by Sir William Howe, has retired from the American lines. He was obliged to relinquish his attempt, and with great delay and danger to adopt a new and distant plan of operations. We shall soon know, and in any event have reason to lament, what may have happened since. As to conquest, therefore, my Lords, I repeat, it is impossible. You may swell every expense and every effort still more extravagantly; pile and accumulate every assistance you can buy or borrow; traffic and barter with every little pitiful German prince that sells and sends his subjects to the shambles of a foreign prince; your efforts are forever vain and impotent — doubly so from this mercenary aid on which you rely; for it irritates to an incurable resentment the minds of your enemies to overrun them with the mercenary sons of rapine and plunder, devoting them and their possessions to the rapacity of hireling cruelty! If I were an American, as I am an Englishman, while a foreign troop was landed in my country, I never would lay down my arms — never — never — never.

Your own army is infected with the contagion of these illiberal allies. The spirit of plunder and of rapine is gone forth among them. I know it; and, notwithstanding what the noble Earl who moved the Address has given as his opinion of the American army, I know from authentic information and the most experienced officers, that our discipline is deeply wounded. While this is notoriously our sinking situation, America grows and flourishes; while our strength and discipline are lowered, hers are rising and improving.

But, my Lords, who is the man that, in addition to these disgraces and mischiefs of our army, has dared to authorize and associate to our arms the tomahawk and scalping-knife of the savage? to call into civilized alliance the wild and inhuman savage of the woods; to delegate to the merciless Indian the defence of disputed rights, and to wage the horrors of his barbarous war against our brethren? My Lords, these enormities cry aloud for redress and punishment. Unless thoroughly done away, it will be a stain on the national character. It is a violation of the Constitution. I believe it is against law. It is not the least of our national misfortunes that the strength and character of our army are thus impaired. Infected with the mercenary spirit of robbery and rapine, familiarized to the horrid scenes of savage cruelty, it can no longer boast of the noble and generous principles which dignify a soldier; no longer sympathize with the dignity of the royal banner, nor feel the pride, pomp, and circumstance of glorious war, "that make ambition virtue!" What makes ambition virtue? — the sense of honor. But is the sense of honor consistent with a spirit of plunder or the practice of murder? Can it flow from mercenary motives, or can it prompt to cruel deeds? Besides these murderers and plunderers, let me ask our Ministers, what other allies have they acquired? What other powers have they associated to their cause? Have they entered into alliance with the king of the gipsies? Nothing, my Lords, is too low or too ludicrous to be consistent with their counsels.

The independent views of America have been stated and asserted as the foundation of this Address. My Lords, no man wishes for the due dependence of America on this country more than I do. To preserve it, and not confirm that state of independence into which your measures hitherto have driven them, is the object which we ought to unite in attaining. The Americans, contending for their rights against arbitrary exactions, I love and admire. It is the struggle of free and virtuous patriots. But, contending for independency and total disconnection from England, as an Englishman, I cannot wish them success; for in a due constitutional dependency, including the ancient supremacy of this country in regulating their commerce and navigation, consists the mutual happiness and prosperity of both England and America. She derived assistance and protection from us, and we reaped from her the most important advantages. She was, indeed, the fountain of our wealth, the nerve of our strength, the nursery and basis of our naval power. It is our duty, therefore, my Lords, if we wish to save our country, most seriously to endeavor the recovery of these most beneficial subjects; and in this perilous crisis, perhaps the present moment may be the only one in which we can hope for success; for in their negotiations with France, they have, or think they have, reason to complain. Though it be notorious that they have received from that power important supplies and assistance of various kinds, yet it is certain they expected it in a more decisive and immediate degree. America is in ill-humor with France; on some points they have not entirely answered her expectations. Let us wisely take advantage of every possible moment of reconciliation. Besides, the natural disposition of America herself still leans toward England; to the old habits of connection and mutual interest that united both countries. This *was* the established sentiment of all the continent; and still, my Lords, in the great and principal part, the sound part of America, this wise and affectionate disposition prevails. And there is a very considerable part of America yet sound — the middle and the southern Provinces. Some parts may be factious and blind to their true interests; but if we express a wise and benevolent disposition to communicate with them those immutable rights of nature and those constitutional liberties to which they are equally entitled with ourselves, by a conduct so just and humane we shall confirm the favorable and conciliate the adverse. I say, my Lords, the rights and liberties to which they are equally entitled with ourselves, *but no more.* I would participate to them every enjoyment and freedom which the colonizing subjects of a free state can possess, or wish to possess; and I do not see why they should not enjoy every fundamental right in their property, and every original substantial liberty, which Devonshire, or Surrey, or the county I live in, or any other county in England, can claim; reserving always, as the sacred right of the Mother Country, the due constitutional dependency of the Colonies. The inherent supremacy of the state in regulating and protecting the navigation and commerce of all her subjects, is necessary for the mutual benefit and preservation of every part, to constitute and preserve the prosperous arrangement of the whole empire.

The sound parts of America, of which I have spoken, must be sensible of these great truths and of their real interests. America is not in that state of desperate and contemptible rebellion which this country has been deluded to believe. It is not a wild and lawless banditti, who, having nothing to lose, might hope to snatch something from public convulsions. Many of their leaders and great men have a great stake in this great contest. The gentleman who conducts their armies, I am told, has an estate of four or five thousand pounds a year; and when I consider these things, I cannot but lament the inconsiderate violence of our penal acts, our declarations of treason and rebellion, with all the fatal effects of attainder and confiscation.

As to the disposition of foreign powers which is asserted to be pacific and friendly, let us judge, my Lords, rather by their actions and the nature of things than by interested assertions. The uniform assistance supplied to America by France suggests a different conclusion. The most important interests of France in aggrandizing and enriching herself with what she most wants, supplies of every naval store from America, must inspire her with different sentiments. The extraordinary preparations of the house of Bourbon, by land and by sea, from Dunkirk to the Straits, equally ready and willing to overwhelm these defenceless islands, should rouse us to a sense of their real disposition and our own danger. Not five thousand troops in England! hardly three thousand in Ireland! What can we oppose to the combined force of our enemies? Scarcely twenty ships of the line so fully or sufficiently manned that any admiral's reputation would permit him to take the command of. The river of Lisbon in the possession of our enemies! The seas swept by American privateers! Our Channel trade torn to pieces by them! In this complicated crisis of danger — weakness at home, and calamity abroad, terrified and insulted by the neighboring powers, unable to act in America, or acting only to be destroyed — where is the man with the forehead to promise or hope for success in such a situation, or from perseverance in the measures that have driven us to it? Who has the forehead to do so? Where is that man? I should be glad to see his face.

You cannot conciliate America by your present measures. You cannot subdue her by your present or by any measures. What, then, can you do? You cannot conquer; you cannot gain; but you can address — you can lull the fears and anxieties of the moment into an ignorance of the danger that should produce them. But, my Lords, the time demands the language of truth. We must not now apply the flattering unction of servile compliance or blind complaisance. In a just and necessary war to maintain the rights or honor of my country, I would strip the shirt from my back to support it. But in such a war as this, unjust in its principle, impracticable in its means, and ruinous in its consequences, I would not contribute a single effort nor a single shilling. I do not call for vengeance on the heads of those who have been guilty; I only recommend to them to make their retreat. Let them walk off; and let them make haste, or they may be assured that speedy and condign punishment will overtake them.

My Lords, I have submitted to you, with the freedom and truth which I think my duty, my sentiments on your present awful situation. I have laid before you the ruin of your power, the disgrace of your reputation, the pollution of your discipline, the contamination of your morals, the complication of calamities, foreign and domestic, that overwhelm your sinking country. Your dearest interests, your own liberties, the Constitution itself, totters to the foundation. All this disgraceful danger, this multitude of misery, is the monstrous offspring of this unnatural war. We have been deceived and deluded too long. Let us now stop short. This is the crisis — the only crisis of time and situation — to give us a possibility of escape from the fatal effects of our delusions. But if, in an obstinate and infatuated perseverance in folly, we slavishly echo the peremptory words this day presented to us, nothing can save this devoted country from complete and final ruin. We madly rush into multiplied miseries, and "confusion worse confounded."

Is it possible, can it be believed, that Ministers are yet blind to this impending destruction? I did hope that instead of this false and empty vanity, this overweening pride, engendering high conceits and presumptuous imaginations, Ministers would have humbled themselves in their errors, would have confessed and retracted them, and by an active though a late repentance, have endeavored to redeem them. But, my Lords, since they had neither sagacity to foresee, nor justice nor humanity to shun these oppressive calamities — since not even severe experience can make them feel, nor the imminent ruin of their country awaken them from their stupefaction, the guardian care of Parliament must interpose. I shall therefore, my Lords, propose to you an amendment of the Address to his Majesty, to be inserted immediately after the two first paragraphs of congratulation on the birth of a princess, to recommend an immediate cessation of hostilities, and the commencement of a treaty to restore peace and liberty to America, strength and happiness to England, security and permanent prosperity to both countries. This, my Lords, is yet in our power; and let not the wisdom and justice of your Lordships neglect the happy, and, perhaps, the only opportunity. By the establishment of irrevocable law founded on mutual rights, and ascertained by treaty, these glorious enjoyments may be firmly perpetuated. And let me repeat to your Lordships that the strong bias of America, at least of the wise and sounder parts of it, naturally inclines to this happy and constitutional reconnection with you. Notwithstanding the temporary intrigues with France, we may still be assured of their ancient and confirmed partiality to us. America and France cannot be congenial. There is something decisive and confirmed in the honest American that will not assimilate to the futility and levity of Frenchmen.

My Lords, to encourage and confirm that innate inclination to this country, founded on every principle of affection as well as consideration of interest; to restore that favorable disposition into a permanent and powerful reunion with this country; to revive the mutual strength of the empire; again to awe the house of Bourbon, instead of meanly truckling, as our present calamities compel us, to every insult of French caprice and Spanish punctilio; to re-establish our commerce; to reassert our rights and our honor; to confirm our interests, and renew our glories forever — a consummation most devoutly to be endeavored! and which, I trust, may yet arise from reconciliation with America — I have the honor of submitting to you the following amendment, which I move to be inserted after the two first paragraphs of the Address:

"And that this House does most humbly advise and supplicate his Majesty to be pleased to cause the most speedy and effectual measures to be taken for restoring peace in America; and that no time may be lost in proposing an immediate cessation of hostilities there, in order to the opening of a treaty for the final settlement of the tranquillity of these invaluable Provinces, by a removal of the unhappy causes of this ruinous civil war, and by a just and adequate security against the return of the like calamities in times to come. And this House desire to offer the most dutiful assurances to his Majesty that they will, in due time, cheerfully co-operate with the magnanimity and tender goodness of his Majesty for the preservation of his people, by such explicit and most solemn declarations, and provisions of fundamental and irrevocable laws, as may be judged necessary for the ascertaining and fixing forever the respective rights of Great Britain and her Colonies.

[In the course of this debate, Lord Suffolk, secretary for the Northern Department, undertook to defend the employment of the Indians in the war. His Lordship contended that, besides its policy and necessity, the measure was also allowable on principle; for that "it was perfectly justifiable to use all the means that God and nature put into our hands!"]

I am astonished [exclaimed Lord Chatham as he rose], shocked to hear such principles confessed — to hear them avowed in this House, or in this country; principles equally unconstitutional, inhuman, and unchristian!

My Lords, I did not intend to have encroached again upon your attention, but I cannot repress my indignation. I feel myself impelled by every duty. My Lords, we are called upon as members of this House, as men, as Christian men, to protest against such notions standing near the Throne, polluting the ear of Majesty. "That God and nature put into our hands!" I know not what ideas that lord may entertain of God and nature, but I know that such abominable principles are equally abhorrent to religion and humanity. What! to attribute the sacred sanction of God and nature to the massacres of the Indian scalping-knife — to the cannibal savage torturing, murdering, roasting, and eating — literally, my Lords, eating the mangled victims of his barbarous battles! Such horrible notions shock every precept of religion, divine or natural, and every generous feeling of humanity. And, my Lords, they shock every sentiment of honor; they shock me as a lover of honorable war, and a detester of murderous barbarity.

These abominable principles, and this more abominable avowal of them, demand the most decisive indignation. I call upon that right reverend bench, those holy ministers of the Gospel, and pious pastors of our Church — I conjure them to join in the holy work, and vindicate the religion of their God. I appeal to the wisdom and the law of this learned bench to defend and support the justice of their country. I call upon the Bishops to interpose the unsullied sanctity of their lawn; upon the learned Judges, to interpose the purity of their ermine, to save us from this pollution. I call upon the honor of your Lordships to reverence the dignity of your ancestors, and to maintain your own. I call upon the spirit and humanity of my country to vindicate the national character. I invoke the genius of the Constitution. From the tapestry that adorns these walls, the immortal ancestor of this noble lord frowns with indignation at the disgrace of his country. In vain he led your victorious fleets against the boasted Armada of Spain; in vain he defended and established the honor, the liberties, the religion — the Protestant religion — of this country, against the arbitrary cruelties of Popery and the Inquisition, if these more than popish cruelties and inquisitorial practices are let loose among us — to turn forth into our settlements, among our ancient connections, friends, and relations, the merciless cannibal, thirsting for the blood of man, woman, and child! to send forth the infidel savage — against whom? against your Protestant brethren; to lay waste their country, to desolate their dwellings, and extirpate their race and name with these horrible hell-hounds of savage war — hell-hounds, I say, of savage war! Spain armed herself with blood-hounds to extirpate the wretched natives of America, and we improve on the inhuman example even of Spanish cruelty; we turn loose these savage hell-hounds against our brethren and countrymen in America, of the same language, laws, liberties, and religion, endeared to us by every tie that should sanctify humanity.

My Lords, this awful subject, so important to our honor, our Constitution, and our religion, demands the most solemn and effectual inquiry; and I again call upon your Lordships, and the united powers of the state, to examine it thoroughly and decisively, and to stamp upon it an indelible stigma of the public abhorrence. And I again implore those holy prelates of our religion to do away these iniquities from among us. Let them perform a lustration; let them purify this House, and this country, from this sin.

My Lords, I am old and weak, and at present unable to say more; but my feelings and indignation were too strong to have said less. I could not have slept this night in my bed, nor reposed my head on my pillow, without giving this vent to my eternal abhorrence of such preposterous and enormous principles.

EDMUND BURKE.

SPEECH PREVIOUS TO THE BRISTOL ELECTION; A DEFENCE OF HIS CONDUCT IN PARLIAMENT. AT THE GUILDHALL, BRISTOL, SEPTEMBER 6, 1780.

MR. MAYOR, AND GENTLEMEN,

I am extremely pleased at the appearance of this large and respectable meeting. The steps I may be obliged to take will want the sanction of a considerable authority; and in explaining anything which may appear doubtful in my public conduct, I must naturally desire a very full audience.

I have been backward to begin my canvass. The dissolution of the Parliament was uncertain; and it did not become me, by an unseasonable importunity, to appear diffident of the fact of my six years' endeavors to please you. I had served the city of Bristol honorably; and the city of Bristol had no reason to think that the means of honorable service to the public were become indifferent to me.

I found on my arrival here that three gentlemen had been long in eager pursuit of an object which but two of us can obtain. I found that they had all met with encouragement. A contested election, in such a city as this, is no light thing. I paused on the brink of the precipice. These three gentlemen, by various merits and on various titles, I made no doubt were worthy of your favor. I shall never attempt to raise myself by depreciating the merits of my competitors. In the complexity and confusion of these cross pursuits, I wished to take the authentic public sense of my friends upon a business of so much delicacy. I wished to take your opinion along with me; that if I should give up the contest at the very beginning, my surrender of my post may not seem the effect of inconstancy, or timidity, or anger, or disgust, or indolence, or any other temper unbecoming a man who has engaged in the public service. If, on the contrary, I should undertake the election, and fail of success, I was full as anxious that it should be manifest to the whole world that the peace of the city had not been broken by my rashness, presumption, or fond conceit of my own merit.

I am not come, by a false and counterfeit show of deference to your judgment, to seduce it in my favor. I ask it seriously and unaffectedly. If you wish that I should retire, I shall not consider that advice as a censure upon my conduct, or an alteration in your sentiments; but as a rational submission to the circumstances of affairs. If, on the contrary, you should think it proper for me to proceed on my canvass, if you will risk the trouble on your part, I will risk it on mine. My pretensions are such as you cannot be ashamed of, whether they succeed or fail.

If you call upon me, I shall solicit the favor of the city upon manly ground. I come before you with the plain confidence of an honest servant in the equity of a candid and discerning master. I come to claim your approbation, not to amuse you with vain apologies, or with professions still more vain and senseless. I have lived too long to be served by apologies, or to stand in need of them. The part I have acted has been in open day; and to hold out to a conduct which stands in that clear and steady light for all its good and all its evil, to hold out to that conduct the paltry winking tapers of excuses and promises — I never will do it. They may obscure it with their smoke; but they never can illumine sunshine by such a flame as theirs.

I am sensible that no endeavors have been left untried to injure me in your opinion. But the use of character is to be a shield against calumny. I could wish, undoubtedly, if idle wishes were not the most idle of all things, to make every part of my conduct agreeable to every part of my constituents. But in so great a city, and so greatly divided as this, it is weak to expect it.

In such a discordancy of sentiments, it is better to look to the nature of things than to the humors of men. The very attempt towards pleasing everybody discovers a temper always flashy, and often false and insincere. Therefore, as I have proceeded straight onward in my conduct, so I will proceed in my account of those parts of it which have been most excepted to. But I must first beg leave just to hint to you that we may suffer very great detriment by being open to every talker. It is not to be imagined how much of service is lost from spirits full of activity and full of energy, who are pressing, who are rushing, forward to great and capital objects, when you oblige them to be continually looking back. Whilst they are defending one service, they defraud you of an hundred. Applaud us when we run; console us when we fall; cheer us when we recover; but let us pass on — for God's sake, let us pass on.

Do you think, gentlemen, that every public act in the six years since I stood in this place before you — that all the arduous things which have been done in this eventful period, which has crowded into a few years' space the revolutions of an age, can be opened to you on their fair grounds in half an hour's conversation?

But it is no reason, because there is a bad mode of inquiry, that there should be no examination at all. Most certainly it is our duty to examine — it is our interest, too; but it must be with discretion — with an attention to all the circumstances, and to all the motives; like sound judges, and not like cavilling pettifoggers and quibbling pleaders, prying into flaws and hunting for exceptions. Look, gentlemen, to the whole tenor of your member's conduct. Try whether his ambition or his avarice have justled him out of the straight line of duty; or whether that grand foe of the offices of active life, that master-vice in men of business, a degenerate and inglorious sloth, has made him flag and languish in his course? This is the object of our inquiry. If our member's conduct can bear this touch, mark it for sterling. He may have fallen into errors; he must have faults; but our error is greater, and our fault is radically ruinous to ourselves, if we do not bear, if we do not even applaud, the whole compound and mixed mass of such a character. Not to act thus is folly; I had almost said it is impiety. He censures God who quarrels with the imperfections of man.

Gentlemen, we must not be peevish with those who serve the people. For none will serve us, whilst there is a court to serve, but those who are of a nice and jealous honor. They who think everything, in comparison of that honor, to be dust and ashes, will not bear to have it soiled and impaired by those for whose sake they make a thousand sacrifices to preserve it immaculate and whole. We shall either drive such men from the public stage, or we shall send them to the court for protection; where, if they must sacrifice their reputation, they will at least secure their interest. Depend upon it that the lovers of freedom will be free. None will violate their conscience to please us, in order afterwards to discharge that conscience, which they have violated, by doing us faithful and affectionate service. If we degrade and deprave their minds by servility, it will be absurd to expect that they who are creeping and abject towards us will ever be bold and incorruptible assertors of our freedom against the most seducing and the most formidable of all powers. No! human nature is not so formed; nor shall we improve the faculties or better the morals of public men by our possession of the most infallible receipt in the world for making cheats and hypocrites.

Let me say with plainness, I who am no longer in a public character, that if by a fair, by an indulgent, by a gentlemanly behavior to our representatives, we do not give confidence to their minds, and a liberal scope to their understandings; if we do not permit our members to act upon a very enlarged view of things; we shall at length infallibly degrade our national representation into a confused and scuffling bustle of local agency. When the popular member is narrowed in his ideas, and rendered timid in his proceedings, the service of the Crown will be the sole nursery of statesmen. Among the frolics of the court it may at length take that of attending to its business. Then the monopoly of mental power will be added to the power of all other kinds it possesses. On the side of the people there will be nothing but impotence: for ignorance is impotence; narrowness of mind is impotence; timidity is itself impotence, and makes all other qualities that go along with it impotent and useless.

At present it is the plan of the court to make its servants insignificant. If the people should fall into the same humor, and should choose their servants on the same principles of mere obsequiousness, and flexibility, and total vacancy or indifference of opinion in all public matters, then no part of the state will be sound; and it will be in vain to think of saving it.

I thought it very expedient at this time to give you this candid counsel; and with this counsel I would willingly close, if the matters which at various times have been objected to me in this city concerned only myself, and my own election. These charges, I think, are four in number: my neglect of a due attention to my constituents, the not paying more frequent visits here; my conduct on the affairs of the first Irish Trade Acts; my opinion and mode of proceeding on Lord Beauchamp's Debtors Bills; and my votes on the late affairs of the Roman Catholics. All of these (except perhaps the first) relate to matters of very considerable public concern; and it is not lest you should censure me improperly, but lest you should form improper opinions on matters of some moment to you, that I trouble you at all upon the subject. My conduct is of small importance.

With regard to the first charge, my friends have spoken to me of it in the style of amicable expostulation; not so much blaming the thing, as lamenting the effects. Others, less partial to me, were less kind in assigning the motives. I admit there is a decorum and propriety in a member of Parliament's paying a respectful court to his constituents. If I were conscious to myself that pleasure or dissipation, or low, unworthy occupations, had detained me from personal attendance on you, I would readily admit my fault, and quietly submit to the penalty. But, gentlemen, I live at a hundred miles' distance from Bristol; and at the end of a session I come to my own house, fatigued in body and in mind, to a little repose, and to a very little attention to my family and my private concerns. A visit to Bristol is always a sort of canvass; else it will do more harm than good. To pass from the toils of a session to the toils of a canvass is the furthest thing in the world from repose. I could hardly serve you as I have done, and court you too. Most of you have heard that I do not very remarkably spare myself in public business; and in the private business of my constituents I have done very nearly as much as those who have nothing else to do. My canvass of you was not on the 'Change, nor in the county meetings, nor in the clubs of this city. It was in the House of Commons; it was at the custom-house; it was at the council; it was at the treasury; it was at the admiralty. I canvassed you through your affairs, and not your persons. I was not only your representative as a body; I was the agent, the solicitor of individuals; I ran about wherever your affairs could call me; and in acting for you, I often appeared rather as a ship-broker than as a member of Parliament. There was nothing too laborious or too low for me to undertake. The meanness of the business was raised by the dignity of the object. If some lesser matters have slipped through my fingers, it was because I filled my hands too full, and, in my eagerness to serve you, took in more than any hands could grasp. Several gentlemen stand round me who are my willing witnesses; and there are others who, if they were here, would be still better, because they would be unwilling witnesses to the same truth. It was in the middle of a summer residence in London, and in the middle of a negotiation at the admiralty for your trade, that I was called to Bristol; and this late visit, at this late day, has been possibly in prejudice to your affairs.

Since I have touched upon this matter, let me say, gentlemen, that if I had a disposition or a right to complain, I have some cause of complaint on my side. With a petition of the city in my hand, passed through the corporation without a dissenting voice, a petition in unison with almost the whole voice of the kingdom (with whose formal thanks I was covered over)—while I labored on no less than five bills for a public reform, and fought, against the opposition of great abilities and of the greatest power, every clause and every word of the largest of those bills almost to the very last day of a very long session;—all this time a canvass in Bristol was as calmly carried on as if I were dead. I was considered as a man wholly out of the question. Whilst I watched, and fasted, and sweated in the House of Commons, by the most easy and ordinary arts of election—by dinners and visits, by "How do you do's," and "My worthy friends,"—I was to be quietly moved out of my seat; and promises were made and engagements entered into, without any exception or reserve, as if my laborious zeal in my duty had been a regular abdication of my trust.

To open my whole heart to you on this subject, I do confess, however, that there were other times besides the two years in which I did visit you, when I was not wholly without leisure for repeating that mark of my respect. But I could not bring my mind to see you. You remember, that in the beginning of this American war (that era of calamity, disgrace, and downfall, an era which no feeling mind will ever mention without a tear for England) you were greatly divided; and a very strong body, if not the strongest, opposed itself to the madness which every art and every power were employed to render popular, in order that the errors of the rulers might be lost in the general blindness of the nation. This opposition continued until after our great, but most unfortunate, victory at Long Island. Then all the mounds and banks of our constancy were borne down at once; and the frenzy of the American war broke in upon us like a deluge. This victory, which seemed to put an immediate end to all difficulties, perfected us in that spirit of domination, which our unparalleled prosperity had but too long nurtured. We had been so very powerful, and so very prosperous, that even the humblest of us were degraded into the vices and follies of kings. We lost all measure between means and ends; and our headlong desires became our politics and our morals. All men who wished for peace, or retained any sentiments of moderation, were overborne or silenced; and this city was led by every artifice (and probably with the more management, because I was one of your members) to distinguish itself by its zeal for that fatal cause. In this temper of your and of my mind, I should have sooner fled to the extremities of the earth, than have shown myself here. I, who saw in every American victory (for you have had a long series of these misfortunes) the germ and seed of the naval power of France and Spain, which all our heat and warmth against America was only hatching into life, — I should not have been a welcome visitant with the brow and the language of such feelings. When, afterwards, the other face of your calamity was turned upon you, and showed itself in defeat and distress, I shunned you full as much. I felt sorely this variety in our wretchedness; and I did not wish to have the least appearance of insulting you with that show of superiority, which, though it may not be assumed, is generally suspected in a time of calamity from those whose previous warnings have been despised. I could not bear to show you a representative whose face did not reflect that of his constituents; a face that could not joy in your joys, and sorrow in your sorrows. But time at length has made us all of one opinion; and we have all opened our eyes on the true nature of the American war, to the true nature of all its successes and all its failures.

In that public storm, too, I had my private feelings. I had seen blown down and prostrate on the ground several of those houses to whom I was chiefly indebted for the honor this city has done me. I confess that, whilst the wounds of those I loved were yet green, I could not bear to show myself in pride and triumph in that place into which their partiality had brought me, and to appear at feasts and rejoicings, in the midst of the grief and calamity of my warm friends, my zealous supporters, my generous benefactors. This is a true, unvarnished, undisguised state of the affair. You will judge of it.

This is the only one of the charges in which I am personally concerned. As to the other matters objected against me, which in their turn I shall mention to you, remember once more I do not mean to extenuate or excuse. Why should I, when the things charged are among those upon which I found all my reputation? What would be left to me, if I myself was the man who softened, and blended, and diluted, and weakened, all the distinguishing colors of my life, so as to leave nothing distinct and determinate in my whole conduct?

It has been said, and it is the second charge, that in the questions of the Irish trade, I did not consult the interest of my constituents; or, to speak out strongly, that I rather acted as a native of Ireland, than as an English member of Parliament.

I certainly have very warm good wishes for the place of my birth. But the sphere of my duties is my true country. It was as a man attached to your interests, and zealous for the conservation of your power and dignity, that I acted on that occasion, and on all occasions. You were involved in the American war. A new world of policy was opened, to which it was necessary we should conform, whether we would or not; and my only thought was how to conform to our situation in such a manner as to unite to this kingdom, in prosperity and in affection, whatever remained of the empire. I was true to my old, standing, invariable principle, that all things, which came from Great Britain, should issue as a gift of her bounty and beneficence, rather than as claims recovered against a struggling litigant; or at least, that if your beneficence obtained no credit in your concessions, yet that they should appear the salutary provisions of your wisdom and foresight, not as things wrung from you with your blood by the cruel gripe of a rigid necessity. The first concessions, by being (much against my will) mangled and stripped of the parts which were necessary to make out their just correspondence and connection in trade, were of no use. The next year a feeble attempt was made to bring the thing into better shape. This attempt (countenanced by the Minister) on the very first appearance of some popular uneasiness, was, after a considerable progress through the House, thrown out by him.

What was the consequence? The whole kingdom of Ireland was instantly in a flame. Threatened by foreigners, and, as they thought, insulted by England, they resolved at once to resist the power of France, and to cast off yours. As for us, we were able neither to protect nor to restrain them. Forty thousand men were raised and disciplined without commission from the Crown. Two illegal armies were seen with banners displayed at the same time and in the same country. No executive magistrate, no judicature in Ireland, would acknowledge the legality of the army which bore the King's commission; and no law, or appearance of law, authorized the army commissioned by itself. In this unexampled state of things, which the least error, the least trespass on the right or left, would have hurried down the precipice into an abyss of blood and confusion, the people of Ireland demand a freedom of trade with arms in their hands. They interdict all commerce between the two nations.

They deny all new supply in the House of Commons, although in time of war. They stint the trust of the old revenue, given for two years to all the King's predecessors, to six months. The British Parliament, in a former session, frightened into a limited concession by the menaces of Ireland, frightened out of it by the menaces of England, were now frightened back again, and made a universal surrender of all that had been thought the peculiar, reserved, uncommunicable rights of England; — the exclusive commerce of America, of Africa, of the West Indies — all the enumerations of the Acts of Navigation — all the manufactures — iron, glass — even the last pledge of jealousy and pride, the interest hid in the secret of our hearts, the inveterate prejudice moulded into the constitution of our frame, even the sacred fleece itself, all went together. No reserve; no exception; no debate; no discussion. A sudden light broke in upon us all. It broke in, not through well-contrived and well-disposed windows, but through flaws and breaches; through the yawning chasms of our ruin. We were taught wisdom by humiliation. No town in England presumed to have a prejudice, or dared to mutter a petition. What was worse, the whole Parliament of England, which retained authority for nothing but surrenders, was despoiled of every shadow of its superintendence. It was, without any qualification, denied in theory, as it had been trampled upon in practice. This scene of shame and disgrace has, in a manner whilst I am speaking, ended by the perpetual establishment of a military power in the dominions of this Crown, without consent of the British legislature, contrary to the policy of the Constitution, contrary to the Declaration of Right; and by this your liberties are swept away along with your supreme authority — and both, linked together from the beginning, have, I am afraid, both together perished forever.

What! gentlemen, was I not to foresee, or foreseeing, was I not to endeavor to save you from all these multiplied mischiefs and disgraces? Would the little, silly, canvass prattle of obeying instructions, and having no opinions but yours, and such idle senseless tales, which amuse the vacant ears of unthinking men, have saved you from "the pelting of that pitiless storm," to which the loose improvidence, the cowardly rashness, of those who dare not look danger in the face so as to provide against it in time, and therefore throw themselves headlong into the midst of it, have exposed this degraded nation, beaten down and prostrate on the earth, unsheltered, unarmed, unresisting? Was I an Irishman on that day that I boldly withstood our pride? or on the day that I hung down my head, and wept in shame and silence over the humiliation of Great Britain? I became unpopular in England for the one, and in Ireland for the other. What then? What obligation lay on me to be popular? I was bound to serve both kingdoms. To be pleased with my service was their affair, not mine.

I was an Irishman in the Irish business, just as much as I was an American, when, on the same principles, I wished you to concede to America, at a time when she prayed concession at our feet. Just as much was I an American, when I wished Parliament to offer terms in victory, and not to wait the well-chosen hour of defeat for making good by weakness, and by supplication, a claim of prerogative, pre-eminence, and authority.

Instead of requiring it from me, as a point of duty, to kindle with your passions, had you all been as cool as I was, you would have been saved from disgraces and distresses that are unutterable. Do you remember our Commission? We sent out a solemn embassy across the Atlantic Ocean, to lay the Crown, the Peerage, the Commons of Great Britain, at the feet of the American

Congress. That our disgrace might want no sort of brightening and burnishing, observe who they were that composed this famous embassy! My Lord Carlisle is among the first ranks of our nobility. He is the identical man who, but two years before, had been put forward, at the opening of the session in the House of Lords, as the mover of a haughty and rigorous Address against America. He was put in the front of the embassy of submission. Mr. Eden was taken from the office of Lord Suffolk, to whom he was then Under-Secretary of State; from the office of that Lord Suffolk, who but a few weeks before, in his place in Parliament, did not deign to inquire where a congress of vagrants was to be found. This Lord Suffolk sent Mr. Eden to find these vagrants, without knowing where this King's generals were to be found, who were joined in the same commission of supplicating those whom they were sent to subdue. They enter the capital of America only to abandon it; and these assertors and representatives of the dignity of England, at the tail of a flying army, let fly their Parthian shafts of memorials and remonstrances at random behind them. Their promises and their offers, their flatteries and their menaces, were all despised; and we were saved from the disgrace of their formal reception, only because the Congress scorned to receive them; whilst the state-house of independent Philadelphia opened her doors to the public entry of the ambassador of France. From war and blood we went to submission; and from submission plunged back again to war and blood; to desolate and be desolated, without measure, hope, or end. I am a Royalist; I blushed for this degradation of the Crown. I am a Whig; I blushed for the dishonor of Parliament. I am a true Englishman; I felt to the quick for the disgrace of England. I am a man; I felt for the melancholy reverse of human affairs, in the fall of the first power in the world.

To read what was approaching in Ireland, in the black and bloody characters of the American war, was a painful, but it was a necessary, part of my public duty. For, gentlemen, it is not your fond desires or mine that can alter the nature of things; by contending against which, what have we got, or shall ever get, but defeat and shame? I did not obey your instructions: No. I conformed to the instructions of truth and nature, and maintained your interest, against your opinions, with a constancy that became me. A representative worthy of you ought to be a person of stability. I am to look, indeed, to your opinions; but to such opinions as you and I must have five years hence. I was not to look to the flash of the day. I knew that you chose me, in my place, along with others, to be a pillar of the state, and not a weathercock on the top of the edifice, exalted for my levity and versatility, and of no use but to indicate the shiftings of every fashionable gale. Would to God the value of my sentiments on Ireland and on America had been at this day a subject of doubt and discussion! No matter what my sufferings had been, so that this kingdom had kept the authority I wished it to maintain, by a grave foresight, and by an equitable temperance in the use of its power.

The next article of charge on my public conduct, and that which I find rather the most prevalent of all, is Lord Beauchamp's bill. I mean his bill of last session for reforming the law-process concerning imprisonment. It is said, to aggravate the offence, that I treated the petition of this city with contempt even in presenting it to the House, and expressed myself in terms of marked disrespect. Had this latter part of the charge been true, no merits on the side of the question which I took could possibly excuse me. But I am incapable of treating this city with disrespect. Very fortunately, at this minute (if my bad eyesight does not deceive me) the worthy gentleman deputed on this business stands directly before me. To him I appeal, whether I did not, though it militated with my oldest and my most recent public opinions, deliver the petition with a strong and more than usual recommendation to the consideration of the House, on account of the character and consequence of those who signed it. I believe the worthy gentleman will tell you, that the very day I received it, I applied to the Solicitor, now the Attorney-General, to give it an immediate consideration; and he most obligingly and instantly consented to employ a great deal of his very valuable time to write an explanation of the bill. I attended the committee with all possible care and diligence, in order that every objection of yours might meet with a solution, or produce an alteration. I entreated your learned Recorder (always ready in business in which you take a concern) to attend. But what will you say to those who blame me for supporting Lord Beauchamp's bill, as a disrespectful treatment of your petition, when you hear that out of respect to you, I myself was the cause of the loss of that very bill? For the noble lord who brought it in, and who, I must say, has much merit for this and some other measures, at my request consented to put it off for a week, which the Speaker's illness lengthened to a fortnight; and then the frantic tumult about Popery drove that and every rational business from the House. So that if I choose to make a defence of myself on the little principles of a culprit pleading in his exculpation, I might not only secure my acquittal, but make merit with the opposers of the bill. But I shall do no such thing. The truth is, that I did occasion the loss of the bill, and by a delay caused by my respect to you. But such an event was never in my contemplation. And I am so far from taking credit for the defeat of that measure, that I cannot sufficiently lament my misfortune, if but one man who ought to be at large, has passed a year in prison by my means. I am a debtor to the debtors. I confess judgment. I owe what, if ever it be in my power, I shall most certainly pay, — ample atonement and usurious amends to liberty and humanity for my unhappy lapse. For, gentlemen, Lord Beauchamp's bill was a law of justice and policy, as far as it went; I say as far as it went, for its fault was its being, in the remedial part, miserably defective.

There are two capital faults in our law with relation to civil debts. One is, that every man is presumed solvent — a presumption, in innumerable cases, directly against truth. Therefore the debtor is ordered, on a supposition of ability and fraud, to be coerced his liberty until he makes payment. By this means, in all cases of civil insolvency, without a pardon from his creditor, he is to be imprisoned for life; — and thus a miserable, mistaken invention of artificial science operates to change the civil into a criminal judgment, and to scourge misfortune or indiscretion with a punishment which the law does not inflict on the greatest crimes.

The next fault is, that the inflicting of that punishment is not on the opinion of an equal and public judge; but is referred to the arbitrary discretion of a private, nay interested and irritated, individual. He who formally is, and substantially ought to be, the judge, is in reality no more than ministerial, a mere executive instrument of a private man, who is at once judge and party. Every idea of judicial order is subverted by this procedure. If the insolvency be no crime, why is it punished with arbitrary imprisonment? If it be a crime, why is it delivered into private hands to pardon without discretion, or to punish without mercy and without measure?

To these faults, gross and cruel faults in our law, the excellent principle of Lord Beauchamp's bill applied some sort of remedy. I know that credit must be preserved; but equity must be preserved too; and it is impossible that anything should be necessary to commerce which is inconsistent with justice. The principle of credit was not weakened by that bill. God forbid! The enforcement of that credit was only put into the same public judicial hands on which we depend for our lives, and all that makes life dear to us. But, indeed, this business was taken up too warmly both here and elsewhere. The bill was extremely mistaken. It was supposed to enact what it never enacted; and complaints were made of clauses in it as novelties, which existed before the noble lord that brought in the bill was born. There was a fallacy that ran through the whole of the objections. The gentlemen who opposed the bill always argued, as if the option lay between that bill and the ancient law. — But this is a grand mistake. For, practically, the option is between, not that bill and the old law, but between that bill and those occasional laws, called Acts of Grace. For the operation of the old law is so savage, and so inconvenient to society, that for a long time past, once in every Parliament, and lately twice, the legislature has been obliged to make a general arbitrary jail-delivery, and at once to set open, by its sovereign authority, all the prisons in England.

Gentlemen, I never relished Acts of Grace; nor ever submitted to them but from despair of better. They are a dishonorable invention, by which, not from humanity, not from policy, but merely because we have not room enough to hold these victims of the absurdity of our laws, we turn loose upon the public three or four thousand naked wretches, corrupted by the habits, debased by the ignominy, of a prison. If the creditor had a right to those carcasses as a natural security for his property, I am sure we have no right to deprive him of that security. But if the few pounds of flesh were not necessary to his security, we had not a right to detain the unfortunate debtor, without any benefit at all to the person who confined him. Take it as you will, we commit injustice. Now Lord Beauchamp's bill intended to do deliberately, and with great caution and circumspection, upon each several case, and with all attention to the just claimant, what Acts of Grace do in a much greater measure, and with very little care, caution, or deliberation.

I suspect that here too, if we contrive to oppose this bill, we shall be found in a struggle against the nature of things. For, as we grow enlightened, the public will not bear, for any length of time, to pay for the maintenance of whole armies of prisoners, nor, at their own expense, submit to keep jails as a sort of garrisons, merely to fortify the absurd principle of making men judges in their own cause. For credit has little or no concern in this cruelty. I speak in a commercial assembly. You know that credit is given, because capital *must* be employed; that men calculate the chances of insolvency; and they either withhold the credit, or make the debtor pay the risk in the price. The counting-house has no alliance with the jail. Holland understands trade as well as we, and she has done much more than this obnoxious bill intended to do. There was not, when Mr. Howard visited Holland, more than one prisoner for debt in the great city of Rotterdam. Although Lord Beauchamp's Act (which was previous to this bill, and intended to feel the way for it) has already preserved liberty to thousands, and though it is not three years since the last Act of Grace passed, yet by Mr. Howard's last account, there were near three thousand again in jail. I cannot name this gentleman without remarking that his labors and writings have done much to open the eyes and hearts of mankind. He has visited all Europe,— not to survey the sumptuousness of palaces, or the stateliness of temples; not to make accurate measurements of the remains of ancient grandeur, nor to form a scale of the curiosity of modern art; not to collect medals, or collate manuscripts: — but to dive into the depths of dungeons; to plunge into the infection of hospitals; to survey the mansions of sorrow and pain; to take the gauge and dimensions of misery, depression, and contempt; to remember the forgotten, to attend to the neglected, to visit the forsaken, and to compare and collate the distresses of all men in all countries. His plan is original; and it is as full of genius as it is of humanity. It was a voyage of discovery; a circumnavigation of charity. Already the benefit of his labor is felt more or less in every country; — I hope he will anticipate his final reward by seeing all its effects fully realized in his own. He will receive, not by detail, but in gross, the reward of those who visit the prisoner; and he has so forestalled and monopolized this branch of charity, that there will be, I trust, little room to merit by such acts of benevolence hereafter.

Nothing now remains to trouble you with but the fourth charge against me — the business of the Roman Catholics. It is a business closely connected with the rest. They are all on one and the same principle. My little scheme of conduct, such as it is, is all arranged. I could do nothing but what I have done on this subject, without confounding the whole train of my ideas, and disturbing the whole order of my life. Gentlemen, I ought to apologize to you for seeming to think anything at all necessary to be said upon this matter. The calumny is fitter to be scrawled with the midnight chalk of incendiaries, with "No Popery," on walls and doors of devoted houses, than to be mentioned in any civilized company. I had heard that the spirit of discontent on that subject was very prevalent here. With pleasure I find that I have been grossly misinformed. If it exists at all in this city, the laws have crushed its exertions, and our morals have shamed its appearance in daylight. I have pursued this spirit wherever I could trace it; but it still fled from me. It was a ghost which all had heard of, but none had seen. None would acknowledge that he thought the public proceeding with regard to our Catholic dissenters to be blamable; but several were sorry it had made an ill impression upon others, and that my interest was hurt by my share in the business. I find with satisfaction and pride, that not above four or five in this city (and I dare say these misled by some gross misrepresentation) have signed that symbol of delusion and bond of sedition, that libel on the national religion and English character, the Protestant Association. It is therefore, gentlemen, not by way of cure, but of prevention, and lest the arts of wicked men may prevail over the integrity of any one amongst us, that I think it necessary to open to you the merits of this transaction pretty much at large; and I beg your patience upon it: for, although the reasonings that have been used to depreciate the Act are of little force, and though the authority of the men concerned in this ill design is not very imposing; yet the audaciousness of these conspirators against the national honor, and the extensive wickedness of their attempts, have raised persons of little importance to a degree of evil eminence, and imparted a sort of sinister dignity to proceedings that had their origin in only the meanest and blindest malice.

In explaining to you the proceedings of Parliament which have been complained of, I will state to you, first, the thing that was done; next, the persons who did it; and lastly, the grounds and reasons upon which the legislature proceeded in this deliberate act of public justice and public prudence.

Gentlemen, the condition of our nature is such, that we buy our blessings at a price. The Reformation, one of the greatest periods of human improvement, was a time of trouble and confusion. The vast structure of superstition and tyranny, which had been for ages in rearing, and which was combined with the interest of the great and of the many, which was moulded into the laws, the manners, and civil institutions of nations, and blended with the frame and policy of states, could not be brought to the ground without a fearful struggle; nor could it fall without a violent concussion of itself and all about it. When this great revolution was attempted in a more regular mode by government, it was opposed by plots and seditions of the people; when by popular efforts, it was repressed as rebellion by the hand of power; and bloody executions (often bloodily returned) marked the whole of its progress through all its stages. The affairs of religion, which are no longer heard of in the tumult of our present contentions, made a principal ingredient in the wars and politics of that time; the enthusiasm of religion threw a gloom over the politics; and political interests poisoned and perverted the spirit of religion upon all sides. The Protestant religion in that violent struggle, infected, as the Popish had been before, by worldly interests and worldly passions, became a persecutor in its turn, — sometimes of the new sects, which carried their own principles further than it was convenient to the original reformers, and always of the body from whom they parted; — and this persecuting spirit arose, not only from the bitterness of retaliation, but from the merciless policy of fear.

It was long before the spirit of true piety and true wisdom, involved in the principles of the Reformation, could be depurated from the dregs and feculence of the contention with which it was carried through. However, until this be done, the Reformation is not complete; and those who think themselves good Protestants, from their animosity to others, are in that respect no Protestants at all. It was at first thought necessary, perhaps, to oppose to Popery another Popery, to get the better of it. Whatever was the cause, laws were made in many countries, and in this kingdom in particular, against Papists, which are as bloody as any of those which had been enacted by the Popish princes and states; and where those laws were not bloody, in my opinion they were worse; as they were slow, cruel outrages on our nature, and kept men alive only to insult in their persons every one of the rights and feelings of humanity. I pass those statutes, because I would spare your pious ears the repetition of such shocking things; and I come to that particular law, the repeal of which has produced so many unnatural and unexpected consequences.

A statute was fabricated in the year 1699, by which the saying mass (a church-service in the Latin tongue, not exactly the same as our liturgy, but very near it, and containing no offence whatsoever against the laws, or against good morals) was forged into a crime punishable with perpetual imprisonment. The teaching school, a useful and virtuous occupation, even the teaching in a private family, was in every Catholic subjected to the same unproportioned punishment. Your industry, and the bread of your children, was taxed for a pecuniary reward to stimulate avarice to do what nature refused, to inform and prosecute on this law. Every Roman Catholic was, under the same Act, to forfeit his estate to his nearest Protestant relation, until, through a profession of what he did not believe, he redeemed by his hypocrisy what the law had transferred to the kinsman as the recompense of his profligacy. When thus turned out of doors from his paternal estate, he was disabled from acquiring any other by any industry, donation, or charity; but was rendered a foreigner in his native land, only because he retained the religion, along with the property, handed down to him from those who had been the old inhabitants of that land before him.

Does any one who hears me approve this scheme of things, or think there is common justice, common sense, or common honesty in any part of it? If any does, let him say it, and I am ready to discuss the point with temper and candor. But instead of approving, I perceive a virtuous indignation beginning to rise in your minds on the mere cold stating of the statute.

But what will you feel, when you know from history how this statute passed, and what were the motives, and what the mode of making it? A party in this nation, enemies to the system of the Revolution, were in opposition to the government of King William. They knew that our glorious deliverer was an enemy to all persecution. They knew that he came to free us from slavery and Popery, out of a country where a third of the people are contented Catholics under a Protestant government. He came with a part of his army composed of those very Catholics, to overset the power of a Popish prince. Such is the effect of a tolerating spirit; and so much is liberty served in every way, and by all persons, by a manly adherence to its own principles. Whilst freedom is true to itself, everything becomes subject to it; and its very adversaries are an instrument in its hands.

The party I speak of (like some amongst us who would disparage the best friends of their country) resolved to make the King either violate his principles of toleration, or incur the odium of protecting Papists. They therefore brought in this bill, and made it purposely wicked and absurd that it might be rejected. The then court-party, discovering their game, turned the tables on them, and returned their bill to them stuffed with still greater absurdities, that its loss might lie upon its original authors. They, finding their own ball thrown back to them, kicked it back again to their adversaries. And thus this Act, loaded with the double injustice of two parties, neither of whom intended to pass what they hoped the other would be persuaded to reject, went through the legislature, contrary to the real wish of all parts of it, and of all the parties that composed it. In this manner these insolent and profligate factions, as if they were playing with balls and counters, made a sport of the fortunes and the liberties of their fellow-creatures. Other acts of persecution have been acts of malice. This was a subversion of justice from wantonness and petulance. Look into the History of Bishop Burnet. He is a witness without exception.

The effects of the Act have been as mischievous as its origin was ludicrous and shameful. From that time every person of that communion, lay and ecclesiastic, has been obliged to fly from the face of day. The clergy, concealed in garrets of private houses, or obliged to take a shelter (hardly safe to themselves, but infinitely dangerous to their country) under the privileges of foreign Ministers, officiated as their servants, and under their protection. The whole body of the Catholics, condemned to beggary and to ignorance in their native land, have been obliged to learn the principles of letters, at the hazard of all their other principles, from the charity of your enemies. They have been taxed to their ruin at the pleasure of necessitous and profligate relations, and according to the measure of their necessity and profligacy. Examples of this are many and affecting. Some of them are known by a friend who stands near me in this hall. It is but six or seven years since a clergyman of the name of Malony, a man of morals, neither guilty nor accused of anything noxious to the state, was condemned to perpetual imprisonment for exercising the functions of his religion; and after lying in jail two or three years, was relieved by the mercy of government from perpetual imprisonment on condition of perpetual banishment. A brother of the Earl of Shrewsbury, a Talbot, a name respectable in this country whilst its glory is any part of its concern, was hauled to the bar of the Old Bailey among common felons, and only escaped the same doom, either by some error in the process, or that the wretch who brought him there could not correctly describe his person — I now forget which. In short, the persecution would never have relented for a moment, if the judges, superseding (though with an ambiguous example) the strict rule of their artificial duty by the higher obligation of their conscience, did not constantly throw every difficulty in the way of such informers. But so ineffectual is the power of legal evasion against legal iniquity, that it was but the other day that a lady of condition, beyond the middle of life, was on the point of being stripped of her whole fortune by a near relation, to whom she had been a friend and benefactor; and she must have been totally ruined, without a power of redress or mitigation from the courts of law, had not the legislature itself rushed in, and by a special Act of Parliament rescued her from the injustice of its own statutes. One of the Acts authorizing such things was that which we in part repealed, knowing what our duty was, and doing that duty as men of honor and virtue, as good Protestants, and as good citizens. Let him stand forth that disapproves what we have done!

Gentlemen, bad laws are the worst sort of tyranny. In such a country as this they are of all bad things the worst — worse by far than anywhere else; and they derive a particular malignity even from the wisdom and soundness of the rest of our institutions. For very obvious reasons you cannot trust the Crown with a dispensing power over any of your laws. However, a government, be it as bad as it may, will, in the exercise of a discretionary power, discriminate times and persons; and will not ordinarily pursue any man when its own safety is not concerned. A mercenary informer knows no distinction. Under such a system, the obnoxious people are slaves, not only to the government, but they live at the mercy of every individual; they are at once the slaves of the whole community, and of every part of it; and the worst and most unmerciful men are those on whose goodness they most depend.

In this situation men not only shrink from the frowns of a stern magistrate, but they are obliged to fly from their very species. The seeds of destruction are sown in civil intercourse, in social habitudes. The blood of wholesome kindred is infected. Their tables and beds are surrounded with snares. All the means given by Providence to make life safe and comfortable are perverted into instruments of terror and torment. This species of universal subserviency, that makes the very servant who waits behind your chair the arbiter of your life and fortune, has such a tendency to degrade and abase mankind, and to deprive them of that assured and liberal state of mind which alone can make us what we ought to be, that I vow to God I would sooner bring myself to put a man to immediate death for opinions I disliked, and so to get rid of the man and his opinions at once, than to fret him with a feverish being, tainted with the jail-distemper of a contagious servitude, to keep him above ground an animated mass of putrefaction, corrupted himself, and corrupting all about him.

The Act repealed was of this direct tendency; and it was made in the manner which I have related to you. I will now tell you by whom the bill of repeal was brought into Parliament. I find it has been industriously given out in this city (from kindness to me, unquestionably) that I was the mover or the seconder. The fact is, I did not once open my lips on the subject during the whole progress of the bill. I do not say this as disclaiming my share in that measure. Very far from it. I inform you of this fact, lest I should seem to arrogate to myself the merits which belong to others. To have been the man chosen out to redeem our fellow-citizens from slavery, to purify our laws from absurdity and injustice, and to cleanse our religion from the blot and stain of persecution, would be an honor and happiness to which my wishes would undoubtedly aspire; but to which nothing but my wishes could possibly have entitled me. That great work was in hands in every respect far better qualified than mine. The mover of the bill was Sir George Savile.

When an act of great and signal humanity was to be done, and done with all the weight and authority that belonged to it, the world could cast its eyes upon none but him. I hope that few things which have a tendency to bless or to adorn life have wholly escaped my observation in my passage through it. I have sought the acquaintance of that gentleman, and have seen him in all situations. He is a true genius; with an understanding vigorous, and acute, and refined, and distinguishing even to excess, and illuminated with a most unbounded, peculiar, and original cast of imagination. With these he possesses many external and instrumental advantages, and he makes use of them all. His fortune is among the largest; a fortune which, wholly unencumbered, as it is, with one single charge from luxury, vanity, or excess, sinks under the benevolence of its dispenser. This private benevolence, expanding itself into patriotism, renders his whole being the estate of the public, in which he has not reserved a *peculium* for himself of profit, diversion, or relaxation. During the session the first in and the last out of the House of Commons, he passes from the senate to the camp; and seldom seeing the seat of his ancestors, he is always in the senate to serve his country, or in the field to defend it. But in all well-wrought compositions some particulars stand out more eminently than the rest, and the things which will carry his name to posterity are his two bills — I mean that for a limitation of the claims of the Crown upon landed estates, and this for the relief of the Roman Catholics. By the former he has emancipated property; by the latter he has quieted conscience; and by both he has taught that grand lesson to government and subject, — no longer to regard each other as adverse parties.

Such was the mover of the Act that is complained of by men who are not quite so good as he is; an Act most assuredly not brought in by him from any partiality to that sect which is the object of it. For, among his faults, I really cannot help reckoning a greater degree of prejudice against that people than becomes so wise a man. I know that he inclines to a sort of disgust, mixed with a considerable degree of asperity, to the system; and he has few, or rather no habits with any of its professors. What he has done was on quite other motives. The motives were these, which he declared in his excellent speech on his motion for the bill; namely, his extreme zeal to the Protestant religion, which he thought utterly disgraced by the Act of 1699, and his rooted hatred to all kind of oppression, under any color, or upon any pretence whatsoever.

The seconder was worthy of the mover, and of the

motion. I was not the seconder; it was Mr. Dunning, Recorder of this city. I shall say the less of him, because his near relation to you makes you more particularly acquainted with his merits. But I should appear little acquainted with them, or little sensible of them, if I could utter his name on this occasion without expressing my esteem for his character. I am not afraid of offending a most learned body, and most jealous of its reputation for that learning, when I say he is the first of his profession. It is a point settled by those who settle everything else: and I must add (what I am enabled to say from my own long and close observation) that there is not a man of any profession, or in any situation, of a more erect and independent spirit; of a more proud honor; a more manly mind; a more firm and determined integrity. Assure yourselves, that the names of two such men will bear a great load of prejudice in the other scale before they can be entirely outweighed.

With this mover and this seconder agreed the whole House of Commons; the whole House of Lords; the whole bench of bishops; the King; the Ministry; the Opposition; all the distinguished clergy of the establishment; all the eminent lights (for they were consulted) of the dissenting churches. This according voice of national wisdom ought to be listened to with reverence. To say that all these descriptions of Englishmen unanimously concurred in a scheme for introducing the Catholic religion, or that none of them understood the nature and effects of what they were doing so well as a few obscure clubs of people whose names you never heard of, is shamelessly absurd. Surely it is paying a miserable compliment to the religion we profess, to suggest that everything eminent in the kingdom is indifferent, or even adverse, to that religion, and that its security is wholly abandoned to the zeal of those who have nothing but their zeal to distinguish them. In weighing this unanimous concurrence of whatever the nation has to boast of, I hope you will recollect that all these concurring parties do by no means love one another enough to agree in any point which was not both evidently and importantly right.

To prove this; to prove that the measure was both clearly and materially proper, I will next lay before you, as I promised, the political grounds and reasons for the repeal of that penal statute, and the motives to its repeal at that particular time.

Gentlemen, America—when the English nation seemed to be dangerously, if not irrecoverably, divided; when one, and that the most growing branch, was torn from the parent stock, and ingrafted on the power of France, a great terror fell upon this kingdom. On a sudden we awakened from our dreams of conquest, and saw ourselves threatened with an immediate invasion, which we were at that time very ill prepared to resist. You remember the cloud that gloomed over us all. In that hour of our dismay, from the bottom of the hiding-places into which the indiscriminate rigor of our statutes had driven them, came out the body of the Roman Catholics. They appeared before the steps of a tottering throne with one of the most sober, measured, steady, and dutiful addresses that was ever presented to the Crown. It was no holiday ceremony; no anniversary compliment of parade and show. It was signed by almost every gentleman of that persuasion, of note or property, in England. At such a crisis, nothing but a decided resolution to stand or fall with their country could have dictated such an address, the direct tendency of which was to cut off all retreat, and to render them peculiarly obnoxious to an invader of their own communion. The address showed what I long languished to see, that all the subjects of England had cast off all foreign views and connections, and that every man looked for his relief from every grievance at the hands only of his own natural government.

It was necessary, on our part, that the natural government should show itself worthy of that name. It was necessary, at the crisis I speak of, that the supreme power of the state should meet the conciliatory dispositions of the subject. To delay protection would be to reject allegiance. And why should it be rejected, or even coldly and suspiciously received? If any independent Catholic state should choose to take part with this kingdom in a war with France and Spain, that bigot (if such a bigot could be found) would be heard with little respect, who could dream of objecting his religion to an ally whom the nation would not only receive with its freest thanks, but purchase with the last remains of its exhausted treasure. To such an ally we should not dare to whisper a single syllable of those base and invidious topics upon which some unhappy men would persuade the state to reject the duty and allegiance of its own members. Is it then because foreigners are in a condition to set our malice at defiance, that with them we are willing to contract engagements of friendship, and to keep them with fidelity and honor; but that, because we conceive some descriptions of our countrymen are not powerful enough to punish our malignity, we will not permit them to support our common interest? Is it on that ground that our anger is to be kindled by their offered kindness? Is it on that ground that they are to be subjected to penalties, because they are willing, by actual merit, to purge themselves from imputed crimes? Lest by an adherence to the cause of their country they should acquire a title to fair and equitable treatment, are we resolved to furnish them with causes of eternal enmity; and rather supply them with just and founded motives to disaffection, than not to have that disaffection in existence to justify an oppression, which, not from policy, but disposition, we have predetermined to exercise?

What shadow of reason could be assigned, why, at a time when the most Protestant part of this Protestant empire found it for its advantage to unite with the two principal Popish states, to unite itself in the closest bonds with France and Spain, for our destruction, that we should refuse to unite with our own Catholic countrymen for our own preservation? Ought we, like madmen, to tear off the plasters that the lenient hand of prudence had spread over the wounds and gashes which in our delirium of ambition we had given to our own body? No person ever reprobated the American war more than I did, and do, and ever shall. But I never will consent that we should lay additional voluntary penalties on ourselves for a fault which carries but too much of its own punishment in its own nature. For one, I was delighted with the proposal of internal peace. I accepted the blessing with thankfulness and transport; I was truly happy to find one good effect of our civil distractions, that they had put an end to all religious strife and heart-burning in our own bowels. What must be the sentiments of a man who would wish to perpetuate domestic hostility when the causes of dispute are at an end, and who, crying out for peace with one part of the nation on the most humiliating terms, should deny it to those who offer friendship without any terms at all?

But if I was unable to reconcile such a denial to the contracted principles of local duty, what answer could I give to the broad claims of general humanity? I confess to you freely that the sufferings and distresses of the people of America, in this cruel war, have at times affected me more deeply than I can express. I felt every

Gazette of triumph as a blow upon my heart, which has an hundred times sunk and fainted within me at all the mischiefs brought upon those who bear the whole brunt of war in the heart of their country. Yet the Americans are utter strangers to me; a nation among whom I am not sure that I have a single acquaintance. Was I to suffer my mind to be so unaccountably warped; was I to keep such iniquitous weights and measures of temper and of reason, as to sympathize with those who are in open rebellion against an authority which I respect, at war with a country which by every title ought to be, and is, most dear to me; and yet to have no feeling at all for the hardships and indignities suffered by men who, by their very vicinity, are bound up in a nearer relation to us; who contribute their share, and more than their share, to the common prosperity; who perform the common offices of social life, and who obey the laws, to the full as well as I do? Gentlemen, the danger to the state being out of the question (of which, let me tell you, statesmen themselves are apt to have but too exquisite a sense), I could assign no one reason of justice, policy, or feeling, for not concurring most cordially, as most cordially I did concur, in softening some part of that shameful servitude under which several of my worthy fellow-citizens were groaning.

Important effects followed this act of wisdom. They appeared at home and abroad to the great benefit of this kingdom; and, let me hope, to the advantage of mankind at large. It betokened union among ourselves. It showed soundness, even on the part of the persecuted, which generally is the weak side of every community. But its most essential operation was not in England. The Act was immediately, though very imperfectly, copied in Ireland; and this imperfect transcript of an imperfect Act, this first faint sketch of toleration, which did little more than disclose a principle, and mark out a disposition, completed in a most wonderful manner the re-union to the state of all the Catholics of that country. It made us what we ought always to have been, one family, one body, one heart and soul, against the family combination, and all other combinations, of our enemies. We have indeed obligations to that people who received such small benefits with so much gratitude, and for which gratitude and attachment to us, I am afraid they have suffered not a little in other places.

I dare say you have all heard of the privileges indulged to the Irish Catholics residing in Spain. You have likewise heard with what circumstances of severity they have been lately expelled from the seaports of that kingdom, driven into the inland cities, and there detained as a sort of prisoners of state. I have good reason to believe that it was the zeal to our government and our cause (somewhat indiscreetly expressed in one of the addresses of the Catholics of Ireland) which has thus drawn down on their heads the indignation of the court of Madrid, to the inexpressible loss of several individuals, and in future, perhaps, to the great detriment of the whole of their body. Now that our people should be persecuted in Spain for their attachment to this country, and persecuted in this country for their supposed enmity to us, is such a jarring reconciliation of contradictory distresses — is a thing at once so dreadful and ridiculous — that no malice short of diabolical would wish to continue any human creatures in such a situation. But honest men will not forget either their merit or their sufferings. There are men (and many, I trust, there are) who, out of love to their country and their kind, would torture their invention to find excuses for the mistakes of their brethren, and who, to stifle dissension, would construe even doubtful appearances with the utmost favor; such men will never persuade themselves to be ingenious and refined in discovering disaffection and treason in the manifest, palpable signs of suffering loyalty. Persecution is so unnatural to them that they gladly snatch the very first opportunity of laying aside all the tricks and devices of penal politics, and of returning home, after all their irksome and vexatious wanderings, to our natural family mansion, to the grand social principle that unites all men, in all descriptions, under the shadow of an equal and impartial justice.

Men of another sort, I mean the bigoted enemies to liberty, may perhaps, in their politics, make no account of the good or ill affection of the Catholics of England, who are but a handful of people (enough to torment, but not enough to fear), perhaps not so many, of both sexes and of all ages, as fifty thousand. But, gentlemen, it is possible you may not know that the people of that persuasion in Ireland amount at least to sixteen or seventeen hundred thousand souls. I do not at all exaggerate the number. A Nation to be persecuted! Whilst we were masters of the sea, embodied with America, and in alliance with half the powers of the continent, we might perhaps, in that remote corner of Europe, afford to tyrannize with impunity. But there is a revolution in our affairs which makes it prudent to be just. In our late awkward contest with Ireland about trade, had religion been thrown in to ferment and imbitter the mass of discontents, the consequences might have been truly dreadful; but, very happily, that cause of quarrel was previously quieted by the wisdom of the Acts I am commending.

Even in England, where I admit the danger from the discontent of that persuasion to be less than in Ireland; yet even here, had we listened to the counsels of fanaticism and folly, we might have wounded ourselves very deeply, and wounded ourselves in a very tender part. You are apprised that the Catholics of England consist mostly of our best manufacturers. Had the legislature chosen, instead of returning their declarations of duty with correspondent good-will, to drive them to despair, there is a country at their very door to which they would be invited, a country in all respects as good as ours, and with the finest cities in the world ready built to receive them. And thus the bigotry of a free country, and in an enlightened age, would have repeopled the cities of Flanders, which, in the darkness of two hundred years ago, had been desolated by the superstition of a cruel tyrant. Our manufacturers were the growth of the persecutions in the Low Countries. What a spectacle would it be to Europe to see us at this time of day balancing the account of tyranny with those very countries, and by our persecutions driving back trade and manufacture, as a sort of vagabonds, to their original settlement! But I trust we shall be saved this last of disgraces.

So far as to the effect of the Act on the interest of this nation. With regard to the interests of mankind at large I am sure the benefit was very considerable. Long before this Act, indeed, the spirit of toleration began to gain ground in Europe. In Holland, the third part of the people are Catholics; they live at ease, and are a sound part of the State. In many parts of Germany, Protestants and Papists partake the same cities, the same councils, and even the same churches. The unbounded liberality of the King of Prussia's conduct on this occasion is known to all the world; and it is of a piece with the other grand maxims of his reign. The magnanimity of the imperial court, breaking through the narrow principles of its predecessors, has indulged its Protestant subjects — not only with property, with worship, with liberal education — but with honors and trusts, both civil and military. A worthy Protestant gentleman of this country now fills, and fills with credit, a high office in the Austrian Netherlands. Even the Lutheran obstinacy of Sweden has thawed at length, and opened a toleration to all religions. I know myself that in France the Protestants begin to be at rest. The army, which in that country is everything, is open to them; and some of the military rewards and decorations which the laws deny, are supplied by others to make the service acceptable and honorable. The first Minister of Finance in that country is a Protestant. Two years' war without a tax is among the first-fruits of their liberality. Tarnished as the glory of this nation is, and as far as it has waded into the shades of an eclipse, some beams of its former illumination still play upon its surface; and what is done in England is still looked to as argument and as example. It is certainly true that no law of this country ever met with such universal applause abroad, or was so likely to produce the perfection of that tolerating spirit, which, as I observed, has been long gaining ground in Europe; for abroad, it was universally thought that we had done what, I am sorry to say, we had not; they thought we had granted a full toleration. That opinion was, however, so far from hurting the Protestant cause that I declare, with the most serious solemnity, my firm belief that no one thing done for these fifty years past was so likely to prove deeply beneficial to our religion at large as Sir George Savile's act. In its effects it was "an Act for tolerating and protecting Protestantism throughout Europe;" and I hope that those who were taking steps for the quiet and settlement of our Protestant brethren in other countries will, even yet, rather consider the steady equity of the greater and better part of the people of Great Britain, than the vanity and violence of a few.

I perceive, gentlemen, by the manner of all about me, that you look with horror on the wicked clamor which has been raised on this subject; and that instead of an apology for what was done, you rather demand from me an account why the execution of the scheme of toleration was not made more answerable to the large and liberal grounds on which it was taken up? The question is natural and proper; and I remember that a great and learned magistrate, distinguished for his strong and systematic understanding, and who at that time was a member of the House of Commons, made the same objection to the proceeding. The statutes, as they now stand, are, without doubt, perfectly absurd. But I beg leave to explain the cause of this gross imperfection in the tolerating plan, as well and as shortly as I am able. It was universally thought that the session ought not to pass over without doing something in this business. To revise the whole body of the penal statutes was conceived to be an object too big for the time. The penal statute, therefore, which was chosen for repeal (chosen to show our disposition to conciliate, not to perfect a toleration) was this Act of ludicrous cruelty, of which I have just given you the history. It is an Act which, though not by a great deal so fierce and bloody as some of the rest, was infinitely more ready in the execution. It was the Act which gave the greatest encouragement to those pests of society, mercenary informers and interested disturbers of household peace; and it was observed with truth that the prosecutions, either carried to conviction or compounded, for many years, had been all commenced upon that Act. It was said that, whilst we were deliberating on a more perfect scheme, the spirit of the age would never come up to the execution of the statutes which remained, especially as more steps, and a co-operation of more minds and powers were required towards a mischievous use of them, than for the execution of the Act to be repealed; that it was better to unravel this texture from below than from above, beginning with the latest, which, in general practice, is the severest evil. It was alleged that this slow proceeding would be attended with the advantage of a progressive experience; and that the people would grow reconciled to toleration, when they should find by the effects that justice was not so irreconcilable an enemy to convenience as they had imagined.

These, gentlemen, were the reasons why we left this good work in the rude, unfinished state in which good works are commonly left through the tame circumspection with which a timid prudence so frequently enervates beneficence. In doing good, we are generally cold, and languid, and sluggish; and of all things afraid of being too much in the right. But the works of malice and injustice are quite in another style. They are finished with a bold, masterly hand, touched as they are with the spirit of those vehement passions that call forth all our energies whenever we oppress and persecute.

Thus this matter was left for the time, with a full determination in Parliament not to suffer other and worse statutes to remain for the purpose of counteracting the benefits proposed by the repeal of one penal law; for nobody then dreamed of defending what was done for a benefit, on the ground of its being no benefit at all. We were not then ripe for so mean a subterfuge.

I do not wish to go over the horrid scene that was afterwards acted. Would to God it could be expunged forever from the annals of this country! But since it must subsist for our shame, let it subsist for our instruction. In the year 1780, there were found in this nation men deluded enough (for I give the whole to their delusion), on pretences of zeal and piety, without any sort of provocation whatsoever, real or pretended, to make a desperate attempt, which would have consumed all the glory and power of this country in the flames of London, and buried all law, order, and religion under the ruins of the metropolis of the Protestant world. Whether all this mischief done, or in the direct train of doing, was in their original scheme, I cannot say — I hope it was not; but this would have been the unavoidable consequence of their proceedings had not the flames they had lighted up in their fury been extinguished in their blood.

All the time that this horrid scene was acting or avenging, as well as for sometime before, and ever since, the wicked instigators of this unhappy multitude, guilty, with every aggravation, of all their crimes, and screened in a cowardly darkness from their punishment, continued without interruption, pity, or remorse, to blow up the blind rage of the populace with a continued blast of pestilential libels, which infected and poisoned the very air we breathed in.

The main drift of all the libels, and all the riots, was to force Parliament (to persuade us was hopeless) into an act of national perfidy which has no example. For, gentlemen, it is proper you should all know what infamy we escaped by refusing that repeal, for a refusal of which, it seems, I, among others, stand somewhere or other accused. When we took away, on the motives which I had the honor of stating to you, a few of the innumerable penalties upon an oppressed and injured people, the relief was not absolute, but given on a stipulation and compact between them and us; for we bound down the Roman Catholics with the most solemn oaths to bear true allegiance to this government, to abjure all sort of temporal power in any other, and to renounce, under the same solemn obligations, the doctrines of systematic perfidy with which they stood (I conceive very unjustly) charged. Now our modest petitioners came up to us most humbly praying nothing more than that we should break our faith, without any one cause whatsoever of forfeiture assigned; and when the subjects of this kingdom had, on their part, fully performed their engagement, we should refuse, on our part, the benefit we had stipulated on the performance of those very conditions that were prescribed by our own authority, and taken on the sanction of our public faith — that is to say, when we had inveigled them with fair promises within our door, we were to shut it on them; and, adding mockery to outrage, to tell them, "Now we have got you fast; your consciences are bound to a power resolved on your destruction. We have made you swear that your religion obliges you to keep your faith: fools as you are! we will now let you see that our religion enjoins us to keep no faith with you." They who would advisedly call upon us to do such things must certainly have thought us not only a convention of treacherous tyrants, but a gang of the lowest and dirtiest wretches that ever disgraced humanity. Had we done this, we should have indeed proved that there were some in the world whom no faith could bind; and we should have convicted ourselves of that odious principle of which Papists stood accused by those very savages who wished us, on that accusation, to deliver them over to their fury.

In this audacious tumult, when our very name and character as gentlemen was to be cancelled forever along with the faith and honor of the nation, I, who had exerted myself very little on the quiet passing of the bill, thought it necessary then to come forward. I was not alone; but though some distinguished members on all sides, and particularly on ours, added much to their high reputation by the part they took on that day — a part which will be remembered as long as honor, spirit, and eloquence have estimation in the world — I may and will value myself so far that, yielding in abilities to many, I yielded in zeal to none. With warmth and with vigor, and animated with a just and natural indignation, I called forth every faculty that I possessed, and I directed it in every way in which I could possibly employ it. I labored night and day. I labored in Parliament; I labored out of Parliament. If therefore the resolution of the House of Commons, refusing to commit this act of unmatched turpitude, be a crime, I am guilty among the foremost. But, indeed, whatever the faults of that House may have been, no one member was found hardy enough to propose so infamous a thing; and on full debate we passed the resolution against the petitions with as much unanimity as we had formerly passed the law of which these petitions demanded the repeal.

There was a circumstance (justice will not suffer me to pass it over) which, if anything could enforce the reasons I have given, would fully justify the Act of Relief, and render a repeal, or anything like a repeal, unnatural, impossible. It was the behavior of the persecuted Roman Catholics under the acts of violence and brutal insolence which they suffered. I suppose there are not in London less than four or five thousand of that persuasion, from my country, who do a great deal of the most laborious works in the metropolis; and they chiefly inhabit those quarters which were the principal theatre of the fury of the bigoted multitude. They are known to be men of strong arms and quick feelings, and more remarkable for a determined resolution than clear ideas or much foresight. But though provoked by everything that can stir the blood of men, their houses and chapels in flames, and with the most atrocious profanations of everything which they hold sacred before their eyes, not a hand was moved to retaliate, or even to defend. Had a conflict once begun, the rage of their persecutors would have redoubled. Thus fury increasing by the reverberation of outrages, house being fired for house, and church for chapel, I am convinced that no power under heaven could have prevented a general conflagration; and at this day London would have been a tale. But I am well informed, and the thing speaks it, that their clergy exerted their whole influence to keep their people in such a state of forbearance and quiet as, when I look back, fills me with astonishment; but not with astonishment only. Their merits on that occasion ought not to be forgotten; nor will they, when Englishmen come to recollect themselves. I am sure it were far more proper to have called them forth, and given them the thanks of both Houses of Parliament, than to have suffered those worthy clergymen and excellent citizens to be hunted into holes and corners, whilst we are making low-minded inquisitions into the number of their people; as if a tolerating principle was never to prevail, unless we were very sure that only a few could possibly take advantage of it. But indeed we are not yet well recovered of our fright. Our reason, I trust, will return with our security; and this unfortunate temper will pass over like a cloud.

Gentlemen, I have now laid before you a few of the reasons for taking away the penalties of the Act of 1699, and for refusing to establish them on the riotous requisition of 1780. Because I would not suffer anything which may be for your satisfaction to escape, permit me just to touch on the objections urged against our act and our resolves, and intended as a justification of the violence offered to both Houses. "Parliament," they assert, "was too hasty, and they ought, in so essential and alarming a change, to have proceeded with a far greater degree of deliberation." The direct contrary. Parliament was too slow. They took fourscore years to deliberate on the repeal of an Act which ought not to have survived a second session. When at length, after a procrastination of near a century, the business was taken up, it proceeded in the most public manner, by the ordinary stages, and as slowly as a law so evidently right as to be resisted by none would naturally advance. Had it been read three times in one day we should have shown only a becoming readiness to recognize, by protection, the undoubted dutiful behavior of those whom we had but too long punished for offences of presumption or conjecture. But for what end was that bill to linger beyond the usual period of an unopposed measure? Was it to be delayed until a rabble in Edinburgh should dictate to the Church of England what measure of persecution was fitting for her safety? Was it to be adjourned until a fanatical force could be collected in London sufficient to frighten us out of all our ideas of policy and justice? Were we to wait for the profound lectures on the reason of state, ecclesiastical and political, which the Protestant Association have since condescended to read to us? Or were we, seven hundred Peers and Commoners, the only persons ignorant of the ribald invectives which occupy the place of argument in those remonstrances, which every man of common observation had heard a thousand times over, and a thousand times over had despised? All men had before heard what they have to say; and all men at this day know what they dare to do; and, I trust, all honest men are equally influenced by the one, and by the other.

But they tell us that those our fellow-citizens whose chains we have a little relaxed, are enemies to liberty and our free Constitution. Not enemies, I presume, to their own liberty. And as to the Constitution, until we give them some share in it, I do not know on what pretence we can examine into their opinions about a business in which they have no interest or concern. But after all, are we equally sure that they are adverse to our Constitution, as that our statutes are hostile and destructive to them? For my part, I have reason to believe their opinions and inclinations in that respect are various, exactly like those of other men; and if they lean more to the Crown than I and than many of you think *we* ought, we must remember that he who aims at another's life is not to be surprised if he flies into any sanctuary that will receive him. The tenderness of the executive power is the natural asylum of those upon whom the laws have declared war; and to complain that men are inclined to favor the means of their own safety is so absurd that one forgets the injustice in the ridicule.

I must fairly tell you, that, so far as my principles are concerned — principles that I hope will only depart with my last breath — I have no idea of a liberty unconnected with honesty and justice. Nor do I believe that any good constitutions of government, or of freedom, can find it necessary for their security to doom any part of the people to a permanent slavery. Such a constitution of freedom, if such can be, is in effect no more than another name for the tyranny of the strongest faction; and factions in republics have been, and are, full as capable as monarchs of the most cruel oppression and injustice. It is but too true that the love, and even the very idea, of genuine liberty is extremely rare. It is but too true that there are many whose whole scheme of freedom is made up of pride, perverseness, and insolence. They feel themselves in a state of thraldom, they imagine that their souls are cooped and cabined in, unless they have some man, or some body of men, dependent on their mercy. This desire of having some one below them descends to those who are the very lowest of all, — and a Protestant cobbler, debased by his poverty, but exalted by his share of the ruling church, feels a pride in knowing it is by his generosity alone that the peer, whose footman's instep he measures, is able to keep his chaplain from a jail. This disposition is the true source of the passion which many men, in very humble life, have taken to the American war. *Our* subjects in America; *our* Colonies; *our* dependents. This lust of party power is the liberty they hunger and thirst for; and this siren song of ambition has charmed ears that one would have thought were never organized to that sort of music.

This way of proscribing the citizens by denominations and general descriptions, dignified by the name of reason of state and security for constitutions and commonwealths, is nothing better, at bottom, than the miserable invention of an ungenerous ambition, which would fain hold the sacred trust of power without any of the virtues or any of the energies that give a title to it: a receipt of policy made up of a detestable compound of malice, cowardice, and sloth. They would govern men against their will; but in that government they would be discharged from the exercise of vigilance, providence, and fortitude; and therefore, that they may sleep on their watch, they consent to take some one division of the society into partnership of the tyranny over the rest. But let government, in what form it may be, comprehend the whole in its justice, and restrain the suspicious by its vigilance; let it keep watch and ward; let it discover by its sagacity, and punish by its firmness, all delinquency against its power, whenever delinquency exists in the overt acts; and then it will be as safe as ever God and nature intended it should be. Crimes are the acts of individuals, and not of denominations; and therefore arbitrarily to class men under general descriptions in order to proscribe and punish them in the lump for a presumed delinquency, of which perhaps but a part, perhaps none at all, are guilty, is indeed a compendious method, and saves a world of trouble about proof; but such a method, instead of being law, is an act of unnatural rebellion against the legal dominion of reason and justice; and this vice, in any constitution that entertains it, at one time or other will certainly bring on its ruin.

We are told that this is not a religious persecution; and its abettors are loud in disclaiming all severities on account of conscience. Very fine indeed! Then let it be so: they are not persecutors; they are only tyrants. With all my heart. I am perfectly indifferent concerning the pretexts upon which we torment one another; or whether it be for the Constitution of the Church of England, or for the Constitution of the State of England, that people choose to make their fellow-creatures wretched. When we were sent into a place of authority, you that sent us had yourselves but one commission to give. You could give us none to wrong or oppress, or even to suffer any kind of oppression or wrong, on any grounds whatsoever; not on political, as in the affairs of America; not on commercial, as in those of Ireland; not in civil, as in the laws for debt; not in religious, as in the statutes against Protestant or Catholic dissenters. The diversified but connected fabric of universal justice is well cramped and bolted together in all its parts; and, depend upon it, I never have employed, and I never shall employ, any engine of power which may come into my hands to wrench it asunder. All shall stand, if I can help it, and all shall stand connected. After all, to complete this work much remains to be done; much in the East, much in the West. But, great as the work is, if our will be ready, our powers are not deficient.

Since you have suffered me to trouble you so much on

this subject, permit me, gentlemen, to detain you a little longer. I am indeed most solicitous to give you perfect satisfaction. I find there are some of a better and softer nature than the persons with whom I have supposed myself in debate, who neither think ill of the Act of Relief, nor by any means desire the repeal; yet who, not accusing but lamenting what was done, on account of the consequences, have frequently expressed their wish that the late Act had never been made. Some of this description, and persons of worth, I have met with in this city. They conceive that the prejudices, whatever they might be, of a large part of the people ought not to have been shocked; that their opinions ought to have been previously taken, and much attended to; and that thereby the late horrid scenes might have been prevented.

I confess my notions are widely different, and I never was less sorry for any action of my life. I like the bill the better on account of the events of all kinds that followed it. It relieved the real sufferers; it strengthened the state; and, by the disorders that ensued, we had clear evidence that there lurked a temper somewhere which ought not to be fostered by the laws. No ill consequences whatever could be attributed to the Act itself. We knew beforehand, or we were poorly instructed, that toleration is odious to the intolerant; freedom to oppressors; property to robbers; and all kinds and degrees of prosperity to the envious. We knew that all these kinds of men would gladly gratify their evil dispositions under the sanction of law and religion if they could; if they could not, yet, to make way to their objects, they would do their utmost to subvert all religion and all law. This we certainly knew but, knowing this, is there any reason, because thieves break in and steal, and thus bring detriment to you, and draw ruin on themselves, that I am to be sorry that you are in the possession of shops, and of warehouses, and of wholesome laws to protect them? Are you to build no houses because desperate men may pull them down upon their own heads? Or, if a malignant wretch will cut his own throat because he sees you give alms to the necessitous and deserving, shall his destruction be attributed to your charity, and not to his own deplorable madness? If we repent of our good actions, what, I pray you, is left for our faults and follies? It is not the beneficence of the laws; it is the unnatural temper, which beneficence can fret and sour, that is to be lamented. It is this temper which, by all rational means, ought to be sweetened and corrected. If froward men should refuse this cure, can they vitiate anything but themselves? Does evil so react upon good as not only to retard its motion, but to change its nature? If it can so operate, then good men will always be in the power of the bad; and virtue, by a dreadful reverse of order, must lie under perpetual subjection and bondage to vice.

As to the opinion of the people, which some think, in such cases, is to be implicitly obeyed.—Nearly two years' tranquillity which followed the Act, and its instant imitation in Ireland, proved abundantly that the late horrible spirit was, in a great measure, the effect of insidious art, and perverse industry, and gross misrepresentation. But suppose that the dislike had been much more deliberate and much more general than I am persuaded it was. When we know that the opinions of even the greatest multitudes are the standard of rectitude, I shall think myself obliged to make those opinions the masters of my conscience; but if it may be doubted whether Omnipotence itself is competent to alter the essential constitution of right and wrong, sure I am that such *things* as they and I are possessed of no such power.

No man carries further than I do the policy of making government pleasing to the people; but the widest range of this politic complaisance is confined within the limits of justice. I would not only consult the interest of the people, but I would cheerfully gratify their humors. We are all a sort of children that must be soothed and managed. I think I am not austere or formal in my nature. I would bear, I would even myself play my part in, any innocent buffooneries to divert them; but I never will act the tyrant for their amusement. If they will mix malice in their sports, I shall never consent to throw them any living sentient creature whatsoever, no, not so much as a kitling, to torment.

"But, if I profess all this impolitic stubbornness, I may chance never to be elected into Parliament." It is certainly not pleasing to be put out of the public service; but I wish to be a member of Parliament to have my share of doing good and resisting evil. It would therefore be absurd to renounce my objects in order to obtain my seat. I deceive myself indeed most grossly if I had not much rather pass the remainder of my life hidden in the recesses of the deepest obscurity, feeding my mind even with the visions and imaginations of such things, than to be placed on the most splendid throne of the universe, tantalized with a denial of the practice of all which can make the greatest situation any other than the greatest curse. Gentlemen, I have had my day. I can never sufficiently express my gratitude to you for having set me in a place wherein I could lend the slightest help to great and laudable designs. If I have had my share in any measure giving quiet to private property and private conscience; if by my vote I have aided in securing to families the best possession, peace; if I have joined in reconciling kings to their subjects, and subjects to their prince; if I have assisted to loosen the foreign holdings of the citizen, and taught him to look for his protection to the laws of his country, and for his comfort to the good-will of his countrymen; if I have thus taken my part with the best of men in the best of their actions, I can shut the book — I might wish to read a page or two more, but this is enough for my measure — I have not lived in vain.

And now, gentlemen, on this serious day, when I come, as it were, to make up my account with you, let me take to myself some degree of honest pride on the nature of the charges that are against me. I do not here stand before you accused of venality, or of neglect of duty. It is not said that, in the long period of my service, I have in a single instance sacrificed the slightest of your interests to my ambition, or to my fortune. It is not alleged that, to gratify any anger or revenge of my own or of my party, I have had a share in wronging or oppressing any description of men, or any one man in any description. No! the charges against me are all of one kind: that I have pushed the principles of general justice and benevolence too far, further than a cautious policy would warrant, and further than the opinions of many would go along with me. In every accident which may happen through life — in pain, in sorrow, in depression, and distress — I will call to mind this accusation, and be comforted.

Gentlemen, I submit the whole to your judgment. Mr. Mayor, I thank you for the trouble you have taken on this occasion; in your state of health, it is particularly obliging. If this company should think it advisable for me to withdraw, I shall respectfully retire; if you think otherwise, I shall go directly to the Council-house and to the 'Change, and, without a moment's delay, begin my canvass.

LORD ERSKINE.

IN BEHALF OF JOHN STOCKDALE WHEN TRIED FOR A LIBEL ON THE HOUSE OF COMMONS; COURT OF THE KING'S BENCH, DECEMBER 9, 1789.

Gentlemen of the Jury, — Mr. Stockdale, who is brought as a criminal before you for the publication of this book, has, by employing me as his advocate, reposed what must appear to many an extraordinary degree of confidence; since, although he well knows that I am personally connected in friendship with most of those whose conduct and opinions are principally arraigned by its author, he nevertheless commits to my hands his defence and justification.

From a trust apparently so delicate and singular, vanity is but too apt to whisper an application to some fancied merit of one's own; but it is proper, for the honor of the English bar, that the world should know that such things happen to all of us daily, and of course; and that the defendant, without any knowledge of me, or any confidence that was personal, was only not afraid to follow up an accidental retainer from the knowledge he has of the general character of the profession. Happy indeed is it for this country that, whatever interested divisions may characterize other places of which I may have occasion to speak to-day, however the counsels of the highest departments of the state may be occasionally distracted by personal considerations, they never enter these walls to disturb the administration of justice; whatever may be our public principles or the private habits of our lives, they never cast even a shade across the path of our professional duties. If this be the characteristic even of the bar of an English court of justice, what sacred impartiality may not every man expect from its jurors and its bench?

As, from the indulgence which the Court was yesterday pleased to give to my indisposition, this information was not proceeded on when you were attending to try it, it is probable you were not altogether inattentive to what passed at the trial of the other indictment, prosecuted also by the House of Commons; and therefore, without a restatement of the same principles, and a similar quotation of authorities to support them, I need only remind you of the law applicable to this subject, as it was then admitted by the Attorney-General, in concession to my propositions, and confirmed by the higher authority of the Court; viz.,

First, that every information or indictment must contain such a description of the crime that the defendant may know what crime it is which he is called upon to answer.

Secondly, that the jury may appear to be warranted in their conclusion of guilty or not guilty.

And, lastly, that the court may see such a precise and definite transgression upon the record, as to be able to apply the punishment which judicial discretion may dictate, or which positive law may inflict.

It was admitted also to follow as a mere corollary from these propositions, that where an information charges a writing to be composed or published of and concerning the Commons of Great Britain, with an intent to bring that body into scandal and disgrace with the public, the author cannot be brought within the scope of such a charge unless the jury, on examination and comparison of the whole matter written or published, shall be satisfied that the particular passages charged as criminal, when explained by the context, and considered as part of one entire work, were meant and intended by the author to vilify the House of Commons *as a body*, and were written of and concerning them *in Parliament assembled.*

These principles being settled, we are now to see what the present information is.

It charges that the defendant — "unlawfully, wickedly, and maliciously devising, contriving, and intending to asperse, scandalize, and vilify the Commons of Great Britain in Parliament assembled; and most wickedly and audaciously to represent their proceedings as corrupt and unjust; and to make it believed and thought as if the Commons of Great Britain in Parliament assembled, were a most wicked, tyrannical, base, and corrupt set of persons, and to bring them into disgrace with the public" — the defendant published — what? Not those latter ends of sentences which the Attorney-General has read from his brief, as if they had followed one another in order in this book; not those scraps and tails of passages which are patched together upon this record, and pronounced in one breath, as if they existed without intermediate matter in the same page, and without context anywhere. No! This is not the accusation, even mutilated as it is: for the information charges that, with intention to vilify the House of Commons, the defendant published the whole book, describing it on the record by its title: "A Review of the principal Charges against Warren Hastings, Esq., late Governor-General of Bengal;" in which, among other things, the matter particularly selected is to be found. Your inquiry, therefore, is not confined to whether the defendant published those selected parts of it, and whether, looking at them as they are distorted by the information, they carry in fair construction the sense and meaning which the innuendoes put upon them; but whether the author of the entire work — I say the author, since, if *he* could defend himself, the publisher unquestionably can — whether the author wrote the volume which I hold in my hand as a free, manly, *bonâ fide* disquisition of criminal charges against his fellow-citizen; or whether the long, eloquent discussion of them, which fills so many pages, was a mere cloak and cover for the introduction of the supposed scandal imputed to the selected passages, the mind of the writer all along being intent on traducing the House of Commons, and not on fairly answering their charges against Mr. Hastings.

This, gentlemen, is the principal matter for your consideration; and therefore, if, after you shall have taken the book itself into the chamber which will be provided for you, and shall have read the whole of it with impartial attention — if, after the performance of this duty, you can return here, and with clear consciences pronounce upon your oaths that the impression made upon you by these pages is, that the author wrote them with the wicked, seditious, and corrupt intentions charged by the information — you have then my full permission to find the defendant guilty; but if, on the other hand, the general tenor of the composition shall impress you with respect for the author, and point him out to you as a man mistaken, perhaps, himself, but not seeking to deceive others — if every line of the work shall present to you an intelligent, animated mind, glowing with a Christian compassion towards a fellowman whom he believed to be innocent, and with a patriot zeal for the liberty of his country, which he considered as wounded through the sides of an oppressed fellow-citizen; — if *this* shall be the impression on your consciences and understandings, when you are called upon to deliver your verdict; then hear from me that you not only work private injustice, but break up the press of England, and surrender her rights and liberties forever, if you convict the defendant.

Gentlemen, to enable you to form a true judgment of the meaning of this book and of the intention of its author, and to expose the miserable juggle that is played off in the information by the combination of sentences which, in the work itself, have no bearing upon one another, I will first give you the publication as it is charged upon the record and presented by the Attorney-General in opening the case for the Crown; and I will then, by reading the interjacent matter, which is studiously kept out of view, convince you of its true interpretation.

The information, beginning with the first page of the book, charges as a libel upon the House of Commons the following sentence: "The House of Commons has now given its final decision with regard to the merits and demerits of Mr. Hastings. The grand inquest of England have delivered their charges, and preferred their impeachment; their allegations are referred to proof; and from the appeal to the collective wisdom and justice of the nation, in the supreme tribunal of the kingdom, the question comes to be determined whether Mr. Hastings be guilty or not guilty?"

It is but fair, however, to admit that this first sentence, which the most ingenious malice cannot torture into a criminal construction, is charged by the information rather as introductory to what is made to follow it than as libellous in itself; for the Attorney-General, from this introductory passage in the first page, goes on at a leap to page thirteenth, and reads, almost without a stop, as if it immediately followed the other, this sentence: "What credit can we give to multiplied and accumulated charges when we find that they originate from misrepresentation and falsehood?"

From these two passages thus standing together, without the intervenient matter which occupies thirteen pages, one would imagine that, instead of investigating the probability or improbability of the guilt imputed to Mr. Hastings; instead of carefully examining the Charges of the Commons, and the defence of them which had been delivered before them, or which was preparing for the Lords; the author had immediately, and in a moment after stating the mere fact of the impeachment, decided that the act of the Commons originated from misrepresentation and falsehood.

Gentlemen, in the same manner a veil is cast over all that is written in the next seven pages; for, knowing that the context would help to the true construction, not only of the passages charged before, but of those in the sequel of this information, the Attorney-General, aware that it would convince every man who read it that there was no intention in the author to calumniate the House of Commons, passes over, by another leap, to page twenty; and in the same manner, without drawing his breath, and as if it directly followed the two former sentences in the first and thirteenth pages, reads from page twentieth, — "An impeachment of error in judgment with regard to the quantum of a fine, and for an intention that never was executed, and never known to the offending party, characterizes a tribunal of inquisition rather than a Court of Parliament."

From this passage, by another vault, he leaps over one-and-thirty pages more, to page fifty-one, where he reads the following sentence, which he mainly relies on, and upon which I shall by and by trouble you with some observations: "Thirteen of them passed in the House of Commons, not only without investigation, but without being read; and the votes were given without inquiry, argument, or conviction. A majority had determined to impeach; opposite parties met each other, and 'jostled in the dark,' to perplex the political drama, and bring the hero to a tragic catastrophe."

From thence, deriving new vigor from every exertion, he makes his last grand stride over forty-four pages more, almost to the end of the book, charging a sentence in the ninety-fifth page.

So that, out of a volume of one hundred and ten pages, the defendant is only charged with a few scattered fragments of sentences, picked out of three or four. Out of a work consisting of about two thousand five hundred and thirty lines of manly, spirited eloquence, only forty or fifty lines are culled from different parts of it, and artfully put together, so as to rear up a libel out of a false context, by a supposed connection of sentences with one another which are not only entirely independent, but which, when compared with their antecedents, bear a totally different construction. In this manner the greatest works upon government, the most excellent books of science, the sacred Scriptures themselves, might be distorted into libel; by forsaking the general context, and hanging a meaning upon selected parts. Thus, as in the text put by Algernon Sidney, "The fool hath said in his heart, There is no God," the Attorney-General, on the principle of the present proceeding against this pamphlet, might indict the publisher of the Bible for blasphemously denying the existence of Heaven in printing, "There is no God;" — these words alone, without the context, would be selected by the information, and the Bible, like this book, would be underscored to meet it· nor could the defendant, in such a case, have any possible defence, unless the jury were permitted to see, by the book itself, that the verse, instead of denying the existence of the Divinity, only imputed that imagination to a fool.

Gentlemen, having now gone through the Attorney-General's reading, the book shall presently come forward and speak for itself; but before I can venture to lay it before you, it is proper to call your attention to how matters stood at the time of its publication, without which the author's meaning and intention cannot possibly be understood.

The Commons of Great Britain, in Parliament assembled, had accused Mr. Hastings, as Governor-General of Bengal, of high crimes and misdemeanors; and their jurisdiction, for that high purpose of national justice, was unquestionably competent; but it is proper you should know the nature of this inquisitorial capacity. The Commons, in voting an impeachment, may be compared to a grand jury finding a bill of indictment for the Crown: neither the one nor the other can be supposed to proceed but upon the matter which is brought before them; neither of them can find guilt without accusation, nor the truth of accusation, without evidence. When, therefore, we speak of the *accuser* or *accusers* of a person indicted for any crime, although the grand jury are the prosecutors in form, by giving effect to the accusation, yet, in common parlance, we do not consider them as the responsible authors of the prosecution. If I were to write of a most wicked indictment, found against an innocent man, which was preparing for trial, nobody who read it would conceive I meant to stigmatize the grand jury that found the bill; but it would be inquired immediately, who was the prosecutor and who were the witnesses on the back of it? In the same manner I mean to contend that if this book is read with only common attention, the whole scope of it will be discovered to be this: that, in the opinion of the author, Mr. Hastings had been accused of mal-administration in India from the heat and spleen of political divisions in Parliament, and not from any zeal for national honor or justice; that the impeachment did not originate from Government, but from a faction banded against it, which, by misrepresentation and violence, had fastened it on an unwilling House of Commons; that, prepossessed with this sentiment — which, however unfounded, makes no part of the present business, since the publisher is not called before you for defaming individual members of the Commons, but for a contempt of the Commons as a body — the author pursues the charges, article by article; enters into a warm and animated vindication of Mr. Hastings, by regular answers to each of them; and that, as far as the mind and soul of a man can be visible — I might almost say embodied — in his writings, his intention throughout the whole volume appears to have been to charge with injustice the private accusers of Mr. Hastings, and not the House of Commons as a body, which undoubtedly rather reluctantly gave way to, than heartily adopted, the impeachment. This will be found to be the palpable scope of the book; and no man who can read English, and who, at the same time, will have the candor and common sense to take up his impressions from what is written in it, instead of bringing his own along with him to the reading of it, can possibly understand it otherwise.

But it may be said, admitting this to be the scope and design of the author, what right had he to canvass the merits of an accusation upon the records of the Commons, more especially while it was in the course of legal procedure? This, I confess, might have been a serious question; but the Commons, as prosecutors of this information, seem to have waived or forfeited their right to ask it. Before they sent the Attorney-General into this place to punish the publication of answers to their charges, they should have recollected that their own want of circumspection in the maintenance of their privileges, and in the protection of persons accused before them, had given to the public the charges themselves, which should have been confined to their own Journals. The course and practice of Parliament might warrant the printing of them for the use of their own members; but there the publication should have stopped, and all further progress been resisted by authority. If they were resolved to consider answers to their charges as a contempt of their privileges, and to punish the publication of them by such severe prosecutions, it would have well become them to have begun first with those printers who, by publishing the charges themselves throughout the whole kingdom, or rather throughout the whole civilized world, were anticipating the passions and judgments of the public against a subject of England upon his trial, so as to make the publication of answers to them not merely a privilege, but a debt and duty to humanity and justice. The Commons of Great Britain claimed and exercised the privilege of questioning the innocence of Mr. Hastings by their impeachment; but as, however questioned, it was still to be presumed and protected until guilt was established by a judgment, he whom they had accused had an equal claim upon their justice to guard him from prejudice and misrepresentation until the hour of trial.

Had the Commons, therefore, by the exercise of their high, necessary, and legal privileges, kept the public aloof from all canvass of their proceedings by an early punishment of printers who, without reserve or secrecy, had sent out the charges into the world from a thousand presses in every form of publication, they would have then stood upon ground to-day from whence no argument of policy or justice could have removed them; because nothing could be more incompatible with either than appeals to the many upon subjects of judicature which, by common consent, a few are appointed to determine, and which must be determined by facts and principles which the multitude have neither leisure nor knowledge to investigate. But then, let it be remembered that it is for those who have the authority to accuse and punish, to set the example of and to enforce this reserve which is so necessary for the ends of justice. Courts of law therefore, in England, never endure the publication of their records; and a prosecutor of an indictment would be attached for such a publication; and upon the same principle, a defendant would be punished for anticipating the justice of his country by the publication of his defence, the public being no party to it until the tribunal appointed for its determination be open for its decision.

Gentlemen, you have a right to take judicial notice of these matters without the proof of them by witnesses, for jurors may not only, without evidence, found their verdicts on facts that are notorious, but upon what they know privately themselves, after revealing it upon oath to one another, and therefore you are always to remember that this book was written when the charges against Mr. Hastings, to which it is an answer, were, to the knowledge of the Commons (for we cannot presume our watchmen to have been asleep), publicly hawked about in every pamphlet, magazine, and newspaper in the kingdom. You well know with what a curious appetite those charges were devoured by the whole public, interesting as they were, not only from their importance, but from the merit of their composition; certainly not so intended by the honorable and excellent composer to oppress the accused, but because the commonest subjects swell into eloquence under the touch of his sublime genius. Thus, by the remissness of the Commons, who are now the prosecutors of this information, a subject of England, who was not even charged with contumacious resistance to authority, much less a proclaimed outlaw, and therefore fully entitled to every security which the customs and statutes of the kingdom hold out for the protection of British liberty, saw himself pierced with the arrows of thousands and ten thousands of libels.

Gentlemen, ere I venture to lay the book before you, it must be yet further remembered (for the fact is equally notorious) that under these inauspicious circumstances the trial of Mr. Hastings at the bar of the Lords had actually commenced long before its publication.

There the most august and striking spectacle was daily exhibited which the world ever witnessed. A vast stage of justice was erected, awful from its high authority, splendid from its illustrious dignity, venerable from the learning and wisdom of its judges, captivating and affecting from the mighty concourse of all ranks and conditions which daily flocked into it, as into a theatre of pleasure; there, when the whole public mind was at once awed and softened to the impression of every human affection, there appeared, day after day, one after another, men of the most powerful and exalted talents, eclipsing by their accusing eloquence the most boasted harangues of antiquity — rousing the pride of national resentment by the boldest invectives against broken faith and violated treaties, and shaking the bosom with alternate pity and horror by the most glowing pictures of insulted nature and humanity; ever animated and energetic from the love of fame, which is the inherent passion of genius; firm and indefatigable from a strong prepossession of the justice of their cause.

Gentlemen, when the author sat down to write the book now before you, all this terrible, unceasing, exhaustless artillery of warm zeal, matchless vigor of understanding, consuming and devouring eloquence, united with the highest dignity, was daily, and without prospect of conclusion, pouring forth upon one private, unprotected man, who was bound to hear it, in the face of the whole people of England, with reverential submission and silence. I do not complain of this, as I did of the publication of the charges, because it was what the law allowed and sanctioned in the course of a public trial; but when it is remembered that we are not angels, but weak fallible men, and that even the noble judges of that high tribunal are clothed beneath their ermines with the common infirmities of man's nature, it will bring us all to a proper temper for considering the book itself, which will in a few moments be laid before you. But first, let me once more remind you that it was under all these circumstances, and amidst the blaze of passion and prejudice which the scene I have been endeavoring faintly to describe to you might be supposed likely to produce, that the author, whose name I will now give to you, sat down to compose the book which is prosecuted to-day as a libel.

The history of it is very short and natural.

The Rev. Mr. Logan, minister of the gospel at Leith, in Scotland, a clergyman of the purest morals, and, as you will see by and by, of very superior talents, well acquainted with the human character, and knowing the difficulty of bringing back public opinion after it is settled on any subject, took a warm, unbought, unsolicited interest in the situation of Mr. Hastings, and determined, if possible, to arrest and suspend the public judgment concerning him. He felt for the situation of a fellow-citizen exposed to a trial which, whether right or wrong, is undoubtedly a severe one; a trial certainly not confined to a few criminal acts like those we are accustomed to, but comprehending the transactions of a whole life, and the complicated policies of numerous and distant nations; a trial which had neither visible limits to its duration, bounds to its expense, nor circumscribed compass for the grasp of memory or understanding; a trial which had therefore broken loose from the common forms of decision, and had become the universal topic of discussion in the world, superseding not only every other grave pursuit, but every fashionable dissipation.

Gentlemen, the question you have therefore to try upon all this matter is extremely simple. It is neither more nor less than this. At a time when the charges against Mr. Hastings were, by the implied consent of the Commons, in every hand and on every table; when, by their managers, the lightning of eloquence was incessantly consuming him, and flashing in the eyes of the public; when every man was, with perfect impunity, saying, and writing, and publishing just what he pleased of the supposed plunderer and devastator of nations; — would it have been criminal in Mr. Hastings himself to have reminded the public that he was a native of this free land, entitled to the common protection of her justice, and that he had a defence, in his turn, to offer to them, the outlines of which he implored them in the mean time to receive, as an antidote to the unlimited and unpunished poison in circulation against him? This is, without color or exaggeration, the true question you are to decide; because I assert, without the hazard of contradiction, that if Mr. Hastings himself could have stood justified or excused in your eyes for publishing this volume in his own defence, the author, if he wrote it *bonâ fide* to defend him, must stand equally excused and justified; and if the author be justified, the publisher cannot be criminal, unless you have evidence that it was published by him with a different spirit and intention from those in which it was written. The question, therefore, is correctly what I just now stated it to be: Could Mr. Hastings have been condemned to infamy for writing this book?

Gentlemen, I tremble with indignation to be driven to put such a question in England. Shall it be endured that a subject of this country (instead of being arraigned and tried for some single act in her ordinary courts, where the accusation, as soon at least as it is made public, is followed within a few hours by the decision) may be impeached by the Commons for the transactions of twenty years, that the accusation shall spread as wide as the region of letters, that the accused shall stand, day after day, and year after year, as a spectacle before the public, which shall be kept in a perpetual state of inflammation against him; yet that he shall not, without the severest penalties, be permitted to submit anything to the judgment of mankind in his defence? If this be law (which it is for you to-day to decide), such a man has no trial. This great hall, built by our fathers for English justice, is no longer a court, but an altar; and an Englishman, instead of being judged in it by God and his country, is a victim and a sacrifice.

You will carefully remember that I am not presuming to question either the right or duty of the Commons of Great Britain to impeach; neither am I arraigning the propriety of their selecting, as they have done, the most extraordinary persons for ability which the age has produced to manage their impeachment. Much less am I censuring the managers themselves, charged with the conduct of it before the Lords, who are undoubtedly bound, by their duty to the House and to the public, to expatiate upon the crimes of the persons whom they had accused. None of these points are questioned by me, nor are in this place questionable. I desire only to have it decided whether — if the Commons, when national expediency happens to call, in their judgment, for an impeachment, shall, instead of keeping it on their own records, and carrying it with due solemnity to the Peers for trial, permit it, without censure and punishment, to be sold like a common newspaper in the shop of my client, so crowded with their own members, that no plain man, without privilege of Parliament, can hope even for the sight of the fire in a winter's day, every man buying it, reading it, and commenting upon it — the gentleman himself who is the object of it, or his friend in his absence, may not, without stepping beyond the bounds of English freedom, put a copy of what is thus published into his pocket, and send back to the very same shop for publication a *bonâ fide*, rational, able answer to it, in order that the bane and antidote may circulate together, and the public be kept straight till the day of decision? If you think, gentlemen, that this common duty of self-preservation in the accused himself, which nature writes as a law upon the hearts of even savages and brutes, is nevertheless too high a privilege to be enjoyed by an impeached and suffering Englishman; or if you think it beyond the offices of humanity and justice, when brought home to the hand of a brother or a friend, you will say so by your verdict of guilty; the decision will then be yours, and the consolation mine, that I have labored to avert it. A very small part of the misery which will follow from it is likely to light upon me; the rest will be divided among yourselves and your children.

Gentlemen, I observe plainly, and with infinite satisfaction, that you are shocked and offended at my even supposing it possible you should pronounce such a detestable judgment, and that you only require of me to make out to your satisfaction, as I promised, that the real scope and object of this book is a *bonâ fide* defence of Mr. Hastings, and not a cloak and cover for scandal on the House of Commons. I engage to do this, and I engage for nothing more. I shall make an open, manly defence. I mean to torture no expressions from their natural constructions; to dispute no innuendoes on the record, should any of them have a fair application; nor to conceal from your notice any unguarded, intemperate expressions which may, perhaps, be found to chequer the vigorous and animated career of the work. Such a conduct might, by accident, shelter the defendant; but it would be the surrender of the very principle on which alone the liberty of the English press can stand, and I shall never defend any man from a temporary imprisonment by the permanent loss of my own liberty, and the ruin of my country. I mean, therefore, to submit to you that, though you should find a few lines in page thirteen or twenty-one, a few more in page fifty-one, and some others in other places, containing expressions bearing on the House of Commons, even as a body, which if written as independent paragraphs by themselves, would be indefensible libels, yet that you have a right to pass them over in judgment, provided the substance clearly appears to be a *bonâ fide* conclusion, arising from the honest investigation of a subject which it was lawful to investigate, and the questionable expressions the visible effusion of a zealous temper engaged in an honorable and legal pursuit. After this preparation, I am not afraid to lay the book in its genuine state before you.

The pamphlet begins thus: "The House of Commons has now given its final decision with regard to the merits and demerits of Mr. Hastings. The grand inquest of

England have delivered their charges, and preferred their impeachment; their allegations are referred to proof; and, from the appeal to the collective wisdom and justice of the nation in the supreme tribunal of the kingdom, the question comes to be determined whether Mr. Hastings be guilty or not guilty?"

Now, if immediately after what I have just read to you (which is the first part charged by the information) the author had said, "Will accusations, built on such a baseless fabric, prepossess the public in favor of the impeachment? What credit can we give to multiplied and accumulated charges, when we find that they originate from misrepresentation and falsehood?" every man would have been justified in pronouncing that he was attacking the House of Commons, because the groundless accusations mentioned in the second sentence could have no reference but to the House itself mentioned by name in the first and only sentence which preceded it.

But, Gentlemen, to your astonishment, I will now read what intervenes between these two passages. From this you will see, beyond a possibility of doubt, that the author never meant to calumniate the House of Commons, but to say that the accusations of Mr. Hastings before the whole House grew out of a Committee of Secrecy established some years before, and were afterwards brought forward by the spleen of private enemies and a faction in the government. This will appear, not only from the grammatical construction of the words, but from what is better than words, from the meaning which a person writing as a friend of Mr. Hastings must be supposed to have intended to convey. Why should such a friend attack the House of Commons? Will any man gravely tell me that the House of Commons, as a body, ever wished to impeach Mr. Hastings? Do we not all know that they constantly hung back from it, and hardly knew where they were, or what to do, when they found themselves entangled with it? My learned friend, the Attorney-General, is a member of this Assembly; perhaps he may tell you by and by what he thought of it, and whether he ever marked any disposition in the majority of the Commons hostile to Mr. Hastings. But why should I distress my friend by the question? The fact is sufficiently notorious; and what I am going to read from the book itself (which is left out in the information) is too plain for controversy.

"Whatever may be the event of the impeachment, the proper exercise of such power is a valuable privilege of the British Constitution, a formidable guardian of the public liberty and the dignity of the nation. The only danger is, that, from the influence of faction, and the awe which is annexed to great names, they may be prompted to determine before they inquire, and to pronounce judgment without examination."

Here is the clue to the whole pamphlet. The author trusts to and respects the House of Commons, but is afraid their mature and just consideration may be disturbed by faction. Now, does he mean government by faction? Does he mean the majority of the Commons by faction? Will the House, which is the prosecutor here, sanction that application of the phrase — or will the Attorney-General admit the majority to be the true innuendo of faction? I wish he would; I should then have gained something at least by this extraordinary debate. But I have no expectation of the sort; such a concession would be too great a sacrifice to any prosecution at a time when every thing is considered as faction that disturbs the repose of the Minister in Parliament. But, indeed, Gentlemen, some things are too plain for argument. The author certainly means my friends, who, whatever qualifications may belong to them, must be contented with the appellation of faction while they oppose the Minister in the House of Commons; but the House having given this meaning to the phrase of faction for its own purposes, cannot in decency change the interpretation in order to convict my client. I take that to be beyond the privilege of Parliament.

The same bearing upon individual members of the Commons, and not on the Commons as a body, is obvious throughout. Thus, after saying, in page nine, that the East India Company had thanked Mr. Hastings for his meritorious services (which is unquestionably true), he adds, "that mankind would abide by their deliberate decision, rather than by the intemperate assertion of a committee."

This he writes after the Impeachment was found by the Commons at large, but he takes no account of their proceedings, imputing the whole to the original committee; *i.e.*, the Committee of Secrecy, so called, I suppose, from their being the authors of twenty volumes in folio, which will remain a secret to all posterity, as nobody will ever read them. The same construction is equally plain from what immediately follows: "The report of the Committee of Secrecy also states that the happiness of the native inhabitants of India has been deeply affected, their confidence in English faith and lenity shaken and impaired, and the character of this nation wantonly and wickedly degraded."

Here, again, you are grossly misled by the omission of near twenty-one pages; for the author, though he is here speaking of this committee by name, which brought forward the charges to the notice of the House, and which he continues to do onward to the next select paragraph, yet, by arbitrarily sinking the whole context, he is taken to be speaking of the House as a body, when, in the passage next charged by the information, he reproaches the accusers of Mr. Hastings; although, so far is he from considering them as the House of Commons, that in the very same page he speaks of the Articles as the charges, not even of the Committee, but of Mr. Burke alone, the most active and intelligent member of that body, having been circulated in India by a relation of that gentleman: "The charges of Mr. Burke have been carried to Calcutta, and carefully circulated in India."

Now, if we were considering these passages of the work as calumniating a body of gentlemen, many of whom I must be supposed highly to respect, or as reflecting upon my worthy friend whose name I have mentioned, it would give rise to a totally different inquiry, which it is neither my duty nor yours to agitate; but surely, the more that consideration obtrudes itself upon us, the more clearly it demonstrates that the author's whole direction was against the individual accusers of Mr. Hastings, and not against the House of Commons, which merely trusted to the matter they had collected.

Although, from a caution which my situation dictates as representing another, I have thought it my duty thus to point out to you the real intention of the author, as it appears by the fair construction of the work, yet I protest that in my own apprehension it is very immaterial whether he speaks of the Committee or of the House, provided you shall think the whole volume a *bonâ fide* defence of Mr. Hastings. This is the great point I am, by all my observations, endeavoring to establish, and which I think no man who reads the following short passages can doubt. Very intelligent persons have indeed considered them, if founded in facts, to render every other amplification unnecessary. The first of them is as follows: "It was known, at that time, that Mr. Hastings had not only descended from a public to a private station, but that he was persecuted with accusations and impeachments. But none of these suffering millions have sent their complaints to this country; not a sigh nor a groan has been wafted from India to Britain. On the contrary, testimonies the most honorable to the character and merit of Mr. Hastings have been transmitted by those very princes whom he has been supposed to have loaded with the deepest injuries."

Here, gentlemen, we must be permitted to pause together a little; for, in examining whether these pages were written as an honest answer to the charges of the Commons, or as a prostituted defence of a notorious criminal whom the writer believed to be guilty, truth becomes material at every step; for if in any instance he be detected of a wilful misrepresentation, he is no longer an object of your attention.

Will the Attorney-General proceed then to detect the hypocrisy of our author, by giving us some details of the proofs by which these personal enormities have been established, and which the writer must be supposed to have been acquainted with? I ask this as the defender of Mr. Stockdale, not of Mr. Hastings, with whom I have no concern. I am sorry, indeed, to be so often obliged to repeat this protest; but I really feel myself embarrassed with those repeated coincidences of defence which thicken on me as I advance, and which were, no doubt, overlooked by the Commons when they directed this interlocutory inquiry into his conduct. I ask, then, as counsel for Mr. Stockdale, whether, when a great state criminal is brought for justice at an immense expense to the public, accused of the most oppressive cruelties, and charged with the robbery of princes and the destruction of nations, it is not open to any one to ask, "Who are his accusers? What are the sources and the authorities of these shocking complaints? Where are the ambassadors or memorials of those princes whose revenues he has plundered? Where are the witnesses for those unhappy men in whose persons the rights of humanity have been violated? How deeply buried is the blood of the innocent, that it does not rise up in retributive judgment to confound the guilty?" These, surely, are questions which, when a fellow-citizen is upon a long, painful, and expensive trial, humanity has a right to propose; which the plain sense of the most unlettered man may be expected to dictate; and which all history must provoke from the more enlightened. When Cicero impeached Verres before the great tribunal of Rome of similar cruelties and depredations in her Provinces, the Roman people were not left to such inquiries. All Sicily surrounded the Forum, demanding justice upon her plunderer and spoiler, with tears and imprecations. It was not by the eloquence of the orator, but by the cries and tears of the miserable, that Cicero prevailed in that illustrious cause. Verres fled from the oaths of his accusers and their witnesses, and not from the voice of Tully. To preserve the fame of his eloquence, he composed his five celebrated speeches, but they were never delivered against the criminal, because he had fled from the city, appalled with the sight of the persecuted and the oppressed. It may be said that the cases of Sicily and India are widely different; perhaps they may be; whether they are or not is foreign to my purpose. I am not bound to deny the possibility of answers to such questions; I am only vindicating the right to ask them.

Gentlemen, the author, in the other passage which I marked out to your attention, goes on thus: — "Lord Cornwallis and Sir John Macpherson, his successors in office, have given the same voluntary tribute of approbation to his measures as Governor-General of India. A letter from the former, dated the 10th of August, 1786, gives the following account of our dominions in Asia:

'The native inhabitants of this kingdom are the happiest and best protected subjects in India; our native allies and tributaries confide in our protection; the country powers are aspiring to the friendship of the English; and from the King of Tidore, toward New Guinea, to Timur Shah, on the banks of the Indus, there is not a state that has not lately given us proofs of confidence and respect.'"

Still pursuing the same test of sincerity, let us examine this defensive allegation.

Will the Attorney-General say that he does not believe such a letter from Lord Cornwallis ever existed? No! for he knows that it is as authentic as any document from India upon the table of the House of Commons. What, then, is the letter? "The native inhabitants of this kingdom," says Lord Cornwallis (writing from the very spot), "are the happiest and best protected subjects in India," etc., etc., etc. The inhabitants of this kingdom! Of what kingdom? Of the very kingdom which Mr. Hastings has just returned from governing for thirteen years, and for the misgovernment and desolation of which he stands every day as a criminal, or rather as a spectacle, before us. This is matter for serious reflection, and fully entitles the author to put the question which immediately follows: "Does this authentic account of the administration of Mr. Hastings, and of the state of India, correspond with the gloomy picture of despotism and despair drawn by the Committee of Secrecy?"

Had that picture been even drawn by the House of Commons itself, he would have been fully justified in asking this question; but you observe it has no bearing on it; the last words not only entirely destroy that interpretation, but also the meaning of the very next passage which is selected by the information as criminal;

namely, "What credit can we give to multiplied and accumulated charges, when we find that they originate from misrepresentation and falsehood?"

This passage, which is charged as a libel on the Commons, when thus compared with its immediate antecedent, can bear but one construction. It is impossible to contend that it charges misrepresentation on the House that found the impeachment, but upon the Committee of Secrecy just before adverted to, who were supposed to have selected the matter, and brought it before the whole House for judgment.

I do not mean, as I have often told you, to vindicate any calumny on that honorable Committee, or upon any individual of it, any more than upon the Commons at large, but the defendant is not charged by this informamation with any such offences.

Let me here pause once more to ask you whether the book in its genuine state, as far as we have advanced in it, makes the same impression on your minds now as when it was first read to you in detached passages; and whether, if I were to tear off the first part of it, which I hold in my hand, and give it to you as an entire work, the first and last passages, which have been selected as libels on the Commons, would now appear to be so when blended with the interjacent parts? I do not ask your answer—I shall have it in your verdict. The question is only put to direct your attention in pursuing the remainder of the volume to this main point,—is it an honest, serious defence? For this purpose, and as an example for all others, I will read the author's entire answer to the first article of charge concerning Cheit Sing, the Zemindar of Benares, and leave it to your impartial judgments to determine whether it be a mere cloak and cover for the slander imputed by the information to the concluding sentence of it, which is the only part attacked; or whether, on the contrary, that conclusion itself, when embodied with what goes before it, does not stand explained and justified?

"The first article of impeachment," continues our author, "is concerning Cheit Sing, the Zemindar of Benares. Bulwant Sing, the father of this Rajah, was merely an *aumil*, or farmer and collector of the revenues for Sujah-ul-Dowlah, Nabob of Oude, and Vizier of the Mogul empire. When, on the decease of his father, Cheit Sing was confirmed in the office of collector for the Vizier, he paid two hundred thousand pounds as a gift, or muzzeranah, and an additional rent of thirty thousand pounds per annum."

"As the father was no more than an *aumil*, the son succeeded only to his rights and pretensions. But by a sunnud granted to him by the Nabob, Sujah Dowlah, in September, 1773, through the influence of Mr. Hastings, he acquired a legal title to property in the land, and was raised from the office of aumil to rank of Zemindar. About four years after the death of Bulwant Sing, the Governor-General and Council of Bengal obtained the sovereignty paramount of the province of Benares. On the transfer of this sovereignty the Governor and Council proposed a new grant to Cheit Sing, confirming his former privileges, and conferring upon him the addition of the sovereign rights of the mint, and the powers of criminal justice with regard to life and death. He was then recognized by the Company as one of their Zemindars; a tributary subject, or feudatory vassal, of the British empire in Hindostan. The feudal system, which was formerly supposed to be peculiar to our Gothic ancestors, has always prevailed in the East. In every description of that form of government, notwithstanding accidental variations, there are two associations expressed or understood; one for internal security, the other for external defence. The King or Nabob confers protection on the feudatory baron as tributary prince, on condition of an annual revenue in the time of peace, and of military service, partly commutable for money, in the time of war. The feudal incidents in the Middle Ages in Europe, the fine paid to the superior on marriage, wardship, relief, etc., correspond to the annual tribute in Asia. Military service in war, and extraordinary aids in the event of extraordinary emergencies, were common to both."

"When the Governor-General of Bengal, in 1778, made an extraordinary demand on the Zemindar of Benares for five lacs of rupees, the British empire, in that part of the world, was surrounded with enemies which threatened its destruction. In 1779, a general confederacy was formed among the great powers of Hindostan for the expulsion of the English from their Asiatic dominions. At this crisis the expectation of a French armament augmented the general calamities of the country. Mr. Hastings is charged by the committee with making his first demand under the false pretence that hostilities had commenced with France. Such an insidious attempt to pervert a meritorious action into a crime is new — even in the history of impeachments. On the 7th of July, 1778, Mr. Hastings received private intelligence from an English merchant at Cairo, that war had been declared by Great Britain on the 23d of March, and by France on the 30th of April. Upon this intelligence, considered as authentic, it was determined to attack all the French settlements in India. The information was afterward found to be premature; but in the latter end of August a secret despatch was received from England, authorizing and appointing Mr. Hastings to take the measures which he had already adopted in the preceding month. The Directors and the Board of Control have expressed their approbation of this transaction by liberally rewarding Mr. Baldwyn, the merchant, for sending the earliest intelligence he could procure to Bengal. It was two days after Mr. Hastings's information of the French war that he formed the resolution of exacting the five lacs of rupees from Cheit Sing, and would have made similar exactions from all the dependencies of the Company in India had they been in the same circumstances. The fact is that the great Zemindars of Bengal pay as much to government as their lands can afford. Cheit Sing's collections were above fifty lacs, and his rent not twenty-four."

"The right of calling for extraordinary aids and military service in times of danger being universally established in India, as it was formerly in Europe during the feudal times, the subsequent conduct of Mr. Hastings is explained and vindicated. The Governor-General and Council of Bengal having made a demand upon a tributary Zemindar for three successive years, and that demand having been resisted by their vassal, they are justified in his punishment. The necessities of the Company, in consequence of the critical situation of their affairs in 1781, calling for a high fine; the ability of the Zemindar, who possessed near two crores of rupees in money and jewels, to pay the sum required; his backwardness to comply with the demands of his superiors; his disaffection to the English interest, and desire of revolt, which even then began to appear, and were afterwards conspicuous — fully justify Mr. Hastings in every subsequent step of his conduct. In the whole of his proceedings it is manifest that he had not early formed a design hostile to the Zemindar, but was regulated by events which he could neither foresee nor control. When the necessary measures which he had taken for supporting the authority of the Company by punishing a refractory vassal were thwarted and defeated by the barbarous massacre of the British troops and by the rebellion of Cheit Sing, the appeal was made to arms; an unavoidable revolution took place in Benares, and the Zemindar became the author of his own destruction."

Here follows the concluding passage, which is arraigned by the information: —

"The decision of the House of Commons on this charge against Mr. Hastings is one of the most singular to be met with in the annals of Parliament. The Minister, who was followed by the majority, vindicated him in every thing that he had done, and found him blamable only for what he intended to do; justified every step of his conduct, and only criminated his proposed intention of converting the crimes of the Zemindar to the benefit of the state by a fine of fifty lacs of rupees. An impeachment of error in judgment with regard to the quantum of a fine, and for an intention that never was executed, and never known to the offending party, characterizes a tribunal of inquisition rather than a court of Parliament."

Gentlemen, I am ready to admit that this sentiment might have been expressed in language more reserved and guarded; but you will look to the sentiment itself, rather than to its dress; to the mind of the writer, and not to the bluntness with which he may happen to express it. It is obviously the language of a warm man, engaged in the honest defence of his friend, and who is brought to what he thinks a just conclusion in argument, which perhaps becomes offensive in proportion to its truth. Truth is undoubtedly no warrant for writing what is reproachful of any private man. If a member of society lives within the law, then, if he offends, it is against God alone, and man has nothing to do with him; and if he transgress the laws, the libeller should arraign him before them, instead of presuming to try him himself. But as to writings on general subjects, which are not charged as an infringement on the rights of individuals, but as of a seditious tendency, it is far otherwise. When, in the progress either of legislation or of high national justice in Parliament, they who are amenable to no law are supposed to have adopted, through mistake or error, a principle which, if drawn into precedent, might be dangerous to the public, I shall not admit it to be a libel in the course of a legal and *bonâ fide* publication to state that such a principle had in fact been adopted. The people of England are not to be kept in the dark touching the proceedings of their own representatives. Let us therefore coolly examine this supposed offence, and see what it amounts to.

First, was not the conduct of the right honorable gentleman, whose name is here mentioned, exactly what it is represented? Will the Attorney-General, who was present in the House of Commons, say that it was not? Did not the Minister vindicate Mr. Hastings in what he had done, and was not his consent to that article of the impeachment founded on the intention only of levying a fine on the Zemindar for the service of the state, beyond the quantum which he, the Minister, thought reasonable? What else is this but an impeachment of error in judgment in the quantum of a fine?

So much for the first part of the sentence, which, regarding Mr. Pitt only, is foreign to our purpose; and as to the last part of it, which imputes the sentiments of the Minister to the majority that followed him with their votes on the question, that appears to me to be giving handsome credit to the majority for having voted from conviction, and not from courtesy to the Minister. To have supposed otherwise I dare not say would have been a more natural libel, but it would certainly have been a greater one. The sum and substance therefore of the paragraph is only this: that an impeachment for error in judgment is not consistent with the theory or the practice of the English Government. So say I. I say without reserve, speaking merely in the abstract, and not meaning to decide upon the merits of Mr. Hastings's cause, that an impeachment for an error in judgment is contrary to the whole spirit of English criminal justice, which, though not binding on the House of Commons, ought to be a guide to its proceedings. I say that the extraordinary jurisdiction of impeachment ought never to be assumed to expose error, or to scourge misfortune, but to hold up a terrible example to corruption and wilful abuse of authority, by extra-legal pains. If public men are always punished with due severity when the source of their misconduct appears to have been selfishly corrupt and criminal, the public can never suffer when their errors are treated with gentleness. From such protection to the magistrate, no man can think lightly of the charge of magistracy itself, when he sees, by the language of the saving judgment, that the only title to it is an honest and zealous intention. If at this moment, gentlemen, or indeed in any other in the whole course of our history, the people of England were to call upon every man in this impeaching House of Commons who had given his voice on public questions, or acted in authority, civil or military, to answer for the issues of our councils and our wars, and if honest, single intentions for the public service were refused as answers to impeachments, we should have many relations to mourn for, and many friends to deplore. For my own part, gentlemen, I feel, I hope, for my country as much as any man that inhabits it; but I would rather see it fall, and be buried in its ruins, than lend my voice to wound any Minister, or other responsible person, however unfortunate, who had fairly followed the lights of his understanding and the dictates of his conscience for its preservation.

Gentlemen, this is no theory of mine; it is the language of English law, and the protection which it affords to every man in office, from the highest to the lowest trust of government. In no one instance that can be named, foreign or domestic, did the Court of King's Bench ever interpose its extraordinary jurisdiction by information against any magistrate for the widest departure from the rule of his duty, without the plainest and clearest proof of corruption. To every such application, not so supported, the constant answer has been, Go to a Grand Jury with your complaint. God forbid that a magistrate should suffer from an error in judgment, if his purpose was honestly to discharge his trust. We cannot stop the ordinary course of justice; but wherever the court has a discretion, such a magistrate is entitled to its protection. I appeal to the noble judge, and to every man who hears me, for the truth and universality of this position; and it would be a strange solecism indeed to assert that in a case where the supreme court of criminal justice in the nation would refuse to interpose an extraordinary though a legal jurisdiction, on the principle that the ordinary execution of the laws should never be exceeded but for the punishment of malignant guilt, the Commons, in their higher capacity, growing out of the same Constitution, should reject that principle, and stretch them yet further by a jurisdiction still more eccentric. Many impeachments have taken place, because the law could not adequately punish the objects of them; but who ever heard of one being set on foot because the law, upon principle, would not punish them? Many impeachments have been adopted for a higher example than a prosecution in the ordinary courts, but surely never for a different example. The matter, therefore, in the offensive paragraph is not only an indisputable truth, but a truth in the propagation of which we are all deeply concerned.

Whether Mr. Hastings, in the particular instance, acted from corruption or from zeal for his employers, is what I have nothing to do with; it is to be decided in judgment; my duty stops with wishing him, as I do, an honorable deliverance. Whether the Minister or the Commons meant to found this article of the impeachment on mere error, without corruption, is likewise foreign to the purpose. The author could only judge from what was said and done on the occasion. He only sought to guard the principle, which is a common interest, and the rights of Mr. Hastings under it. He was, therefore, justified in publishing that an impeachment, founded in error in judgment, was to all intents and purposes illegal, unconstitutional, and unjust.

Gentlemen, it is now time for us to return again to the work under examination. The author having discussed the whole of the first article through so many pages, without even the imputation of an incorrect or intemperate expression, except in the concluding passage (the meaning of which I trust I have explained), goes on with the same earnest disposition to the discussion of the second charge respecting the princesses of Oude, which occupies eighteen pages, not one syllable of which the Attorney-General has read, and in which there is not even a glance at the House of Commons. The whole of this answer is, indeed, so far from being a mere cloak for the introduction of slander, that I aver it to be one of the most masterly pieces of writing I ever read in my life. From thence he goes on to the charge of contracts and salaries, which occupies five pages more, in which there is not a glance at the House of Commons, nor a word read by the Attorney-General. He afterward defends

Mr. Hastings against the charges respecting the opium contract. Not a glance at the House of Commons; not a word by the Attorney-General; and, in short, in this manner he goes on with the others, to the end of the book.

Now, is it possible for any human being to believe that a man, having no other intention than to vilify the House of Commons (as this information charges), should yet keep his mind thus fixed and settled as the needle to the pole, upon the serious merits of Mr. Hastings's defence, without ever straying into matter even questionable, except in the two or three selected parts out of two or three hundred pages? This is a forbearance which could not have existed, if calumny and detraction had been the malignant objects which led him to the inquiry and publication. The whole fallacy, therefore, arises from holding up to view a few detached passages, and carefully concealing the general tenor of the book.

Having now finished most, if not all, of these critical observations which it has been my duty to make upon this unfair mode of prosecution, it is but a tribute of common justice to the Attorney-General (and which my personal regard for him makes it more pleasant to pay), that none of my commentaries reflect in the most distant manner upon him; nor upon the Solicitor for the Crown, who sits near me, who is a person of the most correct honor, — far from it. The Attorney-General having orders to prosecute in consequence of the Address of the House to his Majesty, had no choice in the mode; no means at all of keeping the prosecutors before you in countenance, but by the course which has been pursued. But so far has he been from enlisting into the cause those prejudices which it is not difficult to slide into a business originating from such exalted authority, he has honorably guarded you against them; pressing, indeed, severely upon my client with the weight of his ability, but not with the glare and trappings of his high office.

Gentlemen, I wish that my strength would enable me to convince you of the author's singleness of intention, and of the merit and ability of his work, by reading the whole that remains of it. But my voice is already nearly exhausted; I am sorry my client should be a sufferer by my infirmity. One passage, however, is too striking and important to be passed over; the rest I must trust to your private examination. The author having discussed all the charges, article by article, sums them all up with this striking appeal to his readers: —

"The authentic statement of facts which has been given, and the arguments which have been employed, are, I think, sufficient to vindicate the character and conduct of Mr. Hastings, even on the maxims of European policy. When he was appointed Governor-General of Bengal he was invested with a discretionary power to promote the interests of the India Company and of the British empire in that quarter of the globe. The general instructions sent to him from his constituents were, '*That in all your deliberations and resolutions, you make the safety and prosperity of Bengal your principal object, and fix your attention on the security of the possessions and revenues of the Company.*' His superior genius sometimes acted in the spirit, rather than complied with the letter of the law; but he discharged the trust, and preserved the empire committed to his care in the same way, and with greater splendor and success than any of his predecessors in office; his departure from India was marked with the lamentations of the natives and the gratitude of his countrymen; and, on his return to England, he received the cordial congratulations of that numerous and respectable society whose interests he had promoted, and whose dominions he had protected and extended."

Gentlemen of the Jury, if this be a wilfully false account of the instructions given to Mr. Hastings for his government, and of his conduct under them, the author and publisher of this defence deserve the severest punishment for a mercenary imposition on the public. But if it be true that he was directed to make the safety and prosperity of Bengal the first object of his attention, and that under his administration it has been safe and prosperous; if it be true that the security and preservation of our possessions and revenues in Asia were marked out to him as the great leading principle of his government, and that those possessions and revenues, amidst unexampled dangers, have been secured and preserved; then a question may be unaccountably mixed with your consideration much beyond the consequence of the present prosecution, involving, perhaps, the merit of the impeachment itself which gave it birth; a question which the Commons, as prosecutors of Mr. Hastings, should in common prudence have avoided, unless, regretting the unwieldy length of their proceedings against him, they wished to afford him the opportunity of this strange, anomalous defence; since although I am neither his counsel, nor desire to have anything to do with his guilt or innocence, yet in the collateral defence of my client I am driven to state matter which may be considered by many as hostile to the impeachment. For if our dependencies have been secured, and their interests promoted, I am driven in the defence of my client to remark that it is mad and preposterous to bring to the standard of justice and humanity the exercise of a dominion founded upon violence and terror. It may and must be true that Mr. Hastings has repeatedly offended against the rights and privileges of Asiatic government, if he was the faithful deputy of a power which could not maintain itself for an hour without trampling upon both; he may and must have offended against the laws of God and nature if he was the faithful viceroy of an empire wrested in blood from the people to whom God and nature had given it; he may and must have preserved that unjust dominion over timorous and abject nations by a terrifying, overbearing, insulting superiority, if he was the faithful administrator of your government, which, having no root in consent or affection, no foundation in similarity of interests, no support from any one principle which cements men together in society, could be upheld only by alternate stratagem and force. The unhappy people of India, feeble and effeminate as they are from the softness of their climate, and subdued and broken as they have been by the knavery and strength of civilization, still occasionally start up in all the vigor and intelligence of insulted nature. To be governed at all, they must be governed with a rod of iron; and our empire in the East would long since have been lost to Great Britain if civil skill and military prowess had not united their efforts to support an authority which Heaven never gave, by means which it never can sanction.

Gentlemen, I think I can observe that you are touched with this way of considering the subject, and I can account for it. I have not been considering it through the cold medium of books, but have been speaking of man and his nature, and of human dominion, from what I have seen of them myself amongst reluctant nations submitting to our authority. I know what they feel, and how such feelings can alone be repressed. I have heard them in my youth from a naked savage, in the indignant character of a prince surrounded by his subjects, addressing the governor of a British colony, holding a bundle of sticks in his hand as the notes of his unlettered eloquence: "Who is it," said the jealous ruler over the desert encroached upon by the restless foot of English adventure, — "who is it that causes this river to rise in the high mountains, and to empty itself into the ocean? Who is it that causes to blow the loud winds of winter, and that calms them again in the summer? Who is it that rears up the shade of these lofty forests, and blasts them with the quick lightning at his pleasure? The same Being who gave to you a country on the other side of the waters, and gave ours to us; and by this title we will defend it," said the warrior, throwing down his tomahawk upon the ground, and raising the war-sound of his nation. These are the feelings of subjugated man all round the globe; and, depend upon it, nothing but fear will control where it is vain to look for affection.

These reflections are the only antidotes to those anathemas of superhuman eloquence which have lately shaken the walls that surround us, but which it unaccountably falls to my province, whether I will or no, a little to stem the torrent of by reminding you that you have a mighty sway in Asia which cannot be maintained by the finer sympathies of life, or the practice of its charities and affections. What will they do for you when surrounded by two hundred thousand men, with artillery, cavalry, and elephants, calling upon you for their dominions which you have robbed them of? Justice may, no doubt, in such a case forbid the levying of a fine to pay a revolting soldiery; a treaty may stand in the way of increasing a tribute to keep up the very existence of the government; and delicacy for women may forbid all entrance into a Zenana for money, whatever may be the necessity for taking it. All these things must ever be occurring. But under the pressure of such constant difficulties, so dangerous to national honor, it might be better, perhaps, to think of effectually securing it altogether, by recalling our troops and our merchants, and abandoning our Oriental empire. Until this be done, neither religion nor philosophy can be pressed very far into the aid of reformation and punishment. If England, from a lust of ambition and dominion, will insist on maintaining despotic rule over distant and hostile nations, beyond all comparison more numerous and extended than herself, and gives commission to her viceroys to govern them with no other instructions than to preserve them, and to secure permanently their revenues; with what color of consistency or reason can she place herself in the moral chair, and affect to be shocked at the execution of her own orders; adverting to the exact measure of wickedness and injustice necessary to their execution, and complaining only of the excess as the immorality; considering her authority as a dispensation for breaking the commands of God, and the breach of them as only punishable when contrary to the ordinances of man?

Such a proceeding, gentlemen, begets serious reflections. It would be better perhaps for the masters and the servants of all such governments to join in supplication that the great Author of violated humanity may not confound them together in one common judgment.

Gentlemen, I find, as I said before, I have not sufficient strength to go on with the remaining parts of the book. I hope, however, that notwithstanding my omissions, you are now completely satisfied that whatever errors or misconceptions may have misled the writer of these pages, the justification of a person whom he believed to be innocent, and whose accusers had themselves appealed to the public, was the single object of his contemplation. If I have succeeded in that object, every purpose which I had in addressing you has been answered.

It only now remains to remind you that another consideration has been strongly pressed upon you, and, no doubt, will be insisted on in reply. You will be told that the matters which I have been justifying as legal, and even meritorious, have therefore not been made the subject of complaint; and that whatever intrinsic merit parts of the book may be supposed or even admitted to possess, such merit can afford no justification to the selected passages, some of which, even with the context, carry the meaning charged by the information, and which are indecent animadversions on authority. To this I would answer (still protesting as I do against the application of any one of the innuendoes), that if you are firmly persuaded of the singleness and purity of the author's intentions, you are not bound to subject him to infamy, because, in the zealous career of a just and animated composition, he happens to have tripped with his pen into an intemperate expression in one or two instances of a long work. If this severe duty were binding on your consciences, the liberty of the press would be an empty sound, and no man could venture to write on any subject, however pure his purpose, without an attorney at one elbow and a counsel at the other.

From minds thus subdued by the terrors of punishment there could issue no works of genius to expand the empire of human reason, nor any masterly compositions on the general nature of government, by the help of which the great commonwealths of mankind have founded their establishments; much less any of those useful applications of them to critical conjunctures by which, from time to time, our own Constitution, by the exertion of patriot citizens, has been brought back to its standard. Under such terrors, all the great lights of science and civilization must be extinguished; for men cannot communicate their free thoughts to one another with a lash held over their heads. It is the nature of everything that is great and useful, both in the animate and inanimate world, to be wild and irregular; and we must be contented to take them with the alloys which belong to them, or live without them. Genius breaks from the fetters of criticism; but its wanderings are sanctioned by its majesty and wisdom, when it advances in its path. Subject it to the critic, and you tame it into dullness. Mighty rivers break down their banks in the winter, sweeping away to death the flocks which are fattened on the soil that they fertilize in the summer; the few may be saved by embankments from drowning, but the flock must perish for hunger. Tempests occasionally shake our dwellings and dissipate our commerce; but they scourge before them the lazy elements which, without them, would stagnate into pestilence. In like manner Liberty herself, the last and best gift of God to his creatures, must be taken just as she is: you might pare her down into bashful regularity, and shape her into a perfect model of severe, scrupulous law, but she would then be Liberty no longer; and you must be content to die under the lash of this inexorable justice which you had exchanged for the banners of Freedom.

If it be asked where the line to this indulgence and impunity is to be drawn, the answer is easy. The liberty of the press, on *general* subjects, comprehends and implies as much strict observance of positive law as is consistent with perfect purity of intention and equal and useful society. What that latitude is cannot be promulgated in the abstract, but must be judged of in the particular instance; and consequently, upon this occasion, must be judged of by you without forming any possible precedent for any other case; and where can the judgment be possibly so safe as with the members of that society which alone can suffer, if the writing is calculated to do mischief to the public? You must, therefore, try the book by that criterion, and say whether the publication was premature and offensive; or, in other words, whether the publisher was bound to have suppressed it until the public ear was anticipated and abused, and every avenue to the human heart or understanding secured and blocked up? I see around me those by whom, by and by, Mr. Hastings will be most ably and eloquently defended; but I am sorry to remind my friends that, but for the right of suspending the public judgment concerning him till their season of exertion comes round, the tongues of angels would be insufficient for the task.

Gentlemen, I hope I have now performed my duty to my client — I sincerely hope that I have; for, certainly, if ever there was a man pulled the other way by his interests and affections, if ever there was a man who should have trembled at the situation in which I have been placed on this occasion, it is myself, who not only love, honor, and respect, but whose future hopes and preferments are linked, from free choice, with those who, from the mistakes of the author, are treated with great severity and injustice. These are strong retardments; but I have been urged on to activity by considerations which can never be inconsistent with honorable attachments, either in the political or social world — the love of justice and of liberty, and a zeal for the Constitution of my country, which is the inheritance of our posterity, of the public, and of the world. These are the motives which have animated me in defence of this person, who is an entire stranger to me; whose shop I never go to; and the author of whose publication — or Mr. Hastings, who is the object of it — I never spoke to in my life.

One word more, gentlemen, and I have done. Every human tribunal ought to take care to administer justice as we look hereafter to have justice administered to ourselves. Upon the principle on which the Attorney-General prays sentence upon my client — God have mercy upon us! Instead of standing before him in judgment with the hopes and consolations of Christians, we must call upon the mountains to cover us; for which of us can present, for omniscient examination, a pure, unspotted, and faultless course? But I humbly expect that the benevolent Author of our being will judge us as I have been pointing out for your example. Holding up the great volume of our lives in his hands, and regarding the general scope of them — if he discovers benevolence, charity, and good-will to man beating in the heart, where he alone can look; if he finds that our conduct, though often forced out of the path by our infirmities, has been in general well directed; his all-searching eye will assuredly never pursue us into those little corners of our lives, much less will his justice select them for punishment without the general context of our existence, by which faults may be sometimes found to have grown out of virtues, and very many of our heaviest offences to have been grafted by human imperfection upon the best and kindest of our affections. No, gentlemen, believe me, this is not the course of divine justice, or there is no truth in the Gospels of Heaven. If the general tenor of a man's conduct be such as I have represented it, he may walk through the shadow of death, with all his faults about him, with as much cheerfulness as in the common paths of life; because he knows that, instead of a stern accuser to expose before the Author of his nature those frail passages which, like the scored matter in the book before you, checker the volume of the brightest and best-spent life, his mercy will obscure them from the eye of his purity, and our repentance blot them out forever.

All this would, I admit, be perfectly foreign and irrelevant if you were sitting here in a case of property be-

between man and man, where a strict rule of law must operate, or there would be an end of civil life and society. It would be equally foreign, and still more irrelevant, if applied to those shameful attacks upon private reputation which are the bane and disgrace of the press; by which whole families have been rendered unhappy during life by aspersions cruel, scandalous, and unjust. Let such libellers remember that no one of my principles of defence can, at any time, or upon any occasion, ever apply to shield them from punishment; because such conduct is not only an infringement of the rights of men, as they are defined by strict law, but is absolutely incompatible with honor, honesty, or mistaken good intention. On such men let the Attorney-General bring forth all the artillery of his office, and the thanks and blessings of the whole public will follow him. But this is a totally different case. Whatever private calumny may mark this work, it has not been made the subject of complaint, and we have therefore nothing to do with that, nor any right to consider it. We are trying whether the public could have been considered as offended and endangered if Mr. Hastings himself, in whose place the author and publisher have a right to put themselves, had, under all the circumstances which have been considered, composed and published the volume under examination. That question cannot, in common sense, be anything resembling a question of law, but is a pure question of fact, to be decided on the principles which I have humbly recommended. I therefore ask of the Court that the book itself may now be delivered to you. Read it with attention, and as you shall find it, pronounce your verdict.

DANIEL WEBSTER.

REPLY TO HAYNE; IN THE UNITED STATES SENATE, JANUARY 26, 1830.

Mr. President, — When the mariner has been tossed for many days in thick weather, and on an unknown sea, he naturally avails himself of the first pause in the storm, the earliest glance of the sun, to take his latitude, and ascertain how far the elements have driven him from his true course. Let us imitate this prudence, and before we float farther on the waves of this debate, refer to the point from which we departed, that we may at least be able to conjecture where we now are. I ask for the reading of the resolution before the Senate.

The Secretary read the resolution, as follows: —

> "*Resolved*, That the Committee on Public Lands be instructed to inquire and report the quantity of public lands remaining unsold within each State and Territory, and whether it be expedient to limit for a certain period the sales of the public lands to such lands only as have heretofore been offered for sale, and are now subject to entry at the minimum price. And, also, whether the office of Surveyor-General, and some of the land offices, may not be abolished without detriment to the public interest; or whether it be expedient to adopt measures to hasten the sales and extend more rapidly the surveys of the public lands."

We have thus heard, Sir, what the resolution is which is actually before us for consideration; and it will readily occur to every one that it is almost the only subject about which something has not been said in the speech, running through two days, by which the Senate has been entertained by the gentleman from South Carolina. Every topic in the wide range of our public affairs, whether past or present — everything, general or local, whether belonging to national politics or party politics — seems to have attracted more or less of the honorable member's attention, save only the resolution before the Senate. He has spoken of everything but the public lands; they have escaped his notice. To that subject, in all his excursions, he has not paid even the cold respect of a passing glance.

When this debate, Sir, was to be resumed on Thursday morning, it so happened that it would have been convenient for me to be elsewhere. The honorable member, however, did not incline to put off the discussion to another day. He had a shot, he said, to return, and he wished to discharge it. That shot, Sir, which he thus kindly informed us was coming, that we might stand out of the way, or prepare ourselves to fall by it and die with decency, has now been received. Under all advantages, and with expectation awakened by the tone which preceded it, it has been discharged, and has spent its force. It may become me to say no more of its effect, than that, if nobody is found, after all, either killed or wounded, it is not the first time in the history of human affairs that the vigor and success of the war have not quite come up to the lofty and sounding phrase of the manifesto.

The gentleman, Sir, in declining to postpone the debate, told the Senate, with the emphasis of his hand upon his heart, that there was something rankling *here*, which he wished to relieve.

[Mr. Hayne rose, and disclaimed having used the word *rankling*.]

It would not, Mr. President, be safe for the honorable member to appeal to those around him upon the question whether he did, in fact, make use of that word. But he may have been unconscious of it. At any rate, it is enough that he disclaims it. But still, with or without the use of that particular word, he had yet something *here*, he said, of which he wished to rid himself by an immediate reply. In this respect, Sir, I have a great advantage over the honorable gentleman. There is nothing *here*, Sir, which gives me the slightest uneasiness; neither fear, nor anger, nor that which is sometimes more troublesome than either, the consciousness of having been in the wrong. There is nothing either originating *here*, or now received *here* by the gentleman's shot. Nothing originating here, for I had not the slightest feeling of unkindness towards the honorable member. Some passages, it is true, had occurred since our acquaintance in this body which I could have wished might have been otherwise; but I had used philosophy, and forgotten them. I paid the honorable member the attention of listening with respect to his first speech; and when he sat down, though surprised, and I must even say astonished, at some of his opinions, nothing was farther from my intention than to commence any personal warfare. Through the whole of the few remarks I made in answer, I avoided, studiously and carefully, everything which I thought possible to be construed into disrespect. And, Sir, while there is thus nothing originating *here* which I have wished at any time, or now wish, to discharge, I must repeat, also, that nothing has been received *here* which *rankles*, or in any way gives me annoyance. I will not accuse the honorable member of violating the rules of civilized war — I will not say that he poisoned his arrows. But whether his shafts were, or were not, dipped in that which would have caused rankling, if they had reached their destination, there was not, as it happened, quite strength enough in the bow to bring them to their mark. If he wishes now to gather up those shafts, he must look for them elsewhere; they will not be found fixed and quivering in the object at which they were aimed.

The honorable member complained that I had slept on his speech. I must have slept on it, or not slept at all. The moment the honorable member sat down, his friend from Missouri rose, and, with much honeyed commendation of the speech, suggested that the impressions which it had produced were too charming and delightful to be disturbed by other sentiments or other sounds, and proposed that the Senate should adjourn. Would it have been quite amiable in me, Sir, to interrupt this excellent good feeling? Must I not have been absolutely malicious, if I could have thrust myself forward to destroy sensations thus pleasing? Was it not much better and kinder, both to sleep upon them myself, and to allow others also the pleasure of sleeping upon them? But if it be meant, by sleeping upon his speech, that I took time to prepare a reply to it, it is quite a mistake. Owing to other engagements I could not employ even the interval between the adjournment of the Senate and its meeting the next morning in attention to the subject of this debate. Nevertheless, Sir, the mere matter of fact is undoubtedly true. I did sleep on the gentleman's speech, and slept soundly. And I slept equally well on his speech of yesterday, to which I am now replying. It is quite possible that in this respect, also, I possess some advantage over the honorable member, attributable, doubtless, to a cooler temperament on my part; for, in truth, I slept upon his speeches remarkably well.

But the gentleman inquires why *he* was made the object of such a reply? Why was *he* singled out? If an attack has been made on the East, he, he assures us, did not begin it; it was made by the gentleman from Missouri. Sir, I answered the gentleman's speech because I happened to hear it; and because, also, I chose to give an answer to that speech, which, if unanswered, I thought most likely to produce injurious impressions. I did not stop to inquire who was the original drawer of the bill. I found a responsible indorser before me, and it was my purpose to hold him liable, and to bring him to his just responsibility without delay. But, Sir, this interrogatory of the honorable member was only introductory to another. He proceeded to ask me whether I had turned upon him, in this debate, from the consciousness that I should find an overmatch, if I ventured on a contest with his friend from Missouri. If, Sir, the honorable member, *modestiæ gratia*, had chosen thus to defer to his friend, and to pay him a compliment, without intentional disparagement to others, it would have been quite according to the friendly courtesies of debate, and not at all ungrateful to my own feelings. I am not one of those, Sir, who esteem any tribute of regard, whether light and occasional, or more serious and deliberate, which may be bestowed on others, as so much unjustly withholden from themselves. But the tone and manner of the gentleman's question forbid me thus to interpret it. I am not at liberty to consider it as nothing more than a civility to his friend. It had an air of taunt and disparagement, something of the loftiness of asserted superiority, which does not allow me to pass it over without notice. It was put as a question for me to answer, and so put as if it were difficult for me to answer, whether I deemed the member from Missouri an overmatch for myself in debate here. It seems to me, Sir, that this is extraordinary language, and an extraordinary tone, for the discussions of this body.

Matches and overmatches! Those terms are more applicable elsewhere than here, and fitter for other assemblies than this. Sir, the gentleman seems to forget where and what we are. This is a Senate — a Senate of equals, of men of individual honor and personal character, and of absolute independence. We know no masters, we acknowledge no dictators. This is a hall for mutual consultation and discussion; not an arena for the exhibition of champions. I offer myself, Sir, as a match for no man; I throw the challenge of debate at no man's feet. But then, Sir, since the honorable member has put the question in a manner that calls for an answer, I will give him an answer; and I tell him that, holding myself to be the humblest of the members here, I yet know nothing in the arm of his friend from Missouri, either alone, or when aided by the arm of *his* friend from South Carolina, that need deter even me from espousing whatever opinions I may choose to espouse, from debating whenever I may choose to debate, or from speaking whatever I may see fit to say, on the floor of the Senate. Sir, when uttered as matter of commendation or compliment, I should dissent from nothing which the honorable member might say of his friend. Still less do I put forth any pretensions of my own. But when put to me as matter of taunt, I throw it back, and say to the gentleman that he could possibly say nothing less likely than such a comparison to wound my pride of personal character. The anger of its tone rescued the remark from intentional irony, which otherwise, probably, would have been its general acceptation. But, Sir, if it be imagined that by this mutual quotation and commendation; if it be supposed that, by casting the characters of the drama, assigning to each his part, to one the attack, to another the cry of onset; or if it be thought that, by a loud and empty vaunt of anticipated victory, any laurels are to be won here; if it be imagined, especially, that any or all these things will shake any purpose of mine, I can tell the honorable member, once for all, that he is greatly mistaken, and that he is dealing with one of whose temper and character he has yet much to learn. Sir, I shall not allow myself on this occasion, I hope on no occasion, to be betrayed into any loss of temper; but if provoked, as I trust I never shall be, into crimination and recrimination, the honorable member may perhaps find that in that contest there will be blows to take as well as blows to give; that others can state comparisons as significant, at least, as his own, and that his impunity may possibly demand of him whatever powers of taunt and sarcasm he may possess. I commend him to a prudent husbandry of his resources. . . .

In the course of my observations the other day, Mr. President, I spoke of the Ordinance of 1787, which prohibits slavery, in all future times, north-west of the Ohio, as a measure of great wisdom and foresight, and one which had been attended with highly beneficial and permanent consequences. I supposed that, on this point, no two gentlemen in the Senate could entertain different opinions. But the simple expression of this sentiment has led the gentleman, not only into a labored defence of slavery in the abstract, and on principle, but also into a warm accusation against me, as having attacked the system of domestic slavery now existing in the Southern States. For all this there was not the slightest foundation in anything said or intimated by me. I did not utter a single word which any ingenuity could torture into an attack on the slavery of the South. I said only that it was highly wise and useful, in legislating for the North-western country, while it was yet a wilderness, to prohibit the introduction of slaves; and I added that I presumed there was no reflecting and intelligent person in the neighboring state of Kentucky, who would doubt that, if the same prohibition had been extended at the same early period over that Commonwealth, her strength and population would, at this day, have been far greater than they are. If these opinions be thought doubtful, they are, nevertheless, I trust, neither extraordinary nor disrespectful. They attack nobody, and menace nobody. And yet, Sir, the gentleman's optics have discovered, even in the mere expression of this sentiment, what he calls the very spirit of the Missouri question! He represents me as making an onset on the whole South, and manifesting a spirit which would interfere with, and disturb, their domestic condition!

Sir, this injustice no otherwise surprises me, than as it is committed here, and committed without the slightest pretence of ground for it. I say it only surprises me as being done here; for I know full well that it is, and has been, the settled policy of some persons in the South for years to represent the people of the North as disposed to interfere with them in their own exclusive and peculiar concerns. This is a delicate and sensitive point in Southern feeling; and of late years it has always been touched, and generally with effect, whenever the object has been to unite the whole South against Northern men or Northern measures. This feeling, always carefully kept alive, and maintained at too intense a heat to admit discrimination or reflection, is a lever of great power in our political machine. It moves vast bodies, and gives to them one and the same direction. But it is without adequate cause, and the suspicion which exists is wholly groundless. There is not, and never has been, a disposition in the North to interfere with these interests of the South. Such interference has never been supposed to be within the power of government; nor has it been in any way attempted. The slavery of the South has always been regarded as a matter of domestic policy, left with the States themselves, and with which the fed-era*l* government had nothing to do. Certainly, Sir, I am, and ever have been, of that opinion. The gentleman, indeed, argues that slavery in the abstract is no evil. Most assuredly, I need not say, I differ with him altogether and most widely, on that point. I regard domestic slavery as one of the greatest evils, both moral and political. But whether it be a malady, and whether it be curable, and, if so, by what means; or, on the other hand, whether it be the *vulnus immedicabile* of the social system — I leave it to those whose right and duty it is to inquire and to decide. And this, I believe, Sir, is, and uniformly has been, the sentiment of the North. . . .

[In support of this last statement Mr. Webster appeals to the history of attempts made to enlist the first Congress in the abolition of slavery. These attempts resulted in the famous resolutions reported by a committee composed almost exclusively of Northern men, and adopted by a House two-thirds of whose members were from the North, declaring that Congress has "no authority to interfere in the emancipation of slaves, or in the treatment of them in any of the States."]

The fears of the South, whatever fears they might have entertained, were allayed and quieted by this early decision; and so remained till they were excited afresh, without cause, but for collateral and indirect purposes. When it became necessary, or was thought so by some political persons, to find an unvarying ground for the exclusion of Northern men from confidence and from lead in the affairs of the republic, then, and not till then, the cry was raised, and the feeling industriously excited, that the influence of Northern men in the public councils would endanger the relation of master and slave. For myself, I claim no other merit than that this gross and enormous injustice towards the whole North has not wrought upon me to change my opinions or my political conduct. I hope I am above violating my principles, even under the smart of injury and false imputations. Unjust suspicions and undeserved reproach, whatever pain I may experience from them, will not induce me, I trust, to overstep the limits of constitutional duty, or to encroach on the rights of others. The domestic slavery of the Southern States I leave where I find it, — in the hands of their own governments. It is their affair, not mine. Nor do I complain of the peculiar effect which the magnitude of that population has had in the distribution of power under this federal government. We know, Sir, that the representation of the States in the other House is not equal. We know that great advantage in that respect is enjoyed by the slave-holding States; and we know, too, that the intended equivalent for that advantage, that is to say, the imposition of direct taxes in the same ratio, has become merely nominal, the habit of the government being almost invariably to collect its revenue from other sources and in other modes. Nevertheless, I do not complain; nor would I countenance any movement to alter this arrangement of representation. It is the original bargain, the compact; let it stand; let the advantage of it be fully enjoyed. The Union itself is too full of benefit to be hazarded in propositions for changing its original basis. I go for the Constitution as it is, and for the Union as it is. But I am resolved not to submit in silence to accusations either against myself individually or against the North, wholly unfounded and unjust; accusations which impute to us a disposition to evade the constitutional compact, and to extend the power of the government over the internal laws and domestic condition of the States. All such accusations, wherever and whenever made, all insinuations of the existence of any such purposes, I know and feel to be groundless and injurious.

And we must confide in Southern gentlemen themselves; we must trust to those whose integrity of heart and magnanimity of feeling will lead them to a desire to maintain and disseminate truth, and who possess the means of its diffusion with the Southern public; we must leave it to them to disabuse that public of its prejudices. But in the mean time, for my own part, I shall continue to act justly, whether those towards whom justice is exercised receive it with candor or with contumely. . . .

[Mr. Webster next refutes the charge of inconsistency between his present position regarding the public lands and that taken by him in 1825.]

We approach, at length, Sir, to a more important part of the honorable gentleman's observations. Since it does not accord with my views of justice and policy to give away the public lands altogether, as mere matter of gratuity, I am asked by the honorable gentleman on what ground it is that I consent to vote them away in particular instances. How, he inquires, do I reconcile with these professed sentiments, my support of measures appropriating portions of the lands to particular roads, particular canals, particular rivers, and particular institutions of education in the West? This leads, Sir, to the real and wide difference, in political opinion, between the honorable gentleman and myself. On my part, I look upon all these objects as connected with the common good, fairly embraced in its object and its terms; he, on the contrary, deems them all, if good at all, only local good. This is our difference. The interrogatory which he proceeded to put at once explains this difference. "What interest," asks he, "has South Carolina in a canal in Ohio?" Sir, this very question is full of significance. It develops the gentleman's whole political system; and its answer expounds mine. Here we differ.

I look upon a road over the Alleghanies, a canal round the falls of the Ohio, or a canal or railway from the Atlantic to the Western waters, as being an object large and extensive enough to be fairly said to be for the common benefit. The gentleman thinks otherwise, and this is the key to his construction of the powers of the government. He may well ask what interest has South Carolina in a canal in Ohio. On his system, it is true, she has no interest. On that system Ohio and Carolina are different governments and different countries; connected here, it is true, by some slight and ill-defined bond of union, but in all main respects separate and diverse. On that system Carolina has no more interest in a canal in Ohio than in Mexico. The gentleman, therefore, only follows out his own principles; he does no more than arrive at the natural conclusions of his own doctrines; he only announces the true results of that creed which he has adopted himself, and would persuade others to adopt, when he thus declares that South Carolina has no interest in a public work in Ohio.

Sir, we narrow-minded people of New England do not reason thus. Our notion of things is entirely different. We look upon the States, not as separated, but as united. We love to dwell on that union, and on the mutual happiness which it has so much promoted, and the common renown which it has so greatly contributed to acquire. In our contemplation, Carolina and Ohio are parts of the same country; States, united under the same general government, having interests common, associated, intermingled. In whatever is within the proper sphere of the constitutional power of this government, we look upon the States as one. We do not impose geographical limits to our patriotic feeling or regard; we do not follow rivers and mountains and lines of latitude to find boundaries beyond which public improvements do not benefit us. We who come here as agents and representatives of these narrow-minded and selfish men of New England, consider ourselves as bound to regard with an equal eye the good of the whole, in whatever is within our powers of legislation. Sir, if a railroad or canal, beginning in South Carolina and ending in South Carolina, appeared to me to be of national importance and national magnitude, believing, as I do, that the power of government extends to the encouragement of works of that description, if I were to stand up here and ask, What interest has Massachusetts in a railroad in South Carolina? I should not be willing to face my constituents. These same narrow-minded men would tell me that they had sent me to act for the whole country, and that one who possessed too little comprehension, either of intellect or feeling, one who was not large enough, both in mind and in heart, to embrace the whole, was not fit to be intrusted with the interest of any part.

Sir, I do not desire to enlarge the powers of the government by unjustifiable construction, nor to exercise any not within a fair interpretation. But when it is believed that a power does exist, then it is, in my judgment, to be exercised for the general benefit of the whole. So far as respects the exercise of such a power, the States are one. It was the very object of the Constitution to create unity of interests to the extent of the powers of the general government. In war and peace we are one; in commerce, one; because the authority of the general government reaches to war and peace, and to the regulation of commerce. I have never seen any more difficulty in erecting lighthouses on the lakes, than on the ocean; in improving the harbors of inland seas, than if they were within the ebb and flow of the tide; or in removing obstructions in the vast streams of the West, more than in any work to facilitate commerce on the Atlantic coast.

If there be any power for one, there is power also for the other; and they are all and equally for the common good of the country.

There are other objects, apparently more local, or the benefit of which is less general, towards which, nevertheless, I have concurred with others to give aid by donations of land. It is proposed to construct a road in or through one of the new States in which this government possesses large quantities of land. Have the United States no right, or, as a great and untaxed proprietor, are they under no obligation, to contribute to an object thus calculated to promote the common good of all the proprietors, themselves included? And even with respect to education, which is the extreme case, let the question be considered. In the first place, as we have seen, it was made matter of compact with these States that they should do their part to promote education. In the next place, our whole system of land laws proceeds on the idea that education is for the common good; because in every division a certain portion is uniformly reserved and appropriated for the use of schools. And, finally, have not these new States singularly strong claims founded on the ground already stated, that the government is a great untaxed proprietor, in the ownership of the soil? It is a consideration of great importance, that probably there is in no part of the country, or of the world, so great call for the means of education, as in these new States; owing to the vast number of persons within those ages in which education and instruction are usually received, if received at all. This is the natural consequence of recency of settlement and rapid increase. The census of these States shows how great a proportion of the whole population occupies the classes between infancy and manhood. These are the wide fields, and here is the deep and quick soil for the seeds of knowledge and virtue; and this is the favored season, the very spring-time for sowing them. Let them be disseminated without stint. Let them be scattered with a bountiful hand, broadcast. Whatever the government can fairly do towards these objects, in my opinion, ought to be done.

These, Sir, are the grounds, succinctly stated, on which my votes for grants of lands for particular objects rest; while I maintain at the same time, that it is all a common fund, for the common benefit. And reasons like these, I presume, have influenced the votes of other gentlemen of New England. Those who have a different view of the powers of the government, of course, come to different conclusions on these, as on other questions. I observed, when speaking on this subject before, that if we looked to any measure, whether for a road, a canal, or anything else, intended for the improvement of the West, it would be found that, if the New England *ayes* were struck out of the lists of votes, the Southern *noes* would always have rejected the measure. The truth of this has not been denied, and cannot be denied. In stating this, I thought it just to ascribe it to the constitutional scruples of the South, rather than to any other less favorable or less charitable cause. But no sooner had I done this, than the honorable gentleman asks if I reproach him and his friends with their constitutional scruples. Sir, I reproach nobody. I stated a fact, and gave the most respectful reason for it that occurred to me. The gentleman cannot deny the fact; he may, if he choose, disclaim the reason. It is not long since I had occasion, in presenting a petition from his own State, to account for its being intrusted to my hands, by saying that the constitutional opinions of the gentleman and his worthy colleague prevented them from supporting it. Sir, did I state this as matter of reproach? Far from it.

Did I attempt to find any other cause than an honest one for these scruples? Sir, I did not. It did not become me to doubt or to insinuate that the gentleman had either changed his sentiments, or that he had made up a set of constitutional opinions accommodated to any particular combination of political occurrences. Had I done so, I should have felt that, while I was entitled to little credit in thus questioning other people's motives, I justified the whole world in suspecting my own. But how has the gentleman returned this respect for others' opinions? His own candor and justice, how have they been exhibited towards the motives of others, while he has been at so much pains to maintain, what nobody has disputed, the purity of his own? Why, Sir, he has asked *when*, and *how*, and *why*, New England votes were found going for measures favorable to the West? He has demanded to be informed whether all this did not begin in 1825, and while the election of President was still pending? . . .

[Mr. Webster answers this insinuation by showing that the generous policy of New England toward the West found expression years before the political exigency referred to; and that it was embodied in the two well-known Acts of 1820 and 1821, "by far the most important general measures respecting the public lands which have been adopted in the last twenty years."]

Having recurred to these two important measures, in answer to the gentleman's inquiries, I must now beg permission to go back to a period yet somewhat earlier, for the purpose of still further showing how much, or rather how little, reason there is for the gentleman's insinuation that political hopes or fears, or party associations, were the grounds of these New England votes. And after what has been said, I hope it may be forgiven me if I allude to some political opinions and votes of my own, of very little public importance certainly, but which, from the time at which they were given and expressed, may pass for good witnesses on this occasion.

This government, Mr. President, from its origin to the peace of 1815, had been too much engrossed with various other important concerns to be able to turn its thoughts inward, and look to the development of its vast internal resources. In the early part of President Washington's administration, it was fully occupied with completing its own organization, providing for the public debt, defending the frontiers, and maintaining domestic peace. Before the termination of that administration the fires of the French Revolution blazed forth, as from a new-opened volcano, and the whole breadth of the ocean did not secure us from its effects. The smoke and the cinders reached us, though not the burning lava. Difficult and agitating questions, embarrassing to government and dividing public opinion, sprung out of the new state of our foreign relations, and were succeeded by others, and yet again by others, equally embarrassing and equally exciting division and discord, through the long series of twenty years, till they finally issued in the war with England. Down to the close of that war no distinct, marked, and deliberate attention had been given, or could have been given, to the internal condition of the country, its capacities of improvement, or the constitutional power of the government in regard to objects connected with such improvement.

The peace, Mr. President, brought about an entirely new and a most interesting state of things; it opened to us other prospects and suggested other duties. We ourselves were changed, and the whole world was changed. The pacification of Europe, after June, 1815, assumed a firm and permanent aspect. The nations evidently manifested that they were disposed for peace. Some agitation of the waves might be expected, even after the storm had subsided, but the tendency was, strongly and rapidly, towards settled repose.

It so happened, Sir, that I was at that time a member of Congress, and, like others, naturally turned my thoughts to the contemplation of the recently altered condition of the country and of the world. It appeared plainly enough to me, as well as to wiser and more experienced men, that the policy of the government would naturally take a start in a new direction; because new directions would necessarily be given to the pursuits and occupations of the people. We had pushed our commerce far and fast, under the advantage of a neutral flag. But there were now no longer flags, either neutral or belligerent. The harvest of neutrality had been great, but we had gathered it all. With the peace of Europe it was obvious there would spring up in her circle of nations a revived and invigorated spirit of trade, and a new activity in all the business and objects of civilized life. Hereafter, our commercial gains were to be earned only by success in a close and intense competition. Other nations would produce for themselves, and carry for themselves, and manufacture for themselves, to the full extent of their abilities. The crops of our plains would no longer sustain European armies, nor our ships longer supply those whom war had rendered unable to supply themselves. It was obvious that, under these circumstances, the country would begin to survey itself, and to estimate its own capacity of improvement.

And this improvement — how was it to be accomplished, and who was to accomplish it? We were ten or twelve millions of people, spread over almost half a world. We were more than twenty States, some stretching along the same seaboard, some along the same line of inland frontier, and others on opposite banks of the same vast rivers. Two considerations at once presented themselves with great force in looking at this state of things. One was, that that great branch of improvement which consisted in furnishing new facilities of intercourse, necessarily ran into different States in every leading instance, and would benefit the citizens of all such States. No one State, therefore, in such cases, would assume the whole expense, nor was the co-operation of several States to be expected. Take the instance of the Delaware breakwater. It will cost several millions of money. Would Pennsylvania alone ever have constructed it? Certainly never while this Union lasts, because it is not for her sole benefit. Would Pennsylvania, New Jersey, and Delaware have united to accomplish it at their joint expense? Certainly not, for the same reason. It could not be done, therefore, but by the general government. The same may be said of the large inland undertakings, except that, in them, government, instead of bearing the whole expense, co-operates with others who bear a part. The other consideration is, that the United States have the means. They enjoy the revenues derived from commerce, and the States have no abundant and easy sources of public income. The custom-houses fill the general treasury, while the States have scanty resources, except by resort to heavy direct taxes.

Under this view of things, I thought it necessary to settle, at least for myself, some definite notions with respect to the powers of the government in regard to internal affairs. It may not savor too much of self-commendation to remark that, with this object, I considered the Constitution, its judicial construction, its contemporaneous exposition, and the whole history of the legislation of Congress under it; and I arrived at the conclusion that government had power to accomplish sundry objects, — or aid in their accomplishment, — which are now commonly spoken of as internal improvements. That conclusion, Sir, may have been right, or it may have been wrong. I am not about to argue the grounds of it at large. I say only, that it was adopted and acted on even so early as in 1816. Yes, Mr. President, I made up my opinion, and determined on my intended course of political conduct on these subjects, in the Fourteenth Congress, in 1816. And now, Mr. President, I have further to say, that I made up these opinions, and entered on this course of political conduct *Teucro duce.* Yes, Sir, I pursued in all this a South Carolina track on the doctrines of internal improvement. South Carolina, as she was then represented in the other House, set forth in 1816, under a fresh and leading breeze, and I was among the followers. But if my leader sees new lights, and turns a sharp corner, unless I see new lights also, I keep straight on in the same path. I repeat that leading gentlemen from South Carolina were first and foremost in behalf of the doctrines of internal improvements, when those doctrines came first to be considered and acted upon in Congress. The debate on the bank question, on the tariff of 1816, and on the direct tax, will show who was who, and what was what, at that time. The tariff of 1816 (one of the plain cases of oppression and usurpation, from which, if the government does not recede, individual States may justly secede from the government) is, Sir, in truth, a South Carolina tariff, supported by South Carolina votes. But for those votes, it could not have passed in the form in which it did pass; whereas, if it had depended on Massachusetts votes, it would have been lost. Does not the honorable gentleman well know all this? There are certainly those who do full well know it all. I do not say this to reproach South Carolina. I only state the fact; and I think it will appear to be true, that among the earliest and boldest advocates of the tariff as a measure of protection, and on the express ground of protection, were leading gentlemen of South Carolina in Congress. I did not then, and cannot now, understand their language in any other sense. While this tariff of 1816 was under discussion in the House of Representatives, an honorable gentleman from Georgia, now of this House [Mr. Forsyth], moved to reduce the proposed duty on cotton. He failed by four votes, South Carolina giving three votes (enough to have turned the scale) against his motion. The act, Sir, then passed, and received on its passage the support of a majority of the Representatives of South Carolina present and voting. This act is the first in the order of those now denounced as plain usurpations. We see it daily in the list, by the side of those of 1824 and 1828, as a case of manifest oppression, justifying disunion. I put it home to the honorable member from South Carolina, that his own State was not only "art and part" in this measure, but the *causa causans.* Without her aid this seminal principle of mischief, this root of Upas, could not have been planted. I have already said, and it is true, that this act proceeded on the ground of protection. It interfered directly with existing interests of great value and amount. It cut up the Calcutta cotton trade by the roots; but it passed, nevertheless, and it passed on the principle of protecting manufactures, on the principle against free trade, on the principle opposed to that which lets us alone.

Such, Mr. President, were the opinions of important and leading gentlemen from South Carolina on the subject of internal improvement, in 1816. I went out of Congress the next year, and returning again in 1823, thought I found South Carolina where I had left her.

I really supposed that all things remained as they were, and that the South Carolina doctrine of internal improvements would be defended by the same eloquent voices and the same strong arms as formerly. In the lapse of these six years, it is true, political associations had assumed a new aspect and new divisions. A strong party had arisen in the South hostile to the doctrine of internal improvements. Anti-consolidation was the flag under which this party fought; and its supporters inveighed against internal improvements, much after the manner in which the honorable gentleman has now inveighed against them, as part and parcel of the system of consolidation. Whether this party arose in South Carolina itself, or in the neighborhood, is more than I know. I think the latter. However that may have been, there were those found in South Carolina ready to make war upon it, and who did make intrepid war upon it. Names being regarded as things in such controversies, they bestowed on the anti-improvement gentlemen the appellation of Radicals. Yes, Sir, the appellation of Radicals, as a term of distinction applicable and applied to those who denied the liberal doctrines of internal improvement, originated, according to the best of my recollection, somewhere between North Carolina and Georgia. Well, Sir, these mischievous Radicals were to be put down, and the strong arm of South Carolina was stretched out to put them down. About this time, Sir, I returned to Congress. The battle with the Radicals had been fought, and our South Carolina champions of the doctrines of internal improvement had nobly maintained their ground, and were understood to have achieved a victory. We looked upon them as conquerors. They had driven back the enemy with discomfiture, — a thing, by the way, Sir, which is not always performed when it is promised. A gentleman to whom I have already referred in this debate had come into Congress, during my absence from it, from South Carolina, and had brought with him a high reputation for ability. He came from a school with which we had been acquainted, *et noscitur a sociis.* I hold in my hand, Sir, a printed speech of this distinguished gentleman [Mr. McDuffie] "On Internal Improvements," delivered about the period to which I now refer, and printed with a few introductory remarks upon consolidation; in which, Sir, I think he quite consolidated the arguments of his opponents, the Radicals, if to crush be to consolidate.

[Mr. Webster quotes passages from the speech claiming for the "Republican" party of that time, — the dominant party in the South, — and for the South Carolinian delegation in Congress, led by Mr. Calhoun, the honor of originating the system and policy of internal improvements.]

Such are the opinions, Sir, which were maintained by South Carolina gentlemen in the House of Representatives, on the subject of internal improvements, when I took my seat there as a member from Massachusetts in 1823. But this is not all. We had a bill before us, and passed it in that House, entitled, "An Act to procure the necessary surveys, plans, and estimates upon the subject of roads and canals." It authorized the President to cause surveys and estimates to be made of the routes of such roads and canals as he might deem of national importance in a commercial or military point of view, or for the transportation of the mail, and appropriated thirty thousand dollars out of the treasury to defray the expense. This act, though preliminary in its nature, covered the whole ground. It took for granted the complete power of internal improvement, as far as any of its advocates had ever contended for it. Having passed the other House, the bill came up to the Senate, and was here considered and debated in April, 1824. The honorable member from South Carolina was a member of the Senate at that time. While the bill was under consideration here, a motion was made to add the following proviso: —

"*Provided*, That nothing herein contained shall be construed to affirm or admit a power in Congress, on their own authority, to make roads or canals within any of the States of the Union." The yeas and nays were taken on this proviso, and the honorable member voted in the negative! The proviso failed.

A motion was then made to add this proviso; viz., —

"*Provided*, That the faith of the United States is hereby pledged, that no money shall ever be expended for roads or canals, except it shall be among the several States, and in the same proportion as direct taxes are laid and assessed by the provisions of the Constitution."

The honorable member voted against this proviso also, and it failed. The bill was then put on its passage, and the honorable member voted for it, and it passed, and became a law.

Now, it strikes me, Sir, that there is no maintaining these votes but upon tne power of internal improvement, in its broadest sense. In truth, these bills for surveys and estimates have always been considered as test questions; they show who is for and who against internal improvement. This law itself went the whole length, and assumed the full and complete power. The gentleman's votes sustained that power, in every form in which the various propositions to amend presented it. He went for the entire and unrestrained authority, without consulting the States, and without agreeing to any proportionate distribution. And now suffer me to remind you, Mr. President, that it is this very same power, thus sanctioned in every form by the gentleman's own opinion, that is so plain and manifest a usurpation that the State of South Carolina is supposed to be justified in refusing submission to any laws carrying the power into effect. Truly, Sir, is not this a little too hard? May we not crave some mercy, under favor and protection of the gentleman's own authority? Admitting that a road, or a canal, must be written down flat usurpation as was ever committed, may we find no mitigation in our respect for his place and his vote, as one that knows the law?

The tariff, which South Carolina had an efficient hand in establishing in 1816, and this asserted power of internal improvement, advanced by her in the same year, and, as we have seen, approved and sanctioned by her representatives in 1824 — these two measures are the great grounds on which she is now thought to be justified in breaking up the Union, if she sees fit to break it up!

I may now safely say, I think, that we have had the authority of leading and distinguished gentlemen from South Carolina in support of the doctrine of internal improvement. I repeat that, up to 1824, I, for one, followed South Carolina; but when that star, in its ascension, veered off in an unexpected direction, I relied on its light no longer.

[Here the Vice-President said, "Does the chair understand the gentleman from Massachusetts to say that the person now occupying the chair of the Senate has changed his opinions on the subject of internal improvements?"]

From nothing ever said to me, Sir, have I had reason to know of any change in the opinions of the person filling the chair of the Senate. If such change has taken place, I regret it. I speak generally of the State of South Carolina. Individuals we know there are who hold opinions favorable to the power. An application for its exercise, in behalf of a public work in South Carolina itself, is now pending, I believe, in the other House, presented by members from that State.

I have thus, Sir, perhaps not without some tediousness of detail, shown, if I am in error on the subject of internal improvement, how, and in what company, I fell into that error. If I am wrong, it is apparent who misled me.

I go to other remarks of the honorable member; and I have to complain of an entire misapprehension of what I said on the subject of the national debt, though I can hardly perceive how any one could misunderstand me. What I said was, not that I wished to put off the payment of the debt, but, on the contrary, that I had always voted for every measure for its reduction as uniformly as the gentleman himself. He seems to claim the exclusive merit of a disposition to reduce the public charge. I do not allow it to him. As a debt, I was, I am, for paying it, because it is a charge on our finances and on the industry of the country. But I observed that I thought I perceived a morbid fervor on that subject—an excessive anxiety to pay off the debt, not so much because it is a debt simply, as because, while it lasts, it furnishes one objection to disunion. It is, while it continues, a tie of common interest. I did not impute such motives to the honorable member himself, but that there is such a feeling in existence I have not a particle of doubt. The most I said was, that if one effect of the debt was to strengthen our Union, that effect itself was not regretted by me, however much others might regret it. The gentleman has not seen how to reply to this otherwise than by supposing me to have advanced the doctrine that a national debt is a national blessing. Others, I must hope, will find much less difficulty in understanding me. I distinctly and pointedly cautioned the honorable member not to understand me as expressing an opinion favorable to the continuance of the debt. I repeated this caution, and repeated it more than once; but it was thrown away.

On yet another point I was still more unaccountably misunderstood. The gentleman had harangued against "consolidation." I told him in reply that there was one kind of consolidation to which I was attached, and that was the consolidation of our Union; and that this was precisely that consolidation to which I feared others were not attached, and that such consolidation was the very end of the Constitution, the leading object, as they had informed us themselves, which its framers had kept in view. I turned to their communication, and read their very words, "the consolidation of the Union," and expressed my devotion to this sort of consolidation. I said in terms that I wished not, in the slightest degree, to augment the powers of this government; that my object was to preserve, not to enlarge; and that by consolidating the Union I understood no more than the strengthening of the Union, and perpetuating it. Having been thus explicit, having thus read from the printed book the precise words which I adopted as expressing my own sentiments, it passes comprehension how any man could understand me as contending for an extension of the powers of the government, or for consolidation in that odious sense, in which it means an accumulation in the federal government of the powers properly belonging to the States.

I repeat, Sir, that, in adopting the sentiment of the framers of the Constitution, I read their language audibly, and word for word; and I pointed out the distinction, just as fully as I have now done, between the consolidation of the Union and that other obnoxious consolidation which I disclaimed. And yet the honorable member misunderstood me. The gentleman had said that he wished for no fixed revenue, — not a shilling. If by a word he could convert the Capitol into gold, he would not do it. Why all this fear of revenue? Why, Sir, because, as the gentleman told us, it tends to consolidation. Now, this can mean neither more nor less than that a common revenue is a common interest, and that all common interests tend to preserve the union of the States. I confess I like that tendency; if the gentleman dislikes it, he is right in deprecating a shilling of fixed revenue. So much, Sir, for consolidation. . . .

Professing to be provoked by what he chose to consider a charge made by me against South Carolina, the honorable member, Mr. President, has taken up a new crusade against New England. Leaving altogether the subject of the public lands, in which his success, perhaps, had been neither distinguished nor satisfactory, and letting go, also, of the topic of the tariff, he sallied forth in a general assault on the opinions, politics, and parties of New England, as they have been exhibited in the last thirty years. This is natural. The "narrow policy" of the public lands had proved a legal settlement in South Carolina, and was not to be removed. The "accursed policy" of the tariff, also, had established the fact of its birth and parentage in the same State. No wonder, therefore, the gentleman wished to carry the war, as he expressed it, into the enemy's country. Prudently willing to quit these subjects, he was, doubtless, desirous of fastening on others, which could not be transferred south of Mason and Dixon's line. The politics of New England became his theme; and it was in this part of his speech, I think, that he menaced me with such sore discomfiture. Discomfiture! Why, Sir, when he attacks anything which I maintain, and overthrows it, when he turns the right or left of any position which I take up, when he drives me from any ground I choose to occupy, he may then talk of discomfiture, but not till that distant day. What has he done? Has he maintained his own charges? Has he proved what he alleged? Has he sustained himself in his attack on the government, and on the history of the North, in the matter of the public lands? Has he disproved a fact, refuted a proposition, weakened an argument, maintained by me? Has he come within beat of drum of any position of mine? Oh, no; but he has "carried the war into the enemy's country!" Carried the war into the enemy's country! Yes, Sir, and what sort of a war has he made of it? Why, Sir, he has stretched a drag-net over the whole surface of perished pamphlets, indiscreet sermons, frothy paragraphs, and fuming popular addresses; over whatever the pulpit in its moments of alarm, the press in its heats, and parties in their extravagance, have severally thrown off in times of general excitement and violence. He has thus swept together a mass of such things as, but that they are now old and cold, the public health would have required him rather to leave in their state of dispersion. For a good long hour or two we had the unbroken pleasure of listening to the honorable member, while he recited with his usual grace and spirit, and with evident high gusto, speeches, pamphlets, addresses, and all the *et ceteras* of the political press, such as warm heads produce in warm times; and such as it would be "discomfiture" indeed for any one, whose taste did not delight in that sort of reading, to be obliged to peruse. This is his war. This it is to carry war into the enemy's country. It is in an invasion of this sort that he flatters himself with the expectation of gaining laurels fit to adorn a Senator's brow!

Mr. President, I shall not, it will not, I trust, be expected that I should, either now or at any time, separate this farrago into parts, and answer and examine its components. I shall barely bestow upon it all a general remark or two. In the run of forty years, Sir, under this Constitution, we have experienced sundry successive violent party contests. Party arose, indeed, with the Constitution itself, and, in some form or other, has attended it through the greater part of its history. Whether any other constitution than the old Articles of Confederation was desirable, was itself a question on which parties divided; if a new Constitution were framed, what powers should be given to it was another question; and, when it had been formed, what was, in fact, the just extent of the powers actually conferred was a third. Parties, as we know, existed under the first administration, as distinctly marked as those which have manifested themselves at any subsequent period. The contest immediately preceding the political change in 1801, and that, again, which existed at the commencement of the late war, are other instances of party excitement, of something more than usual strength and intensity. In all these conflicts there was, no doubt, much of violence on both and all sides. It would be impossible, if one had a fancy for such employment, to adjust the relative *quantum* of violence between these contending parties. There was enough in each, as must always be expected in popular governments. With a great deal of proper and decorous discussion there was mingled a great deal, also, of declamation, virulence, crimination, and abuse. In regard to any party, probably, at one of the leading epochs in the history of parties, enough may be found to make out another inflamed exhibition, not unlike that with which the honorable member has edified us. For myself, Sir, I shall not rake among the rubbish of by-gone times to see what I can find, or whether I cannot find something by which I can fix a blot on the escutcheon of any State, any party, or any part of the country. General Washington's administration was steadily and zealously maintained, as we all know, by New England. It was violently opposed elsewhere. We know in what quarter he had the most earnest, constant, and persevering support, in all his great and leading measures. We know where his private and personal character was held in the highest degree of attachment and veneration; and we know, too, where his measures were opposed, his services slighted, and his character vilified. We know, or we might know, if we turned to the journals, who expressed respect, gratitude, and regret when he retired from the chief magistracy, and who refused to express either respect, gratitude, or regret. I shall not open those journals. Publications more abusive or scurrilous never saw the light than were sent forth against Washington and all his leading measures from presses south of New England. But I shall not look them up. I employ no scavengers; no one is in attendance on me, tendering such means of retaliation; and, if there were, with an ass's load of them, with a bulk as huge as that which the gentleman himself has produced, I would not touch one of them. I see enough of the violence of our own times to be no way anxious to rescue from forgetfulness the extravagances of times past.

Besides, what is all this to the present purpose? It has nothing to do with the public lands, in regard to which the attack was begun; and it has nothing to do with those sentiments and opinions which I have thought tend to disunion, and all of which the honorable member seems to have adopted himself, and undertaken to defend. New England has, at times, so argues the gentleman, held opinions as dangerous as those which he now holds. Suppose this were so; why should he therefore abuse New England? If he finds himself countenanced by acts of hers, how is it that, while he relies on these acts, he covers, or seeks to cover, their authors with reproach? But, Sir, if, in the course of forty years, there have been undue effervescences of party in New England, has the same thing happened nowhere else? . . . If the gentleman wishes to increase his stores of party abuse and frothy violence, if he has a determined proclivity to such pursuits, there are treasures of that sort south of the Potomac, much to his taste, yet untouched. . . . The gentleman's purveyors have only catered for him among the productions of one side. I certainly shall not supply the deficiency by furnishing samples of the other. I leave to him, and to them, the whole concern. It is enough for me to say, that if, in any part of this their grateful occupation, if, in all their researches, they find anything in the history of Massachusetts or New England, or in the proceedings of any legislative or other public body, disloyal to the Union, speaking slightly of its value, proposing to break it up, or recommending non-intercourse with neighboring States, on account of difference of political opinion, then, Sir, I give them all up to the honorable gentleman's unrestrained rebuke; expecting, however, that he will extend his buffetings in like manner to all similar proceedings, wherever else found. . . .

Mr. President, in carrying his warfare, such as it is, into New England, the honorable gentleman all along professes to be acting on the defensive. He chooses to consider me as having assailed South Carolina, and insists that he comes forth only as her champion, and in her defence. Sir, I do not admit that I made any attack whatever on South Carolina. Nothing like it. The honorable member, in his first speech, expressed opinions, in regard to revenue and some other topics, which I heard both with pain and with surprise. I told the gentleman I was aware that such sentiments were entertained out of the government, but had not expected to find them advanced in it; that I knew there were persons in the South who speak of our Union with indifference or doubt, taking pains to magnify its evils, and to say nothing of its benefits; that the honorable member himself, I was sure, could never be one of these; and I regretted the expression of such opinions as he had avowed, because I thought their obvious tendency was to encourage feelings of disrespect to the Union, and to impair its strength. This, Sir, is the sum and substance of all I said on the subject. And this constitutes the attack, which called on the chivalry of the gentleman, in his own opinion, to harry us with such a foray among the party pamphlets and party proceedings of Massachusetts! If he means that I spoke with dissatisfaction or disrespect of the ebullitions of individuals in South Carolina, it is true. But if he means that I had assailed the character of the State, her honor, or patriotism, that I reflected on her history or her conduct, he has not the slightest ground for any such assumption. I did not even refer, I think, in my observations, to any collection of individuals. I said nothing of the recent conventions. I spoke in the most guarded and careful manner, and only expressed my regret for the publication of opinions which I presumed the honorable member disapproved as much as myself. In this, it seems, I was mistaken. I do not remember that the gentleman has disclaimed any sentiment, or any opinion, of a supposed anti-union tendency, which on all or any of the recent occasions has been expressed. The whole drift of his speech has been rather to prove that, in divers times and manners, sentiments equally liable to my objection have been avowed in New England. And one would suppose that his object, in this reference to Massachusetts, was to find a precedent to justify proceedings in the South, were it not for the reproach and contumely with which he labors, all along, to load these his own chosen precedents. By way of defending South Carolina from what he chooses to think an attack on her, he first quotes the example of Massachusetts, and then denounces that example in good set terms. This twofold purpose, not very consistent, one would think, with itself, was exhibited more than once in the course of his speech. He referred, for instance, to the Hartford Convention. Did he do this for authority, or for a topic of reproach? Apparently for both; for he told us that he should find no fault with the mere fact of holding such a convention, and considering and discussing such questions as he supposes were then and there discussed; but what rendered it obnoxious was its being held at the time, and under the circumstances of the country then existing. We were in a war, he said, and the country needed all our aid; the hand of government required to be strengthened, not weakened; and patriotism should have postponed such proceedings to another day. The thing itself, then, is a precedent; the time and manner of it only, a subject of censure. Now, Sir, I go much further on this point than the honorable member. Supposing, as the gentleman seems to do, that the Hartford Convention assembled for any such purpose as breaking up the Union, because they thought unconstitutional laws had been passed, or to consult on that subject, or to calculate the value of the Union; supposing this to be their purpose, or any part of it, then, I say, the meeting itself was disloyal, and was obnoxious to censure, whether held in time of peace or time of war, or under whatever circumstances. The material question is the *object*. Is dissolution the object? If it be, external circumstances may make it a more or less aggravated case, but cannot affect the principle. I do not hold, therefore, Sir, that the Hartford Convention was pardonable, even to the extent of the gentleman's admission, if its objects were really such as have been imputed to it. Sir, there never was a time, under any degree of excitement, in which the Hartford Convention, or any other convention, could have maintained itself one moment in New England, if assembled for any such purpose as the gentleman says would have been an allowable purpose. To hold conventions to decide constitutional law! to try the binding validity of statutes, by votes in a convention! Sir, the Hartford Convention, I presume, would not desire that the honorable gentleman should be their defender or advocate, if he puts their case upon such untenable and extravagant grounds.

Then, Sir, the gentleman has no fault to find with these recently promulgated South Carolina opinions. And certainly he need have none; for his own sentiments as now advanced, and advanced on reflection, as far as I have been able to comprehend them, go the full length of all these opinions. I propose, Sir, to say something on these, and to consider how far they are just and constitutional. Before doing that, however, let me observe that the eulogium pronounced by the honorable gentleman on the character of the State of South Carolina, for Revolutionary and other merits, meets my hearty concurrence. I shall not acknowledge that the honorable member goes before me in regard for whatever of distinguished talent, or distinguished character, South Carolina has produced. I claim part of the honor, I partake in the pride, of her great names. I claim them for countrymen, one and all. The Laurenses, the Rutledges, the Pinckneys, the Sumters, the Marions, Americans all, whose fame is no more to be hemmed in by State lines than their talents and patriotism were capable of being circumscribed within the same narrow limits. In their day and generation they served and honored the country, and the whole country; and their renown is of the treasures of the whole country. Him whose honored name the gentleman himself bears, — does he esteem me less capable of gratitude for his patriotism, or sympathy for his sufferings, than if his eyes had first opened upon the light of Massachusetts instead of South Carolina? Sir, does he suppose it in his power to exhibit a Carolina name so bright as to produce envy in my bosom? No, Sir; increased gratification and delight rather. I thank God that, if I am gifted with little of the spirit which is able to raise mortals to the skies, I have yet none, as I trust, of that other spirit, which would drag angels down. When I shall be found, Sir, in my place here in the Senate, or elsewhere, to sneer at public merit, because it happens to spring up beyond the little limits of my own State or neighborhood; when I refuse, for any such cause, or for any cause, the homage due to American talent, to elevated patriotism, to sincere devotion to liberty and the country; or, if I see an uncommon endowment of Heaven, if I see extraordinary capacity and virtue, in any son of the South, and if, moved by local prejudice, or gangrened by State jealousy, I get up here to abate the tithe of a hair from his just character and just fame, may my tongue cleave to the roof of my mouth!

Sir, let me recur to pleasing recollections; let me indulge in refreshing remembrance of the past; — let me remind you that in early times no States cherished greater harmony, both of principle and feeling, than Massachusetts and South Carolina. Would to God that harmony might again return! Shoulder to shoulder they went through the Revolution, hand in hand they stood round the administration of Washington, and felt his own great arm lean on them for support. Unkind feeling, if it exist, alienation and distrust are the growth, unnatural to such soils, of false principles since sown. They are weeds, the seeds of which that same great arm never scattered.

Mr. President, I shall enter on no encomium upon Massachusetts; she needs none. There she is, behold her, and judge for yourselves. There is her history; the world knows it by heart. The past, at least, is secure. There is Boston, and Concord, and Lexington, and Bunker Hill; and there they will remain forever. The bones of her sons, falling in the great struggle for Independence, now lie mingled with the soil of every State from New England to Georgia; and there they will lie forever. And, Sir, where American Liberty raised its first voice, and where its youth was nurtured and sustained, there it still lives in the strength of its manhood and full of its original spirit. If discord and disunion shall wound it; if party strife and blind ambition shall hawk at and tear it; if folly and madness, if uneasiness under salutary and necessary restraint, shall succeed to separate it from that Union by which alone its existence is made sure; it will stand, in the end, by the side of that cradle in which its infancy was rocked; it will stretch forth its arm with whatever of vigor it may still retain, over the friends who gather round it; and it will fall at last, if fall it must, amidst the proudest monuments of its own glory, and on the very spot of its origin.

There yet remains to be performed, Mr. President, by far the most grave and important duty which I feel to be devolved on me by this occasion. It is to state, and to defend, what I conceive to be the true principles of the Constitution under which we are here assembled. I might well have desired that so weighty a task should have fallen into other and abler hands. I could have wished that it should have been executed by those whose character and experience give weight and influence to their opinions such as cannot possibly belong to mine. But, Sir, I have met the occasion, not sought it; and I shall proceed to state my own sentiments, without challenging for them any particular regard, with studied plainness, and as much precision as possible.

I understand the honorable gentleman from South Carolina to maintain that it is a right of the State legislatures to interfere, whenever in their judgment this government transcends its constitutional limits, and to arrest the operation of its laws.

I understand him to maintain this right, as a right existing *under the Constitution*, not as a right to overthrow it on the ground of extreme necessity, such as would justify violent revolution.

I understand him to maintain an authority, on the part of the States, thus to interfere for the purpose of correcting the exercise of power by the general government, of checking it, and of compelling it to conform to their opinion of the extent of its powers.

I understand him to maintain that the ultimate power of judging of the constitutional extent of its own authority is not lodged exclusively in the general government, or any branch of it; but that, on the contrary, the States may lawfully decide for themselves, and each State for itself, whether, in a given case, the act of the general government transcends its power.

I understand him to insist that, if the exigency of the case, in the opinion of any State government, require it, such State government may, by its own sovereign authority, annul an act of the general government which it deems plainly and palpably unconstitutional.

This is the sum of what I understand from him to be the South Carolina doctrine and the doctrine which he maintains. I propose to consider it, and compare it with the Constitution. Allow me to say, as a preliminary remark, that I call this the South Carolina doctrine only because the gentleman himself has so denominated it. I do not feel at liberty to say that South Carolina, as a State, has ever advanced these sentiments. I hope she has not, and never may. That a great majority of her people are opposed to the tariff laws, is doubtless true. That a majority, somewhat less than that just mentioned, conscientiously believe these laws unconstitutional, may probably also be true. But, that any majority holds to the right of direct State interference at State discretion, — the right of nullifying acts of Congress by acts of State legislation, — is more than I know, and what I shall be slow to believe.

That there are individuals besides the honorable gentleman who do maintain these opinions, is quite certain. I recollect the recent expression of a sentiment which circumstances attending its utterance and publication justify us in supposing was not unpremeditated, "The sovereignty of the State — never to be controlled, construed, or decided on, but by her own feelings of honorable justice."

[Mr. Hayne here rose and said that, for the purpose of being clearly understood, he would state that his proposition was in the words of the Virginia resolution as follows: —

"That this assembly doth explicitly and peremptorily declare, that it views the powers of the federal government, as resulting from the compact to which the States are parties, as limited by the plain sense and intention of the instrument constituting that compact, as no farther valid than they are authorized by the grants enumerated in that compact; and that, in case of a deliberate, palpable, and dangerous exercise of other powers, not granted by the said compact, the States who are parties thereto have the right, and are in duty bound, to interpose, for arresting the progress of the evil, and for maintaining within their respective limits the authorities, rights, and liberties appertaining to them."]

Mr. Webster resumed: —

I am quite aware, Mr. President, of the existence of the resolution which the gentleman read, and has now repeated, and that he relies on it as his authority. I know the source, too, from which it is understood to have proceeded. I need not say that I have much respect for the constitutional opinions of Mr. Madison; they would weigh greatly with me always. But, before the authority of his opinion be vouched for the gentleman's proposition, it will be proper to consider what is the fair interpretation of that resolution to which Mr. Madison is understood to have given his sanction. As the gentleman construes it, it is an authority for him. Possibly he may not have adopted the right construction. That resolution declares, that, *in the case of the dangerous exercise of powers not granted by the general government, the States may interpose to arrest the progress of the evil.* But how interpose, and what does this declaration purport? Does it mean no more than that there may be extreme cases, in which the people, in any mode of assembling, may resist usurpation and relieve themselves from a tyrannical government? No one will deny this. Such resistance is not only acknowledged to be just in America, but in England also. Blackstone admits as much, in the theory, and practice, too, of the English constitution. We, Sir, who oppose the Carolina doctrine, do not deny that the people may, if they choose, throw off any government, when it becomes oppressive and intolerable, and erect a better in its stead. We all know that civil institutions are established for the public benefit, and that when they cease to answer the ends of their existence they may be changed. But I do not understand the doctrine now contended for to be that which, for the sake of distinction, we may call the right of revolution. I understand the gentleman to maintain that, without revolution, without civil commotion, without rebellion, a remedy for supposed abuse and transgression of the powers of the general government lies in a direct appeal to the interference of the State governments.

[Mr. Hayne here rose and said: He did not contend for the mere right of revolution, but for the right of constitutional resistance. What he maintained was, that, in case of a plain, palpable violation of the Constitution by the general government, a State may interpose; and that this interposition is constitutional.]

Mr. Webster resumed:

So, Sir, I understood the gentleman, and am happy to find that I did not misunderstand him. What he contends for is, that it is constitutional to interrupt the administration of the Constitution itself, in the hands of those who are chosen and sworn to administer it, by the direct interference, in form of law, of the States, in virtue of their sovereign capacity. The inherent right in the people to reform their government I do not deny; and they have another right, and that is, to resist unconstitutional laws, without overturning the government. It is no doctrine of mine that unconstitutional laws bind the people. The great question is, whose prerogative is it to decide on the constitutionality or unconstitutionality of the laws? On that the main debate hinges. The proposition that, in case of a supposed violation of the Constitution by Congress, the States have a constitutional right to interfere and annul the law of Congress, is the proposition of the gentleman.

I do not admit it. If the gentleman had intended no more than to assert the right of revolution for justifiable cause, he would have said only what all agree to. But I cannot conceive that there can be a middle course, between submission to the laws, when regularly pronounced constitutional, on the one hand, and open resistance, which is revolution or rebellion, on the other. I say, the right of a State to annul a law of Congress cannot be maintained but on the ground of the inalienable right of man to resist oppression; that is to say, upon the ground of revolution. I admit that there is an ultimate violent remedy, above the Constitution and in defiance of the Constitution, which may be resorted to when a revolution is to be justified. But I do not admit that, under the Constitution and in conformity with it, there is any mode in which a State government, as a member of the Union, can interfere and stop the progress of the general government, by force of her own laws, under any circumstances whatever.

This leads us to inquire into the origin of this government and the source of its power. Whose agent is it? Is it the creature of the State legislatures, or the creature of the people? If the government of the United States be the agent of the State governments, then they may control it, provided they can agree in the manner of controlling it; if it be the agent of the people, then the people alone can control it, restrain it, modify, or reform it. It is observable enough, that the doctrine for which the honorable gentleman contends leads him to the necessity of maintaining, not only that this general government is the creature of the States, but that it is the creature of each of the States severally, so that each may assert the power for itself of determining whether it acts within the limits of its authority. It is the servant of four-and-twenty masters, of different wills and different purposes, and yet bound to obey all. This absurdity (for it seems no less) arises from a misconception as to the origin of this government and its true character. It is, Sir, the people's Constitution, the people's government, made for the people, made by the people, and answerable to the people. The people of the United States have declared that this Constitution shall be the supreme law. We must either admit the proposition, or dispute their authority. The States are, unquestionably, sovereign, so far as their sovereignty is not affected by this supreme law. But the State legislatures, as political bodies, however sovereign, are yet not sovereign over the people. So far as the people have given power to the general government, so far the grant is unquestionably good, and the government holds of the people, and not of the State governments. We are all agents of the same supreme power, the people. The general government and the State governments derive their authority from the same source. Neither can, in relation to the other, be called primary, though one is definite and restricted, and the other general and residuary. The national government possesses those powers which it can be shown the people have conferred on it, and no more. All the rest belongs to the State governments, or to the people themselves. So far as the people have restrained State sovereignty, by the expression of their will, in the Constitution of the United States, so far, it must be admitted, State sovereignty is effectually controlled. I do not contend that it is, or ought to be, controlled farther. The sentiment to which I have referred propounds that State sovereignty is only to be controlled by its own "feeling of justice;" that is to say, it is not to be controlled at all; for one who is to follow his own feelings is under no legal control. Now, however men may think this ought to be, the fact is, that the people of the United States have chosen to impose control on State sovereignties. There are those, doubtless, who wish they had been left without restraint; but the Constitution has ordered the matter differently. To make war, for instance, is an exercise of sovereignty; but the Constitution declares that no State shall make war. To coin money is another exercise of sovereign power; but no State is at liberty to coin money. Again, the Constitution says that no sovereign State shall be so sovereign as to make a treaty. These prohibitions, it must be confessed, are a control on the State sovereignty of South Carolina, as well as of the other States, which does not arise "from her own feelings of honorable justice." Such an opinion, therefore, is in defiance of the plainest provisions of the Constitution.

There are other proceedings of public bodies which have already been alluded to, and to which I refer again, for the purpose of ascertaining more fully what is the length and breadth of that doctrine denominated the Carolina doctrine, which the honorable member has now stood up on this floor to maintain. In one of them I find it resolved, that "the tariff of 1828, and every other tariff designed to promote one branch of industry at the expense of others, is contrary to the meaning and intention of the federal compact; and such a dangerous, palpable, and deliberate usurpation of power, by a determined majority, wielding the general government beyond the limits of its delegated powers, as calls upon States which compose the suffering minority, in their sovereign capacity, to exercise the powers which, as sovereigns, necessarily devolve upon them when their compact is violated."

Observe, Sir, that this resolution holds the tariff of 1828, and every other tariff designed to promote one branch of industry at the expense of another, to be such a dangerous, palpable, and deliberate usurpation of power, as calls upon the States, in their sovereign capacity, to interfere by their own authority. This denunciation, Mr. President, you will please to observe, includes our old tariff of 1816, as well as all others; because that was established to promote the interest of the manufacturers of cotton, to the manifest and admitted injury of the Calcutta cotton trade. Observe, again, that all the qualifications are here rehearsed and charged upon the tariff, which are necessary to bring the case within the gentleman's proposition. The tariff is a usurpation: it is a dangerous usurpation; it is a palpable usurpation; it is a deliberate usurpation. It is such a usurpation, therefore, as calls upon the States to exercise their right of interference. Here is a case, then, within the gentleman's principles, and all his qualifications of his principles. It is a case for action. The Constitution is plainly, dangerously, palpably, and deliberately violated; and the States must interpose their own authority to arrest the law. Let us suppose the State of South Carolina to express this same opinion by the voice of her legislature. That would be very imposing; but what then? Is the voice of one State conclusive? It so happens that, at the very moment when South Carolina resolves that the tariff laws are unconstitutional, Pennsylvania and Kentucky resolve exactly the reverse. *They* hold those laws to be both highly proper and strictly constitutional. And now, Sir, how does the honorable member propose to deal with this case? How does he relieve us from this difficulty, upon any principle of his? His construction gets us into it; how does he propose to get us out?

In Carolina, the tariff is a palpable, deliberate usurpation; Carolina, therefore, may nullify it, and refuse to pay the duties. In Pennsylvania, it is both clearly constitutional and highly expedient; and there the duties are to be paid. And yet we live under a government of uniform laws, and under a Constitution, too, which contains an express provision, as it happens, that all duties shall be equal in all the States. Does not this approach absurdity?

If there be no power to settle such questions, independent of either of the States, is not the whole Union a rope of sand? Are we not thrown back again, precisely, upon the old Confederation?

It is too plain to be argued. Four and twenty interpreters of constitutional law, each with a power to decide for itself, and none with authority to bind anybody else, and this constitutional law the only bond of their union! What is such a state of things but a mere connection during pleasure, or, to use the phraseology of the times, *during feeling?* And that feeling, too, not the feeling of the people, who established the Constitution, but the feeling of the State governments.

In another of the South Carolina addresses, having premised that the crisis requires "all the concentrated energy of passion," an attitude of open resistance to the laws of the Union is advised. Open resistance to the laws, then, is the constitutional remedy, the conservative power of the State, which the South Carolina doctrines teach for the redress of political evils, real or imaginary. And its authors further say that, appealing with confidence to the Constitution itself, to justify their opinions, they cannot consent to try their accuracy by the courts of justice. In one sense, indeed, Sir, this is assuming an attitude of open resistance in favor of liberty. But what sort of liberty? The liberty of establishing their own opinions, in defiance of the opinions of all others; the liberty of judging and of deciding exclusively themselves, in a matter in which others have as much right to judge and decide as they; the liberty of placing their own opinions above the judgment of all others, above the laws, and above the Constitution. This is their liberty, and this is the fair result of the proposition contended for by the honorable gentleman. Or it may be more properly said, it is identical with it, rather than a result from it. . . .

And now, Sir, what I have first to say on this subject is, that at no time, and under no circumstances, has New England, or any State in New England, or any respectable body of persons in New England, or any public man of standing in New England, put forth such a doctrine as this Carolina doctrine.

The gentleman has found no case, he can find none, to support his own opinions by New England authority. New England has studied the Constitution in other schools, and under other teachers. She looks upon it with other regards, and deems more highly and reverently both of its just authority and its utility and excellence. The history of her legislative proceedings may be traced. The ephemeral effusions of temporary bodies, called together by the excitement of the occasion, may be hunted up; they have been hunted up. The opinions and votes of her public men, in and out of Congress, may be explored. It will all be in vain. The Carolina doctrine can derive from her neither countenance nor support. She rejects it now; she always did reject it; and, till she loses her senses, she always will reject it. The honorable member has referred to expressions on the subject of the embargo law, made in this place by an honorable and venerable gentleman [Mr. Hillhouse], now favoring us with his presence. He quotes that distinguished Senator as saying that, in his judgment, the embargo law was unconstitutional, and that, therefore, in his opinion, the people were not bound to obey it. That, Sir, is perfectly constitutional language. An unconstitutional law is not binding; but then it does not rest with a resolution or a law of a State legislature to decide whether an act of Congress be, or be not, constitutional. An unconstitutional act of Congress would not bind the people of this District, although they have no legislature to interfere in their behalf; and, on the other hand, a constitutional law of Congress does bind the citizens of every State, although all their legislatures should undertake to annul it by act or resolution. The venerable Connecticut Senator is a constitutional lawyer of sound principles and enlarged knowledge; a statesman practised and experienced, bred in the company of Washington, and holding just views upon the nature of our governments. He believed the embargo unconstitutional, and so did others; but what then? Who did he suppose was to decide that question? The State legislatures? Certainly not. No such sentiment ever escaped his lips.

Let us follow up, Sir, this New England opposition to the embargo laws; let us trace it till we discern the principle which controlled and governed New England throughout the whole course of that opposition. We shall then see what similarity there is between the New England school of constitutional opinions, and this modern Carolina school. . . . No doubt, Sir, a great majority of the people of New England conscientiously believed the embargo law of 1807 unconstitutional; as conscientiously, certainly, as the people of South Carolina hold that opinion of the tariff. They reasoned thus: Congress has power to regulate commerce; but here is a law, they said, stopping all commerce, and stopping it indefinitely. The law is perpetual; that is, it is not limited in point of time, and must, of course, continue until it shall be repealed by some other law. It is as perpetual, therefore, as the law against treason or murder. Now, is this regulating commerce, or destroying it? Is it guiding, controlling, giving the rule to commerce, as a subsisting thing; or is it putting an end to it altogether? Nothing is more certain than that a majority in New England deemed this law a violation of the Constitution. The very case required by the gentleman to justify State interference had then arisen. Massachusetts believed this law to be "a deliberate, palpable, and dangerous exercise of a power not granted by the Constitution." Deliberate it was, for it was long continued; palpable, she thought it, as no words in the Constitution gave the power, and only a construction, in her opinion most violent, raised it; dangerous it was, since it threatened utter ruin to her most important interests. Here, then, was a Carolina case. How did Massachusetts deal with it? It was, as she thought, a plain, manifest, palpable violation of the Constitution, and it brought ruin to her doors. Thousands of families, and hundreds of thousands of individuals, were beggared by it. While she saw and felt all this, she saw and felt, also, that, as a measure of national policy, it was perfectly futile; that the country was no way benefited by that which caused so much individual distress; that it was efficient only for the production of evil, and all that evil inflicted on ourselves. In such a case, under such circumstances, how did Massachusetts demean herself? Sir, she remonstrated, she memorialized, she addressed herself to the general government, not exactly "with the concentrated energy of passion," but with her own strong sense, and the energy of sober conviction. But she did not interpose the arm of her own power to arrest the law, and break the embargo. Far from it. Her principles bound her to two things; and she followed her principles, lead where they might. First, to submit to every constitutional law of Congress; and, secondly, if the constitutional validity of the law be doubted, to refer that question to the decision of the proper tribunals. The first principle is vain and ineffectual without the second. A majority of us in New England believed the embargo law unconstitutional; but the great question was, and always will be, in such cases, Who is to decide this? Who is to judge between the people and the government? And, Sir, it is quite plain that the Constitution of the United States confers on the government itself, to be exercised by its appropriate department, and under its own responsibility to the people, this power of deciding ultimately and conclusively upon the just extent of its own authority. If this had not been done, we should not have advanced a single step beyond the old Confederation.

Being fully of opinion that the embargo law was unconstitutional, the people of New England were yet equally clear in the opinion — it was a matter they did [not] doubt upon — that the question, after all, must be decided by the judicial tribunals of the United States. Before those tribunals, therefore, they brought the question. Under the provisions of the law they had given bonds to millions in amount, and which were alleged to be forfeited. They suffered the bonds to be sued, and thus raised the question. In the old-fashioned way of settling disputes they went to law. The case came to hearing and solemn argument; and he who espoused their cause, and stood up for them against the validity of the embargo act, was none other than that great man of whom the gentleman has made honorable mention, Samuel Dexter. He was then, Sir, in the fullness of his knowledge and the maturity of his strength. He had retired from long and distinguished public service here, to the renewed pursuit of professional duties; carrying with him all that enlargement and expansion, all the new strength and force, which an acquaintance with the more general subjects discussed in the national councils is capable of adding to professional attainment in a mind of true greatness and comprehension. He was a lawyer, and he was also a statesman. . . . He put into his effort his whole heart, as well as all the powers of his understanding; for he had avowed in the most public manner his entire concurrence with his neighbors on the point in dispute. He argued the cause; it was lost, and New England submitted. The established tribunals pronounced the law constitutional, and New England acquiesced. Now, Sir, is not this the exact opposite of the doctrine of the gentleman from South Carolina? According to him, instead of referring to the judicial tribunals, we should have broken up the embargo by laws of our own; we should have repealed it, *quoad* New England; for we had a strong, palpable, and oppressive case. Sir, we believed the embargo unconstitutional; but still that was matter of opinion, and who was to decide it? We thought it a clear case; but, nevertheless, we did not take the law into our own hands, because we did not wish to bring about a revolution, nor to break up the Union; for I maintain that, between submission to the decision of the constituted tribunals and revolution, or disunion, there is no middle ground; there is no ambiguous condition, half allegiance and half rebellion. And, Sir, how futile, how very futile, it is to admit the right of State interference, and then attempt to save it from the character of unlawful resistance, by adding terms of qualification to the causes and occasions, leaving all these qualifications, like the case itself, in the discretion of the State governments. It must be a clear case, it is said, a deliberate case, a palpable case, a dangerous case. But then the State is still left at liberty to decide for herself what is clear, what is deliberate, what is palpable, what is dangerous. Do adjectives and epithets avail anything?

Sir, the human mind is so constituted that the merits of both sides of a controversy appear very clear and very palpable to those who respectively espouse them; and both sides usually grow clearer as the controversy advances. South Carolina sees unconstitutionality in the tariff; she sees oppression there also, and she sees danger. Pennsylvania, with a vision not less sharp, looks at the same tariff, and sees no such thing in it; she sees it all constitutional, all useful, all safe. The faith of South Carolina is strengthened by opposition, and she now not only sees, but resolves, that the tariff is palpably unconstitutional, oppressive, and dangerous; but Pennsylvania, not to be behind her neighbors, and equally willing to strengthen her own faith by a confident asseveration, resolves also, and gives to every warm affirmative of South Carolina, a plain, downright, Pennsylvania negative. South Carolina, to show the strength and unity of her opinion, brings her assembly to a unanimity within seven voices; Pennsylvania, not to be outdone in this respect more than in others, reduces her dissentient fraction to a single vote. Now, Sir, again I ask the gentleman, What is to be done? Are these States both right? Is he bound to consider them both right? If not, which is in the wrong? or, rather, which has the best right to decide? And if he, and if I, are not to know what the Constitution means, and what it is, till those two State legislatures, and the twenty-two others, shall agree in its construction, what have we sworn to when we have sworn to maintain it? I was forcibly struck, Sir, with one reflection, as the gentleman went on in his speech. He quoted Mr. Madison's resolutions to prove that a State may interfere, in a case of deliberate, palpable, and dangerous exercise of a power not granted. The honorable member supposes the tariff law to be such an exercise of power; and that, consequently, a case has arisen in which the State may, if it see fit, interfere by its own law. Now it so happens, nevertheless, that Mr. Madison deems this same tariff law quite constitutional. Instead of a clear and palpable violation, it is, in his judgment, no violation at all. So that, while they use his authority for a hypothetical case, they reject it in the very case before them. All this, Sir, shows the inherent futility, I had almost used a stronger word, of conceding this power of interference to the States, and then attempting to secure it from abuse by imposing qualifications of which the States themselves are to judge. One of two things is true; either the laws of the Union are beyond the discretion and beyond the control of the States, or else we have no Constitution of general government, and are thrust back again to the days of the Confederation.

Let me here say, Sir, that if the gentleman's doctrine had been received and acted upon in New England, in the times of the embargo and non-intercourse, we should probably not now have been here. The government would very likely have gone to pieces, and crumbled into dust. No stronger case can ever arise than existed under those laws; no States can ever entertain a clearer conviction than the New England States then entertained; and if they had been under the influence of that heresy of opinion, as I must call it, which the honorable member espouses, this Union would, in all probability, have been scattered to the four winds. I ask the gentleman, therefore, to apply his principles to that case; I ask him to come forth and declare whether, in his opinion, the New England States would have been justified in interfering to break up the embargo system under the conscientious opinions which they held upon it? Had they a right to annul that law? Does he admit or deny? If that which is thought palpably unconstitutional in South Carolina justifies that State in arresting the progress of the law, tell me whether that which was thought palpably unconstitutional also in Massachusetts would have justified her in doing the same thing. Sir, I deny the whole doctrine. It has not a foot of ground in the Constitution to stand on. No public man of reputation ever advanced it in Massachusetts, in the warmest times, or could maintain himself upon it there at any time.

I wish now, Sir, to make a remark upon the Virginia resolutions of 1798. I cannot undertake to say how these resolutions were understood by those who passed them. Their language is not a little indefinite. In the case of the exercise by Congress of a dangerous power not granted to them, the resolutions assert the right, on the part of the State, to interfere and arrest the progress of the evil. This is susceptible of more than one interpretation. It may mean no more than that the States may interfere by complaint and remonstrance; or by proposing to the people an alteration of the federal Constitution. This would all be quite unobjectionable. Or it may be that no more is meant than to assert the general right of revolution, as against all governments, in cases of intolerable oppression. This no one doubts, and this, in my opinion, is all that he who framed the resolutions could have meant by it; for I shall not readily believe that he was ever of opinion that a State, under the Constitution and in conformity with it, could, upon the ground of her own opinion of its unconstitutionality, however clear and palpable she might think the case, annul a law of Congress so far as it should operate on herself, by her own legislative power.

I must now beg to ask, Sir, whence is this supposed right of the States derived? Where do they find the power to interfere with the laws of the Union? Sir, the opinion which the honorable gentleman maintains is a notion founded in a total misapprehension, in my judgment, of the origin of this government, and of the foundation on which it stands. I hold it to be a popular government, erected by the people; those who administer it, responsible to the people; and itself capable of being amended and modified, just as the people may choose it should be. It is as popular, just as truly emanating from the people, as the State governments. It is created for one purpose; the State governments for another. It has its own powers; they have theirs. There is no more authority with them to arrest the operation of a law of Congress, than with Congress to arrest the operation of their laws. We are here to administer a Constitution emanating immediately from the people, and trusted by them to our administration. It is not the creature of the State governments. It is of no moment to the argument, that certain acts of the State legislatures are necessary to fill our seats in this body. That is not one of their original State powers, a part of the sovereignty of the State. It is a duty which the people, by the Constitution itself, have imposed on the State legislatures, and which they might have left to be performed elsewhere, if they had seen fit. So they have left the choice of President with electors; but all this does not affect the proposition that this whole government, President, Senate, and House of Representatives, is a popular government. It leaves it still all its popular character. The governor of a State (in some of the States) is chosen, not directly by the people, but by those who are chosen by the people for the purpose of performing, among other duties, that of electing a governor. Is the government of the State, on that account, not a popular government? This government, Sir, is the independent offspring of the popular will. It is not the creature of State legislatures; nay more, if the whole truth must be told, the people brought it into existence, established it, and have hitherto supported it, for the very purpose, amongst others, of imposing certain salutary restraints on State sovereignties. The States cannot now make war; they cannot contract alliances; they cannot make, each for itself, separate regulations of commerce; they cannot lay imposts; they cannot coin money. If this Constitution, Sir, be the creature of State legislatures, it must be admitted that it has obtained a strange control over the volitions of its creators.

The people, then, Sir, erected this government. They gave it a Constitution, and in that Constitution they have enumerated the powers which they bestow on it. They have made it a limited government. They have defined its authority. They have restrained it to the exercise of such powers as are granted; and all others, they declare, are reserved to the States or the people. But, Sir, they have not stopped here. If they had, they would have accomplished but half their work. No definition can be so clear as to avoid possibility of doubt; no limitation so precise as to exclude all uncertainty. Who, then, shall construe this grant of the people? Who shall interpret their will, where it may be supposed they have left it doubtful? With whom do they repose this ultimate right of deciding on the powers of the government? Sir, they have settled all this in the fullest manner. They have left it with the government itself in its appropriate branches. Sir, the very chief end, the main design for which the whole Constitution was framed and adopted, was to establish a government that should not be obliged to act through State agency, or depend on State opinion and State discretion. The people had had quite enough of that kind of government under the Confederation. Under that system the legal action, the application of law to individuals, belonged exclusively to the States. Congress could only recommend; their acts were not of binding force, till the States had adopted and sanctioned them. Are we in that condition still? Are we yet at the mercy of State discretion and State construction? Sir, if we are, then vain will be our attempt to maintain the Constitution under which we sit.

But, Sir, the people have wisely provided in the Constitution itself a proper, suitable mode and tribunal for settling questions of constitutional law. There are in the Constitution grants of powers to Congress, and restrictions on these powers. There are, also, prohibitions on the States. Some authority must, therefore, necessarily exist, having the ultimate jurisdiction to fix and ascertain the interpretation of these grants, restrictions, and prohibitions. The Constitution has itself pointed out, ordained, and established that authority. How has it accomplished this great and essential end? By declaring, Sir, that "*the Constitution and the laws of the United States made in pursuance thereof shall be the supreme law of the land, anything in the Constitution or laws of any State to the contrary notwithstanding.*"

This, Sir, was the first great step. By this the supremacy of the Constitution and laws of the United States is declared. The people so will it. No State law is to be valid which comes in conflict with the Constitution or any law of the United States passed in pursuance of it. But who shall decide this question of interference? To whom lies the last appeal? This, Sir, the Constitution itself decides also, by declaring, "*that the judicial power shall extend to all cases arising under the Constitution and laws of the United States.*" These two provisions cover the whole ground. They are, in truth, the keystone of the arch! With these, it is a government; without them it is a confederation. In pursuance of these clear and express provisions, Congress established at its very first session, in the judicial act, a mode for carrying them into full effect, and for bringing all questions of constitutional power to the final decision of the Supreme Court. It then, Sir, became a government. It then had the means of self-protection; and, but for this, it would, in all probability, have been now among things which are past. Having constituted the government and declared its powers, the people have further said that, since somebody must decide on the extent of these powers, the government shall itself decide; subject always, like other popular governments, to its responsibility to the people. And now, Sir, I repeat, how is it that a State legislature acquires any power to interfere? Who, or what, gives them the right to say to the people, "We, who are your agents and servants for one purpose, will undertake to decide that your other agents and servants, appointed by you for another purpose, have transcended the authority you gave them!" The reply would be, I think, not impertinent, — "Who made you a judge over another's servants? To their own masters they stand or fall."

Sir, I deny this power of State legislatures altogether. It cannot stand the test of examination. Gentlemen may say that, in an extreme case, a State government might protect the people from intolerable oppression. Sir, in such a case, the people might protect themselves without the aid of the State governments. Such a case warrants revolution. It must make, when it comes, a law for itself. A nullifying act of a State legislature cannot alter the case, nor make resistance any more lawful. In maintaining these sentiments, Sir, I am but asserting the rights of the people. I state what they have declared, and insist on their right to declare it. They have chosen to repose this power in the general government, and I think it my duty to support it, like other constitutional powers.

For myself, Sir, I do not admit the jurisdiction of South Carolina, or any other State, to prescribe my constitutional duty; or to settle, between me and the people, the validity of laws of Congress, for which I have voted. I decline her umpirage. I have not sworn to support the Constitution according to her construction of its clauses. I have not stipulated, by my oath of office or otherwise, to come under any responsibility, except to the people and those whom they have appointed to pass upon the question, whether laws supported by my votes conform to the Constitution of the country. And, Sir, if we look to the general nature of the case, could anything have been more preposterous than to make a government for the whole Union, and yet leave its powers subject, not to one interpretation, but to thirteen, or twenty-four interpretations? Instead of one tribunal, established by all, responsible to all, with power to decide for all, shall constitutional questions be left to four and twenty popular bodies, each at liberty to decide for itself, and none bound to respect the decisions of others; and each at liberty, too, to give a new construction on every new election of its own members? Would anything, with such a principle in it, or rather with such a destitution of all principle, be fit to be called a government? No, Sir; it should not be denominated a Constitution. It should be called, rather, a collection of topics for everlasting controversy; heads of debate for a disputatious people. It would not be a government. It would not be adequate to any practical good, nor fit for any country to live under. To avoid all possibility of being misunderstood, allow me to repeat again, in the fullest manner, that I claim no powers for the government by forced or unfair construction. I admit that it is a government of strictly limited powers, of enumerated, specified, and particularized powers; and that whatsoever is not granted is withheld. But, notwithstanding all this, and however the grant of powers may be expressed, its limit and extent may yet, in some cases, admit of doubt; and the general government would be good for nothing, it would be incapable of long existing, if some mode had not been provided in which those doubts, as they should arise, might be peaceably, but authoritatively solved.

And now, Mr. President, let me run the honorable gentleman's doctrine a little into its practical application. Let us look at his probable *modus operandi*. If a thing can be done, an ingenious man can tell how it is to be done. And I wish to be informed how this State interference is to be put in practice without violence, bloodshed, and rebellion. We will take the existing case of the tariff law. South Carolina is said to have made up her opinion upon it. If we do not repeal it (as we probably shall not), she will then apply to the case the remedy of her doctrine. She will, we must suppose, pass a law of her legislature declaring the several acts of Congress, usually called the tariff laws, null and void so far as they respect South Carolina or the citizens thereof. So far, all is a paper transaction, and easy enough. But the collector at Charleston is collecting the duties imposed by these tariff laws. He, therefore, must be stopped. The collector will seize the goods if the tariff duties are not paid. The State authorities will undertake their rescue; the marshal with his posse will come to the collector's aid; and here the contest begins. The militia of the State will be called out to sustain the nullifying act. They will march, Sir, under a very gallant leader; for I believe the honorable member himself commands the militia of that part of the State. He will raise the nullifying act on his standard, and spread it out as his banner. It will have a preamble, setting forth that the tariff laws are palpable, deliberate, and dangerous violations of the Constitution. He will proceed, with this banner flying, to the custom-house in Charleston.

> "All the while,
> Sonorous metal blowing martial sounds."

Arrived at the custom-house, he will tell the collector that he must collect no more duties under any of the tariff laws. This he will be somewhat puzzled to say, by the way, with a grave countenance, considering what hand South Carolina herself had in that of 1816. But, Sir, the collector would probably not desist at his bidding. He would show him the law of Congress, the treasury instruction, and his own oath of office. He would say he should perform his duty, come what come might.

Here would ensue a pause, for they say that a certain stillness precedes the tempest. The trumpeter would hold his breath a while, and before all this military array should fall on the custom-house, collector, clerks, and all, it is very probable some of those composing it would request of their gallant commander-in-chief to be informed a little upon the point of law; for they have, doubtless, a just respect for his opinions as a lawyer, as well as for his bravery as a soldier. They know he has read Blackstone and the Constitution, as well as Turenne and Vauban. They would ask him, therefore, something concerning their rights in this matter. They would inquire whether it was not somewhat dangerous to resist a law of the United States. What would be the nature of their offence, they would wish to learn, if they by military force and array resisted the execution in Carolina of a law of the United States, and it should turn out, after all, that the law was constitutional. He would answer, of course, Treason. No lawyer could give any other answer. John Fries, he would tell them, had learned that some years ago. "How then," they would ask, "do you propose to defend us? We are not afraid of bullets, but treason has a way of taking people off that we do not much relish. How do you propose to defend us?" "Look at my floating banner," he would reply; "see there the Nullifying Law!" "Is it your opinion, gallant commander," they would then say, "that, if we should be indicted for treason, that same floating banner of yours would make a good plea in bar?" "South Carolina is a sovereign State," he would reply. "That is true; but would the judge admit our plea?" "These tariff laws," he would repeat, "are unconstitutional, palpably, deliberately, dangerously." "That all may be so; but if the tribunal should not happen to be of that opinion, shall we swing for it? We are ready to die for our country, but it is rather an awkward business, this dying without touching the ground! After all, that is a sort of hemp tax, worse than any part of the tariff."

Mr. President, the honorable gentleman would be in a dilemma like that of another great general. He would have a knot before him which he could not untie. He must cut it with his sword. He must say to his followers, "Defend yourselves with your bayonets!" And this is war, — civil war.

Direct collision, therefore, between force and force is the unavoidable result of that remedy for the revision of unconstitutional laws which the gentleman contends for.

It must happen in the very first case to which it is applied. Is not this the plain result? To resist by force the execution of a law, generally is treason. Can the courts of the United States take notice of the indulgence of a State to commit treason? The common saying, that a State cannot commit treason herself, is nothing to the purpose. Can she authorize others to do it? If John Fries had produced an act of Pennsylvania annulling the law of Congress, would it have helped his case? Talk about it as we will, these doctrines go the length of revolution. They are incompatible with any peaceable administration of the government. They lead directly to disunion and civil commotion; and therefore it is, that at their commencement, when they are first found to be maintained by respectable men, and in a tangible form, I enter my public protest against them all.

The honorable gentleman argues that, if this government be the sole judge of the extent of its own powers, whether that right of judging be in Congress or the Supreme Court, it equally subverts State sovereignty. This the gentleman sees, or thinks he sees, although he cannot perceive how the right of judging in this matter, if left to the exercise of State legislatures, has any tendency to subvert the government of the Union. The gentleman's opinion may be that the right ought not to have been lodged with the general government; he may like better such a Constitution as we should have under the right of State interference; but I ask him to meet me on the plain matter of fact. I ask him to meet me on the Constitution itself. I ask him if the power is not found there — clearly and visibly found there?

But, Sir, what is this danger, and what the grounds of it? Let it be remembered that the Constitution of the United States is not unalterable. It is to continue in its present form no longer than the people who established it shall choose to continue it. If they shall become convinced that they have made an injudicious or inexpedient partition and distribution of power between the State governments and the general government, they can alter that distribution at will.

If anything be found in the national Constitution, either by original provision or subsequent interpretation, which ought not to be in it, the people know how to get rid of it. If any construction unacceptable to them be established, so as to become practically a part of the Constitution, they will amend it at their own sovereign pleasure. But while the people choose to maintain it as it is, while they are satisfied with it, and refuse to change it, who has given, or who can give, to the State legislatures a right to alter it either by interference, construction, or otherwise? Gentlemen do not seem to recollect that the people have any power to do anything for themselves. They imagine there is no safety for them, any longer than they are under the close guardianship of the State legislatures. Sir, the people have not trusted their safety, in regard to the general Constitution, to these hands. They have required other security, and taken other bonds. They have chosen to trust themselves, first, to the plain words of the instrument, and to such construction as the government itself, in doubtful cases, should put on its own powers, under its oaths of office, and subject to its responsibility to them; just as the people of a State trust their own State governments with a similar power. Secondly, they have reposed their trust in the efficacy of frequent elections, and in their own power to remove their own servants and agents whenever they see cause. Thirdly, they have reposed trust in the judicial power, which, in order that it might be trustworthy, they have made as respectable, as disinterested, and as independent as was practicable. Fourthly, they have seen fit to rely, in case of necessity or high expediency, on their known and admitted power to alter or amend the Constitution peaceably and quietly, whenever experience shall point out defects or imperfections. And, finally, the people of the United States have at no time, in no way, directly or indirectly, authorized any State legislature to construe or interpret their high instrument of government; much less to interfere by their own power to arrest its course and operation.

If, Sir, the people in these respects had done otherwise than they have done, their Constitution could neither have been preserved, nor would it have been worth preserving. And if its plain provisions shall now be disregarded, and these new doctrines interpolated in it, it will become as feeble and helpless a being as its enemies, whether early or more recent, could possibly desire. It will exist in every State but as a poor dependant on State permission. It must borrow leave to be; and will be no longer than State pleasure, or State discretion, sees fit to grant the indulgence and to prolong its poor existence.

But, Sir, although there are fears, there are hopes also. The people have preserved this, their own chosen Constitution, for forty years, and have seen their happiness, prosperity, and renown grow with its growth, and strengthen with its strength. They are now, generally, strongly attached to it. Overthrown by direct assault, it cannot be; evaded, undermined, nullified, it will not be, if we, and those who shall succeed us here as agents and representatives of the people, shall conscientiously and vigilantly discharge the two great branches of our public trust, faithfully to preserve, and wisely to administer it.

Mr. President, I have thus stated the reasons of my

dissent to the doctrines which have been advanced and maintained. I am conscious of having detained you and the Senate much too long. I was drawn into the debate with no previous deliberation such as is suited to the discussion of so grave and important a subject. But it is a subject of which my heart is full, and I have not been willing to suppress the utterance of its spontaneous sentiments. I cannot, even now, persuade myself to relinquish it without expressing once more my deep conviction that, since it respects nothing less than the Union of the States, it is of most vital and essential importance to the public happiness. I profess, Sir, in my career hitherto to have kept steadily in view the prosperity and honor of the whole country, and the preservation of our Federal Union. It is to that Union we owe our safety at home, and our consideration and dignity abroad. It is to that Union that we are chiefly indebted for whatever makes us most proud of our country. That Union we reached only by the discipline of our virtues in the severe school of adversity. It had its origin in the necessities of disordered finance, prostrate commerce, and ruined credit. Under its benign influences, these great interests immediately awoke as from the dead, and sprang forth with newness of life. Every year of its duration has teemed with fresh proofs of its utility and its blessings; and although our territory has stretched out wider and wider, and our population spread farther and farther, they have not outrun its protection or its benefits. It has been to us all a copious fountain of national, social, and personal happiness.

I have not allowed myself, Sir, to look beyond the Union to see what might lie hidden in the dark recess behind. I have not coolly weighed the chances of preserving liberty, when the bonds that unite us together shall be broken asunder. I have not accustomed myself to hang over the precipice of disunion, to see whether, with my short sight, I can fathom the depth of the abyss below; nor could I regard him as a safe counsellor in the affairs of this government, whose thoughts should be mainly bent on considering, not how the Union should be best preserved, but how tolerable might be the condition of the people when it should be broken up and destroyed. While the Union lasts, we have high, exciting, gratifying prospects spread out before us, — for us and our children. Beyond that, I seek not to penetrate the veil. God grant that, in my day, at least, that curtain may not rise! God grant that on my vision never may be opened what lies behind! When my eyes shall be turned to behold for the last time the sun in heaven, may I not see him shining on the broken and dishonored fragments of a once glorious Union; on States dissevered, discordant, belligerent; on a land rent with civil feuds, or drenched, it may be, in fraternal blood! Let their last feeble and lingering glance rather behold the gorgeous ensign of the Republic, now known and honored throughout the earth, still full high advanced, its arms and trophies streaming in their original lustre, not a stripe erased or polluted, nor a single star obscured; bearing for its motto, no such miserable interrogatory as "What is all this worth?" nor those other words of delusion and folly, "Liberty first, and Union afterwards;" but everywhere, spread all over in characters of living light, blazing on all its ample folds, as they float over the sea and over the land and in every wind under the whole heavens, that other sentiment, dear to every true American heart, — Liberty *and* Union, now and forever, one and inseparable!

LORD MACAULAY.

ON THE REFORM BILL; HOUSE OF COMMONS, MARCH 2, 1831.

It is a circumstance, Sir, of happy augury for the motion before the House, that almost all those who have opposed it have declared themselves hostile on principle to Parliamentary Reform. Two members, I think, have confessed that, though they disapprove of the plan now submitted to us, they are forced to admit the necessity of a change in the representative system. Yet even those gentlemen have used, as far as I have observed, no arguments which would not apply as strongly to the most moderate change as to that which has been proposed by His Majesty's Government. I say, Sir, that I consider this as a circumstance of happy augury. For what I feared was, not the opposition of those who are averse to all reform, but the disunion of reformers. I knew that, during three months, every reformer had been employed in conjecturing what the plan of the Government would be. I knew that every reformer had imagined in his own mind a scheme differing, doubtless, in some points from that which my noble friend, the Paymaster of the Forces, has developed. I felt, therefore, great apprehension that one person would be dissatisfied with one part of the bill, that another person would be dissatisfied with another part, and that thus our whole strength would be wasted in internal dissensions. That apprehension is now at an end. I have seen with delight the perfect concord which prevails among all who deserve the name of reformers in this House; and I trust that I may consider it as an omen of the concord which will prevail among reformers throughout the country. I will not, Sir, at present express any opinion as to the details of the bill; but, having during the last twenty-four hours given the most diligent consideration to its general principles, I have no hesitation in pronouncing it a wise, noble, and comprehensive measure, skilfully framed for the healing of great distempers, for the securing at once of the public liberties and of the public repose, and for the reconciling and knitting together of all the orders of the State.

The honorable Baronet who has just sat down, has told us that the Ministers have attempted to unite two inconsistent principles in one abortive measure. Those were his very words. He thinks, if I understand him rightly, that we ought either to leave the representative system such as it is, or to make it perfectly symmetrical. I think, Sir, that the Ministers would have acted unwisely if they had taken either course. Their principle is plain, rational, and consistent. It is this, to admit the middle class to a large and direct share in the representation, without any violent shock to the institutions of our country. I understand those cheers; but surely the gentlemen who utter them will allow that the change which will be made in our institutions by this bill is far less violent than that which, according to the honorable Baronet, ought to be made if we make any reform at all. I praise the Ministers for not attempting, at the present time, to make the representation uniform. I praise them for not effacing the old distinction between the towns and the counties, and for not assigning members to districts, according to the American practice, by the Rule of Three. The Government has, in my opinion, done all that was necessary for the removal of a great practical evil, and no more than was necessary.

I consider this, Sir, as a practical question. I rest my opinion on no general theory of government. I distrust all general theories of government. I will not positively say, that there is any form of polity which may not, in some conceivable circumstances, be the best possible. I believe that there are societies in which every man may safely be admitted to vote. Gentlemen may cheer, but such is my opinion. I say, Sir, that there are countries in which the condition of the laboring classes is such that they may safely be entrusted with the right of electing members of the Legislature. If the laborers of England were in that state in which I, from my soul, wish to see them; if employment were always plentiful, wages always high, food always cheap; if a large family were considered not as an encumbrance but as a blessing; the principal objections to universal suffrage would, I think, be removed. Universal suffrage exists in the United States without producing any very frightful consequences; and I do not believe that the people of those States, or of any part of the world, are in any good quality naturally superior to our own countrymen. But, unhappily, the laboring classes in England, and in all old countries, are occasionally in a state of great distress. Some of the causes of this distress are, I fear, beyond the control of the Government. We know what effect distress produces, even on people more intelligent than the great body of the laboring classes can possibly be. We know that it makes even wise men irritable, unreasonable, credulous, eager for immediate relief, heedless of remote consequences. There is no quackery in medicine, religion, or politics, which may not impose even on a powerful mind, when that mind has been disordered by pain or fear. It is therefore no reflection on the poorer class of Englishmen, who are not, and who cannot in the nature of things be, highly educated, to say that distress produces on them its natural effects, those effects which it would produce on the Americans, or on any other people; that it blinds their judgment, that it inflames their passions, that it makes them prone to believe those who flatter them, and to distrust those who would serve them. For the sake, therefore, of the whole society, for the sake of the laboring classes themselves, I hold it to be clearly expedient that, in a country like this, the right of suffrage should depend on a pecuniary qualification.

But, Sir, every argument which would induce me to oppose universal suffrage induces me to support the plan which is now before us. I am opposed to universal suffrage, because I think that it would produce a destructive revolution. I support this plan, because I am sure that it is our best security against a revolution. The noble Paymaster of the Forces hinted, delicately indeed and remotely, at this subject. He spoke of the danger of disappointing the expectations of the nation; and for this he was charged with threatening the House. Sir, in the year 1817, the late Lord Londonderry proposed a suspension of the Habeas Corpus Act. On that occasion he told the House that, unless the measures which he recommended were adopted, the public peace could not be preserved. Was he accused of threatening the House? Again, in the year 1819, he proposed the laws known by the name of the Six Acts. He then told the House that, unless the executive power were reinforced, all the institutions of the country would be overturned by popular violence. Was he then accused of threatening the House? Will any gentleman say that it is parliamentary and decorous to urge the danger arising from popular discontent as an argument for severity; but that it is unparliamentary and indecorous to urge that same danger as an argument for conciliation? I, Sir, do entertain great apprehension for the fate of my country. I do in my conscience believe that, unless the plan proposed, or some similar plan, be speedily adopted, great and terrible calamities will befall us. Entertaining this opinion, I think myself bound to state it, not as a threat, but as a reason. I support this bill because it will improve our institutions; but I support it also because it tends to preserve them. That we may exclude those whom it is necessary to exclude, we must admit those whom it may be safe to admit. At present we oppose the schemes of revolutionists with only one half, with only one quarter, of our proper force. We say, and we say justly, that it is not by mere numbers, but by property and intelligence, that the nation ought to be governed. Yet, saying this, we exclude from all share in the government great masses of property and intelligence, great numbers of those who are most interested in preserving tranquillity, and who know best how to preserve it. We do more. We drive over to the side of revolution those whom we shut out from power. Is this a time when the cause of law and order can spare one of its natural allies?

My noble friend, the Paymaster of the Forces, happily described the effect which some parts of our representative system would produce on the mind of a foreigner, who had heard much of our freedom and greatness. If, Sir, I wished to make such a foreigner clearly understand what I consider as the great defects of our system, I would conduct him through that immense city which lies to the north of Great Russell Street and Oxford Street, a city superior in size and in population to the capitals of many mighty kingdoms; and probably superior in opulence, intelligence, and general respectability, to any city in the world. I would conduct him through that interminable succession of streets and squares, all consisting of well built and well furnished houses. I would make him observe the brilliancy of the shops and the crowd of well-appointed equipages. I would show him that magnificent circle of palaces which surrounds the Regent's Park. I would tell him that the rental of this district was far greater than that of the whole kingdom of Scotland at the time of the Union. And then I would tell him, that this was an unrepresented district. It is needless to give any more instances. It is needless to speak of Manchester, Birmingham, Leeds, Sheffield, with no representation, or of Edinburgh and Glasgow with a mock representation. If a property tax were now imposed on the principle that no person who had less than a hundred and fifty pounds a year should contribute, I should not be surprised to find that one half in number and value of the contributors had no votes at all; and it would, beyond all doubt, be found that one fiftieth part in number and value of the contributors had a larger share of the representation than the other forty-nine fiftieths. This is not government by property. It is government by certain detached portions and fragments of property, selected from the rest, and preferred to the rest, on no rational principle whatever.

To say that such a system is ancient is no defence. My honorable friend, the member for the University of Oxford, challenges us to show that the Constitution was ever better than it is. Sir, we are legislators, not antiquaries. The question for us is, not whether the Constitution was better formerly, but whether we can make it better now. In fact, however, the system was not in ancient times by any means so absurd as it is in our age.

One noble lord has to-night told us that the town of Aldborough, which he represents, was not larger in the time of Edward the First than it is at present. The line of its walls, he assures us, may still be traced. It is now built up to that line. He argues, therefore, that as the founders of our representative institutions gave members to Aldborough when it was as small as it now is, those who would disfranchise it on account of its smallness have no right to say that they are recurring to the original principle of our representative institutions. But does the noble lord remember the change which has taken place in the country during the last five centuries? Does he remember how much England has grown in population, while Aldborough has been standing still? Does he consider, that in the time of Edward the First the kingdom did not contain two millions of inhabitants? It now contains nearly fourteen millions. A hamlet of the present day would have been a town of some importance in the time of our early Parliaments. Aldborough may be absolutely as considerable a place as ever. But, compared with the kingdom, it is much less considerable, by the noble lord's own showing, than when it first elected burgesses. My honorable friend, the member for the University of Oxford, has collected numerous instances of the tyranny which the kings and nobles anciently exercised both over this House and over the electors. It is not strange that, in times when nothing was held sacred, the rights of the people, and of the representatives of the people, should not have been held sacred. The proceedings which my honorable friend has mentioned no more prove that, by the ancient constitution of the realm, this House ought to be a tool of the king and of the aristocracy, than the Benevolences and the Shipmoney prove their own legality, or than those unjustifiable arrests, which took place long after the ratification of the Great Charter, and even after the Petition of Right, prove that the subject was not anciently entitled to his personal liberty. We talk of the wisdom of our ancestors; and in one respect at least they were wiser than we. They legislated for their own times. They looked at the England which was before them. They did not think it necessary to give twice as many members to York as they gave to London, because York had been the capital of Britain in the time of Constantius Chlorus; and they would have been amazed indeed if they had foreseen that a city of more than a hundred thousand inhabitants would be left without representatives in the nineteenth century, merely because it stood on ground which, in the thirteenth century, had been occupied by a few huts. They framed a representative system, which, though not without defects and irregularities, was well adapted to the state of England in their time. But a great revolution took place. The character of the old corporations changed. New forms of property came into existence. New portions of society rose into importance. There were in our rural districts rich cultivators, who were not freeholders. There were in our capital rich traders, who were not liverymen. Towns shrank into villages. Villages swelled into cities larger than the London of the Plantagenets. Unhappily, while the natural growth of society went on, the artificial polity continued unchanged. The ancient form of the representation remained; and precisely because the form remained, the spirit departed. Then came that pressure almost to bursting, the new wine in the old bottles, the new society under the old institutions. It is now time for us to pay a decent, a rational, a manly reverence to our ancestors, not by superstitiously adhering to what they, in other circumstances, did, but by doing what they, in our circumstances, would have done. All history is full of revolutions, produced by causes similar to those which are now operating in England. A portion of the community which had been of no account, expands and becomes strong. It demands a place in the system, suited, not to its former weakness, but to its present power. If this is granted, all is well. If this is refused, then comes the struggle between the young energy of one class and the ancient privileges of another. Such was the struggle between the Plebeians and the Patricians of Rome. Such was the struggle of the Italian allies for admission to the full rights of Roman citizens. Such was the struggle of our North American colonies against the mother country. Such was the struggle which the Third Estate of France maintained against the aristocracy of birth. Such was the struggle which the Roman Catholics of Ireland maintained against the aristocracy of creed. Such is the struggle which the free people of color in Jamaica are now maintaining against the aristocracy of skin. Such, finally, is the struggle which the middle classes in England are maintaining against an aristocracy of mere locality, against an aristocracy, the principle of which is to invest a hundred drunken potwallopers in one place, or the owner of a ruined hovel in another, with powers which are withheld from cities renowned to the furthest ends of the earth for the marvels of their wealth and of their industry.

But these great cities, says my honorable friend, the member for the University of Oxford, are virtually, though not directly, represented. Are not the wishes of Manchester, he asks, as much consulted as those of any town which sends members to Parliament? Now, Sir, I do not understand how a power which is salutary when exercised virtually, can be noxious when exercised directly. If the wishes of Manchester have as much weight with us as they would have under a system which should give representatives to Manchester, how can there be any danger in giving representatives to Manchester? A virtual representative is, I presume, a man who acts as a direct representative would act; for surely it would be absurd to say that a man virtually represents the people of Manchester, who is in the habit of saying No, when a man directly representing the people of Manchester would say Aye. The utmost that can be expected from virtual representation is, that it may be as good as direct representation. If so, why not grant direct representation to places which, as everybody allows, ought, by some process or other, to be represented?

If it be said that there is an evil in change as change, I answer that there is also an evil in discontent as discontent. This, indeed, is the strongest part of our case. It is said that the system works well. I deny it. I deny that a system works well, which the people regard with aversion. We may say here that it is a good system and a perfect system. But if any man were to say so to any six hundred and fifty-eight respectable farmers or shopkeepers, chosen by lot in any part of England, he would be hooted down, and laughed to scorn. Are these the feelings with which any part of the government ought to be regarded? Above all, are these the feelings with which the popular branch of the legislature ought to be regarded? It is almost as essential to the utility of a House of Commons that it should possess the confidence of the people, as that it should deserve that confidence. Unfortunately, that which is in theory the popular part of our government, is in practice the unpopular part. Who wishes to dethrone the king? Who wishes to turn the Lords out of their House? Here and there a crazy radical, whom the boys in the street point at as he walks along. Who wishes to alter the constitution of this

House? The whole people. It is natural that it should be so. The House of Commons is, in the language of Mr. Burke, a check, not on the people, but for the people. While that check is efficient, there is no reason to fear that the king or the nobles will oppress the people. But if that check requires checking, how is it to be checked? If the salt shall lose its savor, wherewith shall we season it? The distrust with which the nation regards this House may be unjust. But what then? Can you remove that distrust? That it exists cannot be denied. That it is an evil cannot be denied. That it is an increasing evil cannot be denied. One gentleman tells us that it has been produced by the late events in France and Belgium; another, that it is the effect of seditious works which have lately been published. If this feeling be of origin so recent, I have read history to little purpose. Sir, this alarming discontent is not the growth of a day, or of a year. If there be any symptoms by which it is possible to distinguish the chronic diseases of the body politic from its passing inflammations, all those symptoms exist in the present case. The taint has been gradually becoming more extensive and more malignant, through the whole lifetime of two generations. We have tried anodynes. We have tried cruel operations. What are we to try now? Who flatters himself that he can turn this feeling back? Does there remain any argument which escaped the comprehensive intellect of Mr. Burke, or the subtlety of Mr. Windham? Does there remain any species of coercion which was not tried by Mr. Pitt and by Lord Londonderry? We have had laws. We have had blood. New treasons have been created. The press has been shackled. The Habeas Corpus Act has been suspended. Public meetings have been prohibited. The event has proved that these expedients were mere palliatives. You are at the end of your palliatives. The evil remains. It is more formidable than ever. What is to be done?

Under such circumstances, a great plan of reconciliation, prepared by the Ministers of the Crown, has been brought before us in a manner which gives additional lustre to a noble name inseparably associated during two centuries with the dearest liberties of the English people. I will not say that this plan is in all its details precisely such as I might wish it to be; but it is founded on a great and a sound principle. It takes away a vast power from a few. It distributes that power through the great mass of the middle order. Every man, therefore, who thinks as I think, is bound to stand firmly by Ministers who are resolved to stand or fall with this measure. Were I one of them, I would sooner, infinitely sooner, fall with such a measure than stand by any other means that ever supported a Cabinet.

My honorable friend, the member for the University of Oxford, tells us, that if we pass this law, England will soon be a republic. The reformed House of Commons will, according to him, before it has sat ten years, depose the King and expel the Lords from their House. Sir, if my honorable friend could prove this, he would have succeeded in bringing an argument for democracy infinitely stronger than any that is to be found in the works of Paine. My honorable friend's proposition is in fact this: that our monarchical and aristocratical institutions have no hold on the public mind of England; that these institutions are regarded with aversion by a decided majority of the middle class. This, Sir, I say, is plainly deducible from his proposition; for he tells us that the representatives of the middle class will inevitably abolish royalty and nobility within ten years; and there is surely no reason to think that the representatives of the middle class will be more inclined to a democratic revolution than their constituents. Now, Sir, if I were convinced that the great body of the middle class in England look with aversion on monarchy and aristocracy, I should be forced, much against my will, to come to this conclusion, that monarchical and aristocratical institutions are unsuited to my country. Monarchy and aristocracy, valuable and useful as I think them, are still valuable and useful as means, and not as ends. The end of government is the happiness of the people; and I do not conceive that, in a country like this, the happiness of the people can be promoted by a form of government in which the middle classes place no confidence, and which exists only because the middle classes have no organ by which to make their sentiments known. But, Sir, I am fully convinced that the middle classes sincerely wish to uphold the royal prerogatives and the constitutional rights of the peers. What facts does my honorable friend produce in support of his opinion? One fact only, and that a fact which has absolutely nothing to do with the question. The effect of this Reform, he tells us, would be to make the House of Commons all powerful. It was all powerful once before, in the beginning of 1649. Then it cut off the head of the King, and abolished the House of Peers. Therefore, if it again has the supreme power, it will act in the same manner. Now, Sir, it was not the House of Commons that cut off the head of Charles the First; nor was the House of Commons then all powerful. It had been greatly reduced in numbers by successive expulsions. It was under the absolute dominion of the army. A majority of the House was willing to take the terms offered by the King. The soldiers turned out the majority; and the minority, not a sixth part of the whole House, passed those votes of which my honorable friend speaks, votes of which the middle classes disapproved then, and of which they disapprove still.

My honorable friend, and almost all the gentlemen who have taken the same side with him in this debate, have dwelt much on the utility of close and rotten boroughs. It is by means of such boroughs, they tell us, that the ablest men have been introduced into Parliament. It is true that many distinguished persons have represented places of this description. But, Sir, we must judge of a form of government by its general tendency, not by happy accidents. Every form of government has its happy accidents. Despotism has its happy accidents. Yet we are not disposed to abolish all constitutional checks, to place an absolute master over us, and to take our chance whether he may be a Caligula or a Marcus Aurelius. In whatever way the House of Commons may be chosen, some able men will be chosen in that way who would not be chosen in any other way. If there were a law that the hundred tallest men in England should be members of Parliament, there would probably be some able men among those who would come into the House by virtue of this law. If the hundred persons whose names stand first in the alphabetical list of the Court Guide were made members of Parliament, there would probably be able men among them. We read in ancient history that a very able king was elected by the neighing of his horse; but we shall scarcely, I think, adopt this mode of election. In one of the most celebrated republics of antiquity, Athens, Senators and Magistrates were chosen by lot; and sometimes the lot fell fortunately. Once, for example, Socrates was in office. A cruel and unjust proposition was made by a demagogue. Socrates resisted it at the hazard of his own life. There is no event in Grecian history more interesting than that memorable resistance. Yet who would have officers appointed by lot, because the accident of the lot may have given to a great and good man a power which he would probably never have attained in any other way? We must judge, as I said, by the general tendency of a system. No person can doubt that a House of Commons, chosen freely by the middle classes, will contain many very able men. I do not say that precisely the same able men who would find their way into the present House of Commons will find their way into the reformed House; but that is not the question. No particular man is necessary to the state. We may depend on it, that if we provide the country with popular institutions, those institutions will provide it with great men.

There is another objection, which, I think, was first raised by the honorable and learned member for Newport. He tells us that the elective franchise is property; that to take it away from a man who has not been judicially convicted of malpractices is robbery; that no crime is proved against the voters in the closed boroughs; that no crime is even imputed to them in the preamble of the bill; and that therefore to disfranchise them without compensation would be an act of revoluntionary tyranny. The honorable and learned gentleman has compared the conduct of the present Ministers, to that of those odious tools of power, who, toward the close of the reign of Charles the Second, seized the charters of the Whig corporations. Now, there was another precedent, which I wonder that he did not recollect, both because it is much more nearly in point than that to which he referred, and because my noble friend, the Paymaster of the Forces, had previously alluded to it. If the elective franchise is property, if to disfranchise voters without a crime proved, or a compensation given, be robbery, was there ever such an act of robbery as the disfranchising of the Irish forty-shilling freeholders? Was any pecuniary compensation given to them? Is it declared in the preamble of the bill which took away their franchise, that they had been convicted of any offence? Was any judicial inquiry instituted into their conduct? Were they even accused of any crime? Or if you say it was a crime in the electors of Clare to vote for the honorable and learned gentleman who now represents the County of Waterford, was a Protestant freeholder in Louth to be punished for the crime of a Catholic freeholder in Clare? If the principle of the honorable and learned member for Newport be sound, the franchise of the Irish peasant was property. That franchise the Ministers under whom the honorable and learned member held office did not scruple to take away. Will he accuse those Ministers of robbery? If not, how can he bring such an accusation against their successors?

Every gentleman, I think, who has spoken from the other side of the House, has alluded to the opinions which some of His Majesty's Ministers formerly entertained on the subject of reform. It would be officious in me, Sir, to undertake the defence of gentlemen who are so well able to defend themselves. I will only say that, in my opinion, the country will not think worse either of their capacity or of their patriotism, because they have shown that they can profit by experience, because they have learned to see the folly of delaying inevitable changes. There are others who ought to have learned the same lesson. I say, Sir, that there are those who, I should have thought, must have had enough to last them all their lives of that humiliation which follows obstinate and boastful resistance to changes rendered necessary by the progress of society, and by the development of the human mind. Is it possible that those persons can wish again to occupy a position which can neither be defended nor surrendered with honor? I well remember, Sir, a certain evening in the month of May, 1827. I had not then the honor of a seat in this

House; but I was an attentive observer of its proceedings. The right honorable Baronet opposite, of whom personally I desire to speak with that high respect which I feel for his talents and his character, but of whose public conduct I must speak with the sincerity required by my public duty, was then, as he is now, out of office. He had just resigned the seals of the Home Department, because he conceived that the recent Ministerial arrangements had been too favorable to the Catholic claims. He rose to ask whether it was the intention of the new Cabinet to repeal the Test and Corporation Acts, and to reform the Parliament. He bound up, I well remember, those two questions together; and he declared that, if the Ministers should either attempt to repeal the Test and Corporation Acts, or bring forward a measure of Parliamentary reform, he should think it his duty to oppose them to the utmost. Since that declaration was made four years have elapsed; and what is now the state of the three questions which then chiefly agitated the minds of men? What is become of the Test and Corporation Acts? They are repealed. By whom? By the right honorable Baronet. What has become of the Catholic disabilities? They are removed. By whom? By the right honorable Baronet. The question of Parliamentary reform is still behind. But signs, of which it is impossible to misconceive the import, do most clearly indicate that, unless that question also be speedily settled, property, and order, and all the institutions of this great monarchy, will be exposed to fearful peril. Is it possible that gentlemen long versed in high political affairs cannot read these signs? Is it possible that they can really believe that the representative system of England, such as it now is, will last till the year 1860? If not, for what would they have us wait? Would they have us wait merely that we may show to all the world how little we have profited by our own recent experience? Would they have us wait that we may once again hit the exact point where we can neither refuse with authority, nor concede with grace? Would they have us wait that the numbers of the discontented party may become larger, its demands higher, its feelings more acrimonious, its organization more complete? Would they have us wait till the whole tragicomedy of 1827 has been acted over again; till they have been brought into office by a cry of "No Reform," to be reformers, as they were once before brought into office by a cry of "No Popery," to be emancipators? Have they obliterated from their minds — gladly, perhaps, would some among them obliterate from their minds — the transactions of that year? And have they forgotten all the transactions of the succeeding year? Have they forgotten how the spirit of liberty in Ireland, debarred from its natural outlet, found a vent by forbidden passages? Have they forgotten how we were forced to indulge the Catholics in all the license of rebels, merely because we chose to withhold from them the liberties of subjects? Do they wait for associations more formidable than that of the Corn Exchange, for contributions larger than the Rent, for agitators more violent than those who, three years ago, divided with the King and the Parliament the sovereignty of Ireland? Do they wait for that last and most dreadful paroxysm of popular rage, for that last and most cruel test of military fidelity? Let them wait, if their past experience shall induce them to think that any high honor or any exquisite pleasure is to be obtained by a policy like this. Let them wait, if this strange and fearful infatuation be indeed upon them, that they should not see with their eyes, or hear with their ears, or understand with their heart. But let us know our interest and our duty better.

Turn where we may, within, around, the voice of great events is proclaiming to us: Reform, that you may preserve. Now, therefore, while everything at home and abroad forebodes ruin to those who persist in a hopeless struggle against the spirit of the age; now, while the crash of the proudest throne of the Continent is still resounding in our ears; now, while the roof of a British palace affords an ignominious shelter to the exiled heir of forty kings; now, while we see on every side ancient institutions subverted, and great societies dissolved; now, while the heart of England is still sound; now, while old feelings and old associations retain a power and a charm which may too soon pass away; now, in this your accepted time, now, in this your day of salvation, take counsel, not of prejudice, not of party spirit, not of the ignominious pride of a fatal consistency, but of history, of reason, of the ages which are past, of the signs of this most portentous time. Pronounce in a manner worthy of the expectation with which this great debate has been anticipated, and of the long remembrance which it will leave behind. Renew the youth of the state. Save property, divided against itself. Save the multitude, endangered by its own ungovernable passions. Save the aristocracy, endangered by its own unpopular power. Save the greatest, and fairest, and most highly civilized community that ever existed, from calamities which may in a few days sweep away all the rich heritage of so many ages of wisdom and glory. The danger is terrible. The time is short. If this bill should be rejected, I pray to God that none of those who concur in rejecting it may ever remember their votes with unavailing remorse, amidst the wreck of laws, the confusion of ranks, the spoliation of property, and the dissolution of social order.

JOHN C. CALHOUN.

ON THE SLAVERY QUESTION; IN THE UNITED STATES SENATE, MARCH 4, 1850.

I HAVE, Senators, believed from the first that the agitation of the subject of slavery would, if not prevented by some timely and effective measure, end in disunion. Entertaining this opinion, I have, on all proper occasions, endeavored to call the attention of both the two great parties which divide the country to adopt some measure to prevent so great a disaster, but without success. The agitation has been permitted to proceed with almost no attempt to resist it, until it has reached a point when it can no longer be disguised or denied that the Union is in danger. You have thus had forced upon you the greatest and the gravest question that can ever come under your consideration — How can the Union be preserved?

To give a satisfactory answer to this mighty question, it is indispensable to have an accurate and thorough knowledge of the nature and the character of the cause by which the Union is endangered. Without such knowledge it is impossible to pronounce with any certainty, by what measure it can be saved; just as it would be impossible for a physician to pronounce in the case of some dangerous disease, with any certainty, by what remedy the patient could be saved, without similar knowledge of the nature and character of the cause which produced it. The first question, then, presented for consideration in the investigation I propose to make in order to obtain such knowledge, is — What is it that has endangered the Union?

To this question there can be but one answer, — That the immediate cause is the almost universal discontent which pervades all the States composing the Southern section of the Union. This widely extended discontent is not of recent origin. It commenced with the agitation of the slavery question, and has been increasing ever since. The next question, going one step further back, is — What has caused this widely diffused and almost universal discontent?

It is a great mistake to suppose, as is by some, that it originated with demagogues, who excited the discontent with the intention of aiding their personal advancement, or with the disappointed ambition of certain politicians, who resorted to it as the means of retrieving their fortunes. On the contrary, all the great political influences of the section were arrayed against excitement, and exerted to the utmost to keep the people quiet. The great mass of the people of the South were divided, as in the other section, into Whigs and Democrats. The leaders and the presses of both parties in the South were very solicitous to prevent excitement and to preserve quiet; because it was seen that the effects of the former would necessarily tend to weaken, if not destroy, the political ties which united them with their respective parties in the other section. Those who know the strength of party ties will readily appreciate the immense force which this cause exerted against agitation, and in favor of preserving quiet. But, great as it was, it was not sufficient to prevent the wide-spread discontent which now pervades the section. No; some cause far deeper and more powerful than the one supposed, must exist, to account for discontent so wide and deep. The question then recurs — What is the cause of this discontent? It will be found in the belief of the people of the Southern States, as prevalent as the discontent itself, that they cannot remain, as things now are, consistently with honor and safety, in the Union. The next question to be considered is — What has caused this belief?

One of the causes is, undoubtedly, to be traced to the long-continued agitation of the slave question on the part of the North, and the many aggressions which they have made on the rights of the South during the time. I will not enumerate them at present, as it will be done hereafter in its proper place.

There is another lying back of it — with which this is intimately connected — that may be regarded as the great and primary cause. This is to be found in the fact that the equilibrium between the two sections in the government as it stood when the Constitution was ratified and the government put in action, has been destroyed. At that time there was nearly a perfect equilibrium between the two, which afforded ample means to each to protect itself against the aggression of the other; but, as it now stands, one section has the exclusive power of controlling the government, which leaves the other without any adequate means of protecting itself against its encroachment and oppression. To place this subject distinctly before you, I have, Senators, prepared a brief statistical statement, showing the relative weight of the two sections in the government under the first census of 1790, and the last census of 1840.

According to the former, the population of the United States — including Vermont, Kentucky, and Tennessee, which then were in their incipient condition of becoming States, but were not actually admitted — amounted to

3,929,827. Of this number the Northern States had 1,997,899, and the Southern 1,952,072, making a difference of only 45,827 in favor of the former States. The number of States, including Vermont, Kentucky, and Tennessee, was sixteen; of which eight, including Vermont, belonged to the Northern section, and eight, including Kentucky and Tennessee, to the Southern, — making an equal division of the States between the two sections under the first census. There was a small preponderance in the House of Representatives and in the Electoral College, in favor of the Northern, owing to the fact that, according to the provisions of the Constitution, in estimating federal numbers five slaves count but three; but it was too small to affect sensibly the perfect equilibrium which, with that exception, existed at the time. Such was the equality of the two sections when the States composing them agreed to enter into a Federal Union. Since then the equilibrium between them has been greatly disturbed.

According to the last census the aggregate population of the United States amounted to 17,063,357, of which the Northern section contained 9,728,920, and the Southern 7,334,437, making a difference in round numbers, of 2,400,000. The number of States had increased from sixteen to twenty-six, making an addition of ten States. In the mean time the position of Delaware had become doubtful as to the section to which she properly belonged. Considering her as neutral, the Northern States will have thirteen and the Southern States twelve, making a difference in the Senate of two senators in favor of the former. According to the apportionment under the census of 1840, there were two hundred and twenty-three members of the House of Representatives, of which the Northern States had one hundred and thirty-five, and the Southern States (considering Delaware as neutral) eighty-seven, making a difference in favor of the former in the House of Representatives of forty-eight. The difference in the Senate of two members, added to this, gives to the North in the Electoral College, a majority of fifty. Since the census of 1840, four States have been added to the Union, — Iowa, Wisconsin, Florida, and Texas. They leave the difference in the Senate as it was when the census was taken; but add two to the side of the North in the House, making the present majority in the House in its favor fifty, and in the Electoral College fifty-two.

The result of the whole is to give the Northern section a predominance in every department of the government, and thereby concentrate in it the two elements which constitute the Federal Government: a majority of States, and a majority of their population, estimated in federal numbers. Whatever section concentrates the two in itself possesses the control of the entire government.

But we are just at the close of the sixth decade, and the commencement of the seventh. The census is to be taken this year, which must add greatly to the decided preponderance of the North in the House of Representatives and in the Electoral College. The prospect is, also, that a great increase will be added to its present preponderance in the Senate, during the period of the decade, by the addition of new States. Two territories, Oregon and Minnesota, are already in progress, and strenuous efforts are making to bring in three additional States from the territory recently conquered from Mexico; which, if successful, will add three other States in a short time to the Northern section, making five States; and increasing the present number of its States from fifteen to twenty, and of its senators from thirty to forty. On the contrary, there is not a single territory in progress in the Southern section, and no certainty that any additional State will be added to it during the decade. The prospect then is, that the two sections in the Senate, should the efforts now made to exclude the South from the newly acquired territories succeed, will stand, before the end of the decade, twenty Northern States to fourteen Southern (considering Delaware as neutral), and forty Northern senators to twenty-eight Southern. This great increase of senators, added to the great increase of members of the House of Representatives and the Electoral College on the part of the North, which must take place under the next decade, will effectually and irretrievably destroy the equilibrium which existed when the government commenced.

Had this destruction been the operation of time, without the interference of government, the South would have had no reason to complain; but such was not the fact. It was caused by the legislation of this government, which was appointed as the common agent of all, and charged with the protection of the interests and security of all. The legislation by which it has been effected may be classed under three heads. The first is that series of acts by which the South has been excluded from the common territory belonging to all the States as members of the Federal Union — which have had the effect of extending vastly the portion allotted to the Northern section, and restricting within narrow limits the portion left the South. The next consists in adopting a system of revenue and disbursements by which an undue proportion of the burden of taxation has been imposed upon the South, and an undue proportion of its proceeds appropriated to the North; and the last is a system of political measures by which the original character of the government has been radically changed. I propose to bestow upon each of these, in the order they stand, a few remarks, with the view of showing that it is owing to the action of this government, that the equilibrium between the two sections has been destroyed, and the whole powers of the system centred in a sectional majority.

The first of the series of acts by which the South was deprived of its due share of the territories, originated with the confederacy which preceded the existence of this government. It is to be found in the provision of the ordinance of 1787. Its effect was to exclude the South entirely from that vast and fertile region which lies between the Ohio and the Mississippi Rivers, now embracing five States and one Territory. The next of the series is the Missouri Compromise, which excluded the South from that large portion of Louisiana which lies north of 36° 30′, excepting what is included in the State of Missouri. The last of the series excluded the South from the whole of the Oregon Territory. All these, in the slang of the day, were what are called slave territories, and not free soil; that is, territories belonging to slaveholding powers and open to the emigration of masters with their slaves. By these several acts, the South was excluded from 1,238,025 square miles — an extent of country considerably exceeding the entire valley of the Mississippi. To the South was left the portion of the Territory of Louisiana lying south of 36° 30′, and the portion north of it included in the State of Missouri, with the portion lying south of 36° 30′, including the States of Louisiana and Arkansas, and the territory lying west of the latter and south of 36° 30′, called the Indian country. These, with the Territory of Florida, now the State, make, in the whole, 283,503 square miles. To this must be added the territory acquired with Texas. If the whole should be added to the Southern section, it would make an increase of 325,520, which would make the whole left to the South 609,023.

But a large part of Texas is still in contest between the two sections, which leaves it uncertain what will be the real extent of the portion of territory that may be left to the South.

I have not included the territory recently acquired by the treaty with Mexico. The North is making the most strenuous efforts to appropriate the whole to herself, by excluding the South from every foot of it. If she should succeed, it will add to that from which the South has already been excluded, 526,078 square miles, and would increase the whole which the North has appropriated to herself, to 1,764,023, not including the portion that she may succeed in excluding us from in Texas. To sum up the whole, the United States, since they declared their independence, have acquired 2,373,046 square miles of territory, from which the North will have excluded the South, if she should succeed in monopolizing the newly acquired territories, about three-fourths of the whole, leaving to the South but about one-fourth.

Such is the first and great cause that has destroyed the equilibrium between the two sections in the government.

The next is the system of revenue and disbursements which has been adopted by the government. It is well known that the government has derived its revenue mainly from duties on imports. I shall not undertake to show that such duties must necessarily fall mainly on the exporting States, and that the South, as the great exporting portion of the Union, has in reality paid vastly more than her due proportion of the revenue; because I deem it unnecessary, as the subject has on so many occasions been fully discussed. Nor shall I, for the same reason, undertake to show that a far greater portion of the revenue has been disbursed at the North, than its due share; and that the joint effect of these causes has been to transfer a vast amount from South to North, which, under an equal system of revenue and disbursements, would not have been lost to her. If to this be added, that many of the duties were imposed, not for revenue, but for protection, — that is, intended to put money, not in the treasury, but directly into the pocket of the manufacturers, — some conception may be formed of the immense amount which, in the long course of sixty years, has been transferred from South to North. There are no data by which it can be estimated with any certainty; but it is safe to say that it amounts to hundreds of millions of dollars. Under the most moderate estimate, it would be sufficient to add greatly to the wealth of the North, and thus greatly increase her population by attracting emigration from all quarters to that section.

This, combined with the great primary cause, amply explains why the North has acquired a preponderance in every department of the government by its disproportionate increase of population and States. The former, as has been shown, has increased, in fifty years, 2,400,000 over that of the South. This increase of population during so long a period, is satisfactorily accounted for by the number of emigrants, and the increase of their descendants, which have been attracted to the Northern section from Europe and the South, in consequence of the advantages derived from the causes assigned. If they had not existed — if the South had retained all the capital which has been extracted from her by the fiscal action of the government; and if it had not been excluded by the ordinance of 1787 and the Missouri Compromise, from the region lying between the Ohio and the Mississippi Rivers, and between the Mississippi and the Rocky Mountains north of 36° 30′ — it scarcely admits of a doubt, that it would have divided the emigration with the North, and by retaining her own people, would have at least equalled the North in population under the census of 1840, and probably under that about to be taken. She would also, if she had retained her equal rights in those territories, have maintained an equality in the number of States with the North, and have preserved the equilibrium between the two sections that existed at the commencement of the government. The loss, then, of the equilibrium is to be attributed to the action of this government.

But while these measures were destroying the equilibrium between the two sections, the action of the government was leading to a radical change in its character, by concentrating all the power of the system in itself. The occasion will not permit me to trace the measures by which this great change has been consummated. If it did, it would not be difficult to show that the process commenced at an early period of the government; and that it proceeded almost without interruption, step by step, until it absorbed virtually its entire powers; but without going through the whole process to establish the fact, it may be done satisfactorily by a very short statement.

That the government claims, and practically maintains, the right to decide in the last resort, as to the extent of its powers, will scarcely be denied by any one conversant with the political history of the country. That it also claims the right to resort to force to maintain whatever power it claims, against all opposition, is equally certain. Indeed it is apparent, from what we daily hear, that this has become the prevailing and fixed opinion of a great majority of the community. Now, I ask, what limitation can possibly be placed upon the powers of a government claiming and exercising such rights? And, if none can be, how can the separate governments of the States maintain and protect the powers reserved to them by the Constitution — or the people of the several States maintain those which are reserved to them, and among others, the sovereign powers by which they ordained and established, not only their separate State Constitutions and governments, but also the Constitution and government of the United States? But, if they have no constitutional means of maintaining them against the right claimed by this government, it necessarily follows, that they hold them at its pleasure and discretion, and that all the powers of the system are in reality concentrated in it. It also follows, that the character of the government has been changed in consequence, from a federal republic, as it originally came from the hands of its framers, into a great national consolidated democracy. It has indeed, at present, all the characteristics of the latter, and not one of the former, although it still retains its outward form.

The result of the whole of those causes combined is, that the North has acquired a decided ascendency over every department of this government, and through it a control over all the powers of the system. A single section governed by the will of the numerical majority, has now, in fact, the control of the government and the entire powers of the system. What was once a constitutional federal republic, is now converted, in reality, into one as absolute as that of the Autocrat of Russia, and as despotic in its tendency as any absolute government that ever existed.

As, then, the North has the absolute control over the government, it is manifest, that on all questions between it and the South, where there is a diversity of interests, the interest of the latter will be sacrificed to the former, however oppressive the effects may be; as the South possesses no means by which it can resist, through the action of the government. But if there was no question of vital importance to the South, in reference to which there was a diversity of views between the two sections, this state of things might be endured without the hazard of destruction to the South. But such is not the fact. There is a question of vital importance to the Southern section, in reference to which the views and feelings of the two sections are as opposite and hostile as they can possibly be.

I refer to the relation between the two races in the Southern section, which constitutes a vital portion of her social organization. Every portion of the North entertains views and feelings more or less hostile to it. Those most opposed and hostile regard it as a sin, and consider themselves under the most sacred obligation to use every effort to destroy it. Indeed, to the extent that they conceive that they have power, they regard themselves as implicated in the sin, and responsible for not suppressing it by the use of all and every means. Those less opposed and hostile, regard it as a crime — an offence against humanity, as they call it; and, although not so fanatical, feel themselves bound to use all efforts to effect the same object; while those who are least opposed and hostile, regard it as a blot and a stain on the character of what they call the Nation, and feel themselves accordingly bound to give it no countenance or support. On the contrary, the Southern section regards the relation as one which cannot be destroyed without subjecting the two races to the greatest calamity, and the section to poverty, desolation, and wretchedness; and accordingly they feel bound by every consideration of interest and safety to defend it.

This hostile feeling on the part of the North towards the social organization of the South long lay dormant, but it only required some cause to act on those who felt most intensely that they were responsible for its continuance, to call it into action. The increasing power of this government, and of the control of the Northern section over all its departments, furnished the cause. It was this which made an impression on the minds of many that there was little or no restraint to prevent the government from doing whatever it might choose to do. This was sufficient of itself to put the most fanatical portion of the North in action, for the purpose of destroying the existing relation between the two races in the South.

The first organized movement towards it commenced in 1835. Then, for the first time, societies were organized, presses established, lecturers sent forth to excite the people of the North, and incendiary publications scattered over the whole South, through the mail. The South was thoroughly aroused. Meetings were held everywhere, and resolutions adopted, calling upon the North to apply a remedy to arrest the threatened evil, and pledging themselves to adopt measures for their own protection, if it was not arrested. At the meeting of Congress, petitions poured in from the North, calling upon Congress to abolish slavery in the District of Columbia, and to prohibit what they called the internal slave trade between the States—announcing at the same time that their ultimate object was to abolish slavery, not only in the District, but in the States and throughout the Union. At this period, the number engaged in the agitation was small, and possessed little or no personal influence.

Neither party in Congress had, at that time, any sympathy with them or their cause. The members of each party presented their petitions with great reluctance. Nevertheless, small and contemptible as the party then was, both of the great parties of the North dreaded them. They felt that, though small, they were organized in reference to a subject which had a great and a commanding influence over the Northern mind. Each party, on that account, feared to oppose their petitions, lest the opposite party should take advantage of the one that might do so, by favoring them. The effect was that both united in insisting that the petitions should be received, and that Congress should take jurisdiction over the subject. To justify their course, they took the extraordinary ground that Congress was bound to receive petitions on every subject, however objectionable they might be, and whether they had, or had not, jurisdiction over the subject. These views prevailed in the House of Representatives, and partially in the Senate; and thus the party succeeded in their first movements, in gaining what they proposed — a position in Congress from which agitation could be extended over the whole Union. This was the commencement of the agitation which has ever since continued, and which, as is now acknowledged, has endangered the Union itself.

As for myself, I believed at that early period, if the party that got up the petitions should succeed in getting Congress to take jurisdiction, that agitation would follow, and that it would in the end, if not arrested, destroy the Union. I then so expressed myself in debate, and called upon both parties to take grounds against assuming jurisdiction; but in vain. Had my voice been heeded, and had Congress refused to take jurisdiction, by the united votes of all parties, the agitation which followed would have been prevented, and the fanatical zeal that gives impulse to the agitation, and which has brought us to our present perilous condition, would have become extinguished from the want of fuel to feed the flame. *That* was the time for the North to have shown her devotion to the Union; but, unfortunately, both of the great parties of that section were so intent on obtaining or retaining party ascendency, that all other considerations were overlooked or forgotten.

What has since followed are but natural consequences. With the success of their first movement, this small fanatical party began to acquire strength; and with that, to become an object of courtship to both the great parties. The necessary consequence was a further increase of power, and a gradual tainting of the opinions of both of the other parties with their doctrines, until the infection has extended over both; and the great mass of the population of the North, who, whatever may be their opinion of the original abolition party, which still preserves its distinctive organization, hardly ever fail, when it comes to acting, to co-operate in carrying out their measures. With the increase of their influence, they extended the sphere of their action. In a short time after the commencement of their first movement, they had acquired sufficient influence to induce the legislatures of most of the Northern States to pass acts, which in effect abrogated the clause of the Constitution that provides for the delivery up of fugitive slaves. Not long after, petitions followed to abolish slavery in forts, magazines, and dockyards, and all other places where Congress had exclusive power of legislation. This was followed by petitions and resolutions of legislatures of the Northern States, and popular meetings, to exclude the Southern States from all territories acquired, or to be acquired, and to prevent the admission of any State hereafter into the Union, which, by its constitution, does not prohibit slavery. And Congress is invoked to do all this, expressly with the view to the final abolition of slavery in the States. That has been avowed to be the ultimate object from the beginning of the agitation until the present time; and yet the great body of both parties of the North, with the full knowledge of the fact, although disavowing the abolitionists, have co-operated with them in almost all their measures.

Such is a brief history of the agitation, as far as it has yet advanced. Now I ask, Senators, what is there to prevent its further progress, until it fulfils the ultimate end proposed, unless some decisive measure should be adopted to prevent it? Has any one of the causes, which has added to its increase from its original small and contemptible beginning until it has attained its present magnitude, diminished in force? Is the original cause of the movement — that slavery is a sin, and ought to be suppressed — weaker now than at the commencement? Or is the abolition party less numerous or influential, or have they less influence with, or control over, the two great parties of the North in elections? Or has the South greater means of influencing or controlling the movements of this government now, than it had when the agitation commenced? To all these questions but one answer can be given: No — no — no. The very reverse is true. Instead of being weaker, all the elements in favor of agitation are stronger now than they were in 1835, when it first commenced, while all the elements of influence on the part of the South are weaker. Unless something decisive is done, I again ask, what is to stop this agitation before the great and final object at which it aims — the abolition of slavery in the States — is consummated? Is it, then, not certain that if something is not done to arrest it, the South will be forced to choose between abolition and secession? Indeed, as events are now moving, it will not require the South to secede, in order to dissolve the Union. Agitation will of itself effect it, of which its past history furnishes abundant proof — as I shall next proceed to show.

It is a great mistake to suppose that disunion can be effected by a single blow. The cords which bind these States together in one common Union, are far too numerous and powerful for that. Disunion must be the work of time. It is only through a long process, and successively, that the cords can be snapped, until the whole fabric falls asunder. Already the agitation of the slavery question has snapped some of the most important, and has greatly weakened all the others, as I shall proceed to show.

The cords that bind the States together are not only many, but various in character. Some are spiritual or ecclesiastical; some political; others social. Some appertain to the benefit conferred by the Union, and others to the feeling of duty and obligation.

The strongest of those of a spiritual and ecclesiastical nature, consisted in the unity of the great religious denominations, all of which originally embraced the whole Union. All these denominations, with the exception, perhaps, of the Catholics, were organized very much upon the principle of our political institutions. Beginning with smaller meetings corresponding with the political divisions of the country, their organization terminated in one great central assemblage corresponding very much with the character of Congress. At these meetings the principal clergymen and lay members of the respective denominations from all parts of the Union, met to transact business relating to their common concerns. It was not confined to what appertained to the doctrines and discipline of the respective denominations, but extended to plans for disseminating the Bible, establishing missions, distributing tracts — and of establishing presses for the publication of tracts, newspapers, and periodicals, with a view of diffusing religious information — and for the support of their respective doctrines and creeds. All this combined contributed greatly to strengthen the bonds of the Union. The ties which held each denomination together formed a strong cord to hold the whole Union together, but, powerful as they were, they have not been able to resist the explosive effect of slavery agitation.

The first of these cords which snapped under its explosive force, was that of the powerful Methodist Episcopal Church. The numerous and strong ties which held it together, are all broken, and its unity is gone. They now form separate churches; and, instead of that feeling of attachment and devotion to the interests of the whole church which was formerly felt, they are now arrayed into two hostile bodies, engaged in litigation about what was formerly their common property.

The next cord that snapped was that of the Baptists — one of the largest and most respectable of the denominations. That of the Presbyterian is not entirely snapped, but some of its strands have given way. That of the Episcopal Church is the only one of the four great Protestant denominations which remains unbroken and entire.

The strongest cord of a political character, consists of the many and powerful ties that have held together the two great parties which have, with some modifications, existed from the beginning of the government. They both extended to every portion of the Union, and strongly contributed to hold all its parts together. But this powerful cord has fared no better than the spiritual. It resisted for a long time the explosive tendency of the agitation, but has finally snapped under its force — if not entirely, in a great measure. Nor is there one of the remaining cords which has not been greatly weakened. To this extent the Union has already been destroyed by agitation, in the only way it can be, by sundering and weakening the cords which bind it together.

If the agitation goes on, the same force, acting with increased intensity, as has been shown, will finally snap every cord, when nothing will be left to hold the States together except force. But, surely, that can with no propriety of language be called a Union, when the only means by which the weaker is held connected with the stronger portion is force. It may, indeed, keep them connected; but the connection will partake much more of the character of subjugation, on the part of the weaker to the stronger, than the union of free, independent, and sovereign States, in one confederation, as they stood in the early stages of the government, and which only is worthy of the sacred name of Union.

Having now, Senators, explained what it is that endangers the Union, and traced it to its cause, and explained its nature and character, the question again recurs — How can the Union be saved? To this I answer, there is but one way by which it can be, and that is by adopting such measures as will satisfy the States belonging to the Southern section, that they can remain in the Union consistently with their honor and their safety. There is, again, only one way by which this can be effected, and that is by removing the causes by which this belief has been produced. Do this, and discontent will cease, harmony and kind feelings between the sections be restored, and every apprehension of danger to the Union removed. The question, then, is — How can this be done? But, before I undertake to answer this question, I propose to show by what the Union cannot be saved.

It cannot, then, be saved by eulogies on the Union, however splendid or numerous. The cry of "Union, Union, the glorious Union!" can no more prevent disunion than the cry of "Health, health, glorious health!" on the part of the physician, can save a patient lying dangerously ill. So long as the Union, instead of being regarded as a protector, is regarded in the opposite character, by not much less than a majority of the States, it will be in vain to attempt to conciliate them by pronouncing eulogies on it.

Besides, this cry of Union comes commonly from those whom we cannot believe to be sincere. It usually comes from our assailants. But we cannot believe them to be sincere; for, if they loved the Union, they would necessarily be devoted to the Constitution. It made the Union, — and to destroy the Constitution would be to destroy the Union. But the only reliable and certain evidence of devotion to the Constitution is to abstain, on the one hand, from violating it, and to repel, on the other, all attempts to violate it. It is only by faithfully performing these high duties that the Constitution can be preserved, and with it the Union.

But how stands the profession of devotion to the Union by our assailants, when brought to this test? Have they abstained from violating the Constitution? Let the many acts passed by the Northern States to set aside and annul the clause of the Constitution providing for the delivery up of fugitive slaves answer. I cite this, not that it is the only instance (for there are many others), but because the violation in this particular is too notorious and palpable to be denied. Again: Have they stood forth faithfully to repel violations of the Constitution? Let their course in reference to the agitation of the slavery question, which was commenced and has been carried on for fifteen years, avowedly for the purpose of abolishing slavery in the States — an object all acknowledged to be unconstitutional — answer. Let them show a single instance, during this long period, in which they have denounced the agitators or their attempts to effect what is admitted to be unconstitutional, or a single measure which they have brought forward for that purpose. How can we, with all these facts before us, believe that they are sincere in their profession of devotion to the Union, or avoid believing their profession is but intended to increase the vigor of their assaults and to weaken the force of our resistance?

Nor can we regard the profession of devotion to the Union, on the part of those who are not our assailants, as sincere, when they pronounce eulogies upon the Union, evidently with the intent of charging us with disunion, without uttering one word of denunciation against our assailants. If friends of the Union, their course should be to unite with us in repelling these assaults, and denouncing the authors as enemies of the Union. Why they avoid this, and pursue the course they do, it is for them to explain.

Nor can the Union be saved by invoking the name of the illustrious Southerner whose mortal remains repose on the western bank of the Potomac. He was one of us — a slave-holder and a planter. We have studied his history, and find nothing in it to justify submission to wrong. On the contrary, his great fame rests on the solid foundation that, while he was careful to avoid doing wrong to others, he was prompt and decided in repelling wrong. I trust that, in this respect, we profited by his example.

Nor can we find anything in his history to deter us from seceding from the Union, should it fail to fulfil the objects for which it was instituted, by being permanently and hopelessly converted into the means of oppressing instead of protecting us. On the contrary, we find much in his example to encourage us, should we be forced to the extremity of deciding between submission and disunion.

There existed then, as well as now, a union — that

between the parent country and her then Colonies. It was a union that had much to endear it to the people of the Colonies. Under its protecting and superintending care, the Colonies were planted and grew up and prospered through a long course of years, until they became populous and wealthy. Its benefits were not limited to them. Their extensive agricultural and other productions gave birth to a flourishing commerce, which richly rewarded the parent country for the trouble and expense of establishing and protecting them. Washington was born and grew up to manhood under that union. He acquired his early distinction in its service, and there is every reason to believe that he was devotedly attached to it. But his devotion was a rational one. He was attached to it, not as an end, but as a means to an end. When it failed to fulfil its end, and, instead of affording protection, was converted into the means of oppressing the Colonies, he did not hesitate to draw his sword, and head the great movement by which that union was forever severed, and the independence of these States established. This was the great and crowning glory of his life, which has spread his fame over the whole globe, and will transmit it to the latest posterity.

Nor can the plan proposed by the distinguished senator from Kentucky, nor that of the administration, save the Union. I shall pass by, without remark, the plan proposed by the senator, and proceed directly to the consideration of that of the administration. I, however, assure the distinguished and able senator, that, in taking this course, no disrespect whatever is intended to him or his plan. I have adopted it because so many senators of distinguished abilities, who were present when he delivered his speech and explained his plan, and who were fully capable to do justice to the side they support, have replied to him.

The plan of the administration cannot save the Union, because it can have no effect whatever towards satisfying the States composing the Southern section of the Union, that they can, consistently with safety and honor, remain in the Union. It is, in fact, but a modification of the Wilmot Proviso. It proposes to effect the same object, — to exclude the South from all the territory acquired by the Mexican treaty. It is well known that the South is united against the Wilmot Proviso, and has committed itself by solemn resolutions to resist, should it be adopted. Its opposition is not to the name, but that which it proposes to effect. That, the Southern States hold to be unconstitutional, unjust, inconsistent with their equality as members of the common Union, and calculated to destroy irretrievably the equilibrium between the two sections. These objections equally apply to what, for brevity, I will call the Executive Proviso. There is no difference between it and the Wilmot, except in the mode of effecting the object; and in that respect, I must say that the latter is much the least objectionable. It goes to its object openly, boldly, and distinctly. It claims for Congress unlimited power over the territories, and proposes to assert it over the territories acquired from Mexico, by a positive prohibition of slavery. Not so the Executive Proviso. It takes an indirect course, and in order to elude the Wilmot Proviso, and thereby avoid encountering the united and determined resistance of the South, it denies, by implication, the authority of Congress to legislate for the territories, and claims the right as belonging exclusively to the inhabitants of the territories. But to effect the object of excluding the South, it takes care, in the meantime, to let in emigrants freely from the Northern States and all other quarters except from the South, which it takes special care to exclude by holding up to them the danger of having their slaves liberated under the Mexican laws. The necessary consequence is to exclude the South from the territory just as effectually as would the Wilmot Proviso. The only difference in this respect is, that what one proposes to effect directly and openly, the other proposes to effect indirectly and covertly.

But the Executive Proviso is more objectionable than the Wilmot in another and more important particular. . . . In claiming the right for the inhabitants, instead of Congress, to legislate for the territories, the Executive Proviso assumes that the sovereignty over the territories is vested in the former; or, to express it in the language used in a resolution offered by one of the Senators from Texas (General Houston, now absent), they have "the same inherent right of self-government as the people in the States." The assumption is utterly unfounded, unconstitutional, without example, and contrary to the entire practice of the government, from its commencement to the present time. . . .

[As a striking example of what such doctrine as this will lead to, Mr. Calhoun takes up the case of California, then seeking admission as a State. The organization of a State government there, and the appointment of senators and representatives by the inhabitants of that region, without having first been clothed by Congress with authority for these acts, he characterizes as "revolutionary and rebellious in its character, anarchical in its tendency, and calculated to lead to the most dangerous consequences." And for it he blames most of all the Executive branch of the government, which openly advocates the doctrine in question, and has openly abetted these proceedings.]

Having now shown what cannot save the Union, I return to the question with which I commenced, — How can the Union be saved? There is but one way by which it can with any certainty; and that is, by a full and final settlement, on the principle of justice, of all the questions at issue between the two sections. The South asks for justice, simple justice, and less she ought not to take. She has no compromise to offer but the Constitution; and no concession or surrender to make. She has already surrendered so much that she has little left to surrender. Such a settlement would go to the root of the evil, and remove all cause of discontent, by satisfying the South that she could remain honorably and safely in the Union, and thereby restore the harmony and fraternal feelings between the sections, which existed anterior to the Missouri agitation. Nothing else can, with any certainty, finally and forever settle the question at issue, terminate agitation, and save the Union.

But can this be done? Yes, easily; not by the weaker party, for it can of itself do nothing — not even protect itself — but by the stronger. The North has only to will it to accomplish it — to do justice by conceding to the South an equal right in the acquired territory, and to do her duty by causing the stipulations relative to fugitive slaves to be faithfully fulfilled — to cease the agitation of the slave question, and to provide for the insertion of a provision in the Constitution, by an amendment, which will restore to the South, in substance, the power she possessed of protecting herself, before the equilibrium between the sections was destroyed by the action of this government. There will be no difficulty in devising such a provision — one that will protect the South, and which, at the same time, will improve and strengthen the government, instead of impairing and weakening it.

But will the North agree to this? It is for her to answer the question. But, I will say, she cannot refuse, if she has half the love of the Union which she professes to have, or without justly exposing herself to the charge that her love of power and aggrandizement is far greater than her love of the Union. At all events, the responsibility of saving the Union rests on the North, and not on the South. The South cannot save it by any act of hers, and the North may save it without any sacrifice whatever, unless to do justice, and to perform her duties under the Constitution, should be regarded by her as a sacrifice.

It is time, Senators, that there should be an open and manly avowal on all sides, as to what is intended to be done. If the question is not now settled, it is uncertain whether it ever can hereafter be; and we, as the representatives of the States of this Union regarded as governments, should come to a distinct understanding as to our respective views, in order to ascertain whether the great questions at issue can be settled or not. If you, who represent the stronger portion, cannot agree to settle them on the broad principle of justice and duty, say so; and let the States we both represent agree to separate and part in peace. If you are unwilling we should part in peace, tell us so; and we shall know what to do when you reduce the question to submission or resistance. If you remain silent, you will compel us to infer by your acts what you intend. In that case, California will become the test question. If you admit her under all the difficulties that oppose her admission, you compel us to infer that you intend to exclude us from the whole of the acquired territories, with the intention of destroying irretrievably the equilibrium between the two sections. We should be blind not to perceive in that case, that your real objects are power and aggrandizement, and infatuated, not to act accordingly.

I have now, Senators, done my duty in expressing my opinions fully, freely, and candidly, on this solemn occasion. In doing so, I have been governed by the motives which have governed me in all the stages of the agitation of the slavery question since its commencement. I have exerted myself during the whole period to arrest it, with the intention of saving the Union, if it could be done; and if it could not, to save the section where it has pleased Providence to cast my lot, and which I sincerely believe has justice and the Constitution on its side. Having faithfully done my duty to the best of my ability, both to the Union and my section, throughout this agitation, I shall have the consolation, let what will come, that I am free from all responsibility.

WILLIAM H. SEWARD

ON THE IRREPRESSIBLE CONFLICT; ROCHESTER, OCTOBER, 25, 1858.

THE unmistakable outbreaks of zeal which occur all around me, show that you are earnest men — and such a man am I. Let us therefore, at least for a time, pass all secondary and collateral questions, whether of a personal or of a general nature, and consider the main subject of the present canvass. The Democratic party — or, to speak more accurately, the party which wears that attractive name — is in possession of the Federal Government. The Republicans propose to dislodge that party, and dismiss it from its high trust.

The main subject, then, is, whether the Democratic party deserves to retain the confidence of the American people. In attempting to prove it unworthy, I think that I am not actuated by prejudices against that party, or by prepossessions in favor of its adversary; for I have learned by some experience that virtue and patriotism, vice and selfishness, are found in all parties, and that they differ less in their motives than in the policies they pursue.

Our country is a theatre which exhibits, in full operation, two radically different political systems; the one resting on the basis of servile or slave labor, the other on the basis of voluntary labor of freemen.

The laborers who are enslaved are all negroes, or persons more or less purely of African derivation. But this is only accidental. The principle of the system is, that labor in every society, by whomsoever performed, is necessarily unintellectual, grovelling, and base; and that the laborer, equally for his own good and for the welfare of the State, ought to be enslaved. The white laboring man, whether native or foreigner, is not enslaved, only because he cannot, as yet, be reduced to bondage.

You need not be told now that the slave system is the older of the two, and that once it was universal. The emancipation of our own ancestors, Caucasians and Europeans as they were, hardly dates beyond a period of five hundred years. The great melioration of human society which modern times exhibit, is mainly due to the incomplete substitution of the system of voluntary labor for the old one of servile labor, which has already taken place. This African slave system is one which, in its origin and in its growth, has been altogether foreign from the habits of the races which colonized these States, and established civilization here. It was introduced on this new continent as an engine of conquest, and for the establishment of monarchical power, by the Portuguese and the Spaniards, and was rapidly extended by them all over South America, Central America, Louisiana, and Mexico. Its legitimate fruits are seen in the poverty, imbecility, and anarchy which now pervade all Portuguese and Spanish America. The free-labor system is of German extraction, and it was established in our country by emigrants from Sweden, Holland, Germany, Great Britain, and Ireland. We justly ascribe to its influences the strength, wealth, greatness, intelligence, and freedom, which the whole American people now enjoy. One of the chief elements of the value of human life is freedom in the pursuit of happiness. The slave system is not only intolerable, unjust, and inhuman towards the laborer, whom, only because he is a laborer, it loads down with chains and converts into merchandise; but is scarcely less severe upon the freeman, to whom, only because he is a laborer from necessity, it denies facilities for employment, and whom it expels from the community because it cannot enslave and convert him into merchandise also. It is necessarily improvident and ruinous, because, as a general truth, communities prosper and flourish, or droop and decline, in just the degree that they practise or neglect to practise the primary duties of justice and humanity. The free-labor system conforms to the divine law of equality which is written in the hearts and consciences of men, and therefore is always and everywhere beneficent.

The slave system is one of constant danger, distrust, suspicion, and watchfulness. It debases those whose toil alone can produce wealth and resources for defence, to the lowest degree of which human nature is capable, to guard against mutiny and insurrection, and thus wastes energies which otherwise might be employed in national development and aggrandizement.

The free-labor system educates all alike, and by opening all the fields of industrial employment, and all the departments of authority, to the unchecked and equal rivalry of all classes of men, at once secures universal contentment, and brings into the highest possible activity all the physical, moral, and social energies of the whole state. In states where the slave system prevails, the masters, directly or indirectly, secure all political power, and constitute a ruling aristocracy. In states where the free-labor system prevails, universal suffrage necessarily obtains, and the state inevitably becomes, sooner or later, a republic or democracy.

Russia yet maintains slavery, and is a despotism.

Most of the other European states have abolished slavery, and adopted the system of free labor. It was the antagonistic political tendencies of the two systems which the first Napoleon was contemplating when he predicted that Europe would ultimately be either all Cossack or all republican. Never did human sagacity utter a more pregnant truth. The two systems are at once perceived to be incongruous. But they are more than incongruous — they are incompatible. They never have permanently existed together in one country, and they never can. It would be easy to demonstrate this impossibility from the irreconcilable contrast between their great principles and characteristics. But the experience of mankind has conclusively established it. Slavery, as I have already intimated, existed in every state in Europe. Free labor has supplanted it everywhere except in Russia and Turkey. State necessities developed in modern times are now obliging even those two nations to encourage and employ free labor; and already, despotic as they are, we find them engaged in abolishing slavery. In the United States, slavery came into collision with free labor at the close of the last century, and fell before it in New England, New York, New Jersey, and Pennsylvania, but triumphed over it effectually, and excluded it for a period yet undetermined, from Virginia, the Carolinas, and Georgia. Indeed, so incompatible are the two systems, that every new State which is organized within our ever-extending domain makes its first political act a choice of the one and the exclusion of the other, even at the cost of civil war if necessary. The slave States, without law, at the last national election successfully forbade, within their own limits, even the casting of votes for a candidate for President of the United States supposed to be favorable to the establishment of the free-labor system in new States.

Hitherto, the two systems have existed in different States, but side by side within the American Union. This has happened because the Union is a confederation of States. But in another aspect the United States constitute only one nation. Increase of population, which is filling the States out to their very borders, together with a new and extended net-work of railroads and other avenues, and an internal commerce which daily becomes more intimate, is rapidly bringing the States into a higher and more perfect social unity or consolidation. Thus, these antagonistic systems are continually coming into closer contact, and collision results.

Shall I tell you what this collision means? They who think that it is accidental, unnecessary, the work of interested or fanatical agitators, and therefore ephemeral, mistake the case altogether. It is an irrepressible conflict between opposing and enduring forces, and it means that the United States must and will, sooner or later, become either entirely a slave-holding nation, or entirely a free-labor nation. Either the cotton and rice-fields of South Carolina and the sugar plantations of Louisiana will ultimately be tilled by free labor, and Charleston and New Orleans become marts for legitimate merchandise alone, or else the rye-fields and wheat-fields of Massachusetts and New York must again be surrendered by their farmers to slave culture and to the production of slaves, and Boston and New York become once more markets for trade in the bodies and souls of men. It is the failure to apprehend this great truth that induces so many unsuccessful attempts at final compromise between the slave and free States, and it is the existence of this great fact that renders all such pretended compromises, when made, vain and ephemeral. Startling as this saying may appear to you, fellow citizens, it is by no means an original or even a modern one. Our forefathers knew it to be true, and unanimously acted upon it when they framed the Constitution of the United States. They regarded the existence of the servile system in so many of the States with sorrow and shame which they openly confessed, and they looked upon the collision between them, which was then just revealing itself, and which we are now accustomed to deplore, with favor and hope. They knew that either the one or the other system must exclusively prevail.

Unlike too many of those who in modern time invoke their authority, they had a choice between the two. They preferred the system of free labor, and they determined to organize the government, and so to direct its activity, that that system should surely and certainly prevail. For this purpose, and no other, they based the whole structure of government broadly on the principle that all men are created equal, and therefore free — little dreaming that within the short period of one hundred years their descendants would bear to be told by any orator, however popular, that the utterance of that principle was merely a rhetorical rhapsody; or by any judge, however venerated, that it was attended by mental reservations, which rendered it hypocritical and false. By the ordinance of 1787, they dedicated all of the national domain not yet polluted by slavery to free labor immediately, thenceforth, and forever; while by the new Constitution and laws they invited foreign free labor from all lands under the sun, and interdicted the importation of African slave labor, at all times, in all places, and under all circumstances whatsoever. It is true that they necessarily and wisely modified this policy of freedom by leaving it to the several States, affected as they were by differing circumstances, to abolish slavery in their own way and at their own pleasure, instead of confiding that duty to Congress; and that they secured to the slave States, while yet retaining the system of slavery, a three-fifths representation of slaves in the Federal Government, until they should find themselves able to relinquish it with safety. But the very nature of these modifications fortifies my position, that the fathers knew that the two systems could not endure within the Union, and expected that within a short period slavery would disappear forever. Moreover, in order that these modifications might not altogether defeat their grand design of a republic maintaining universal equality, they provided that two-thirds of the States might amend the Constitution.

It remains to say on this point only one word, to guard against misapprehension. If these States are to again become universally slave-holding, I do not pretend to say with what violations of the Constitution that end shall be accomplished. On the other hand, while I do confidently believe and hope that my country will yet become a land of universal freedom, I do not expect that it will be made so otherwise than through the action of the several States co-operating with the Federal Government, and all acting in strict conformity with their respective constitutions.

The strife and contentions concerning slavery, which gently-disposed persons so habitually deprecate, are nothing more than the ripening of the conflict which the fathers themselves not only thus regarded with favor, but which they may be said to have instituted.

It is not to be denied, however, that thus far the course of that contest has not been according to their humane anticipations and wishes. In the field of federal politics, slavery — deriving unlooked-for advantages from commercial changes, and energies unforeseen from the facilities of combination between members of the slave-holding class and between that class and other property classes — early rallied, and has at length made a stand, not merely to retain its original defensive position, but to extend its sway throughout the whole Union. It is certain that the slave-holding class of American citizens indulge this high ambition, and that they derive encouragement for it from the rapid and effective political successes which they have already obtained. The plan of operation is this: By continued appliances of patronage and threats of disunion, they will keep a majority favorable to these designs in the Senate, where each State has equal representation. Through that majority they will defeat, as they best can, the admission of free States and secure the admission of slave States. Under the protection of the judiciary, they will, on the principle of the Dred Scott case, carry slavery into all the territories of the United States now existing and hereafter to be organized. By the action of the President and the Senate, using the treaty-making power, they will annex foreign slave-holding States. In a favorable conjuncture they will induce Congress to repeal the act of 1808, which prohibits the foreign slave-trade, and so they will import from Africa, at the cost of only twenty dollars a head, slaves enough to fill up the interior of the continent. Thus relatively increasing the number of slave States, they will allow no amendment to the Constitution prejudicial to their interest; and so, having permanently established their power, they expect the federal judiciary to nullify all State laws which shall interfere with internal or foreign commerce in slaves. When the free States shall be sufficiently demoralized to tolerate these designs, they reasonably conclude that slavery will be accepted by those States themselves. I shall not stop to show how speedy or how complete would be the ruin which the accomplishment of these slave-holding schemes would bring upon the country. For one, I should not remain in the country to test the sad experiment. . . . When that evil day shall come, and all further effort at resistance shall be impossible, then, if there be no better hope of redemption than I can now foresee, I shall say with Franklin, while looking abroad over the whole earth for a new and more congenial home, "Where liberty dwells, there is my country."

You will tell me that these fears are extravagant and chimerical. I answer, they are so; but they are so only because the designs of the slave-holders must and can be defeated. But it is only the possibility of defeat that renders them so. They cannot be defeated by inactivity. There is no escape from them compatible with non-resistance. How, then, and in what way, shall the necessary resistance be made? There is only one way. The Democratic party must be permanently dislodged from the government. The reason is, that the Democratic party is inextricably committed to the designs of the slave-holders, which I have described. Let me be well understood. I do not charge that the Democratic candidates for public office now before the people are pledged to — much less that the Democratic masses who support them really adopt — those atrocious and dangerous designs. Candidates may, and generally do, mean to act justly, wisely, and patriotically when they shall be elected; but they become the ministers and servants, not the dictators, of the power which elects them. . . . It is not more true that "hell is paved with good intentions," than it is that earth is covered with wrecks resulting from innocent and amiable motives.

The very constitution of the Democratic party commits it to execute all the designs of the slave-holders, whatever they may be. It is not a party of the whole Union — of all the free States and of all the slave States; nor yet is it a party of the free States in the North and in the

North-West; but it is a sectional and local party, having practically its seat within the slave States, and counting its constituency chiefly and almost exclusively there. Of all its representatives in Congress and in the electoral colleges, two-thirds uniformly come from these States. Its great element of strength lies in the vote of the slave-holders, augmented by the representation of three-fifths of the slaves. Deprive the Democratic party of this strength, and it would be a helpless and hopeless minority, incapable of continued organization. The Democratic party, being thus local and sectional, acquires new strength from the admission of every new slave State, and loses relatively by the admission of every new free State into the Union.

A party is in one sense a joint stock association, in which those who contribute most direct the action and management of the concern. The slave-holders contributing in an overwhelming proportion to the capital strength of the Democratic party, they necessarily dictate and prescribe its policy. The inevitable caucus system enables them to do so with a show of fairness and justice. If it were possible to conceive for a moment that the Democratic party should disobey the behests of the slave-holders, we should then see a withdrawal of the slave-holders, which would leave the party to perish. The portion of the party which is found in the free States is a mere appendage, convenient to modify its sectional character without impairing its sectional constitution, and is less effective in regulating its movement than the nebulous tail of the comet is in determining the appointed, though apparently eccentric, course of the fiery sphere from which it emanates.

To expect the Democratic party to resist slavery and favor freedom, is as unreasonable as to look for Protestant missionaries to the Catholic Propaganda of Rome.

The history of the Democratic party commits it to the policy of slavery. It has been the Democratic party and no other agency, which has carried that policy up to its present alarming culmination. Without stopping to ascertain critically the origin of the present Democratic party, we may concede its claim to date from the era of good feeling which occurred under the administration of President Monroe. At that time, in this State, and about that time in many others of the free States, the Democratic party deliberately disfranchised the free colored or African citizen, and it has pertinaciously continued this disfranchisement ever since. This was an effective aid to slavery; for, while the slave-holder votes for his slaves against freedom, the freed slave in the free States is prohibited from voting against slavery. . . .

[Here follows a review of measures carried or attempted by the Democratic party, from 1824 up to the date of this speech, to show the singleness of the devotion of that party to the support of slavery. The passage closes as follows: —]

The Democratic party, finally, has procured from a supreme judiciary, fixed in its interest, a decree that slavery exists by force of the Constitution in every territory of the United States, paramount to all legislative authority either within the territory or residing in Congress.

Such is the Democratic party. It has no policy, state or federal, for finance, or trade, or manufacture, or commerce, or education, or internal improvements, or for the protection or even the security of civil or religious liberty. It is positive and uncompromising in the interest of slavery, — negative, compromising, and vacillating, in regard to everything else. It boasts its love of equality; and wastes its strength, and even its life, in fortifying the only aristocracy known in the land. It professes fraternity; and, so often as slavery requires, allies itself with proscription. It magnifies itself for conquests in foreign lands; but it sends the national eagle forth always with chains, and not the olive branch, in his fangs.

This dark record shows you, fellow citizens, what I was unwilling to announce at an earlier stage of this argument, that of the whole nefarious schedule of slaveholding designs which I have submitted to you, the Democratic party has left only one yet to be consummated — the abrogation of the law which forbids the African slave-trade. . . .

I think, fellow citizens, that I have shown you that it is high time for the friends of freedom to rush to the rescue of the Constitution, and that their very first duty is to dismiss the Democratic party from the administration of government. Why shall it not be done?

. . . I know — few, I think, know better than I — the resources and energies of the Democratic party, which is identical with the slave power. I do ample justice to its traditional popularity. I know, further — few, I think, know better than I — the difficulties and disadvantages of organizing a new political force, like the Republican party, and the obstacles it must encounter in laboring without prestige and without patronage. But, understanding all this, I know that the Democratic party must go down, and that the Republican party must rise into its place. The Democratic party derived its strength, originally, from its adoption of the principles of equal and exact justice to all men. So long as it practised this principle faithfully, it was invulnerable. It became vulnerable when it renounced the principle, and since that time it has maintained itself, not by virtue of its own strength, or even of its traditional merits, but because there as yet had appeared in the political field no other party that had the conscience and the courage to take up, and avow, and practise the life-inspiring principle which the Democratic party had surrendered. At last, the Republican party has appeared. It avows, now, as the Republican party of 1800 did, in one word, its faith and its works, "Equal and exact justice to all men." Even when it first entered the field, only half organized, it struck a blow which only just failed to secure complete and triumphant victory. In this, its second campaign, it has already won advantages which render that triumph now both easy and certain.

The secret of its assured success lies in that very characteristic which, in the mouth of scoffers, constitutes its great and lasting imbecility and reproach. It lies in the fact that it is a party of one idea; but that idea is a noble one — an idea that fills and expands all generous souls; the idea of equality — the equality of all men before human tribunals and human laws, as they all are equal before the divine tribunal and divine laws.

I know, and you know, that a revolution has begun. I know, and all the world knows, that revolutions never go backward. Twenty Senators and a hundred Representatives proclaim boldly in Congress to-day sentiments and opinions and principles of freedom which hardly so many men, even in this free State, dared to utter in their own homes twenty years ago. While the Government of the United States, under the conduct of the Democratic party, has been all that time surrendering one plain and castle after another to slavery, the people of the United States have been no less steadily and perseveringly gathering together the forces with which to recover back again all the fields and all the castles which have been lost, and to confound and overthrow, by one decisive blow, the betrayers of the constitution and freedom forever.

ABRAHAM LINCOLN.

THE GETTYSBURG ADDRESS; NOVEMBER 19, 1863.

FOURSCORE and seven years ago our fathers brought forth upon this continent a new nation, conceived in liberty, and dedicated to the proposition that all men are created equal. Now we are engaged in a great civil war, testing whether that nation, or any nation so conceived and so dedicated, can long endure. We are met on a great battle-field of that war. We have come to dedicate a portion of that field as a final resting-place for those who here gave their lives that that nation might live. It is altogether fitting and proper that we should do this. But in a larger sense we cannot dedicate, we cannot consecrate, we cannot hallow this ground. The brave men, living and dead, who struggled here, have consecrated it far above our power to add or detract. The world will little note, nor long remember, what we say here, but it can never forget what they did here. It is for us, the living, rather to be dedicated here to the unfinished work which they who fought here have thus far so nobly advanced. It is rather for us to be here dedicated to the great task remaining before us, that from these honored dead we take increased devotion to that cause for which they gave the last full measure of devotion; that we here highly resolve that these dead shall not have died in vain; that this nation, under God, shall have a new birth of freedom, and that government of the people, by the people, and for the people, shall not perish from the earth.

NOTES.

THE ENGLISH CONSTITUTION AND GOVERNMENT.

THE English speeches contained in this volume make frequent reference to a structure of government and to forms and usages unlike those with which we are familiar in the United States. Information upon these subjects is absolutely necessary to an intelligent reading of these speeches, and yet it is not always readily accessible. It has therefore been thought best to embody in succinct statement the peculiar features of the English Constitution, government, and procedure touched upon in the speeches, and incidentally to point out the pitfalls which lurk under the guise of terms and expressions similar in form to our own, but different in content and meaning. It should be noted that the point of view in the following sketch is that of the present status in England. Historical differences within the period covered will be noticed as they occur in the speeches themselves.

THE BRITISH CONSTITUTION.

When a new organization of government was adopted and put upon trial in the United States in 1789, the special features of that organization were set forth in a well-known document, which, by a natural transfer of meaning, took the name of the order and organization which it described; that is, the Constitution of the United States of America. Ever since that time the extraordinary interest centring in this document has, in the usage of American speakers and writers, tended steadily to shift the meaning of the word Constitution to this narrower base; that is, from the actual order and organization of government to the document in which that order is officially described and promulgated. This limitation of meaning is by no means prevalent outside the realm of American politics; and the young American student should be specially cautioned against interpreting in any such narrow sense the frequent reference made by Englishmen to the British Constitution. England has no written Constitution; nor, under the circumstances, could she well have one. Her government is the outcome of ages of experiment and struggle; of incessant re-adjustment of conflicting powers and interests; sometimes of sharp and decisive action; more frequently of insensible but irresistible drifting upon the current of national tendency. Questions of constitutionality, therefore, are settled in England, not by appeal to a state-paper like ours, since none exists, but by appeal to unchallenged usage, to precedents not reversed, or to legislation not repealed, wherever these are to be found in the centuries between Magna Charta and the present time. Even in cases where we find citation of what is claimed to be the very language of the Constitution, we are not to understand anything more than that the language is that of *some* document of acknowledged authority in determining usage; as, for example, an Act of Parliament. And the English Constitution is altered, not through the formality of an amendment voted upon by the people, but by embodying the innovation directly in legislative act, — subject, of course, to prompt ratification or rejection by the people in their next return of members to Parliament. To Englishmen, then, the Constitution means primarily *the established order of government*, whether this be (1) with reference to its organization, its actual structure, and the relation of its parts; or (2) with reference to usage, precedent, and law; or (3) with reference to its genius and spirit. In the first sense the word is often loosely synonymous with our use of the word government; but for this last word English usage has developed a special meaning (see below), which excludes it in certain connections. Examples of these several uses of the word may be found on p. 257, l. 32; p. 50, l. 15; p. 79, l. 35; and p. 42, l. 25.

THE CABINET.

In England the executive power, as of old, is vested nominally in the Crown, but really in the Cabinet, or Ministry, with which body the sovereign is associated, both as its honorary head and as a permanent councillor; influential indeed, but without vote, responsibility, or place in its sessions. Whenever a decisive change of party or of policy becomes apparent in the votes of the House of Commons, the old Cabinet resigns, and a new one is formed to put the new policy into operation. Theoretically the Queen is free to choose whom she will to become Prime Minister and form the new Cabinet; but practically the choice is limited to a single person, the acknowledged leader of the party which has become uppermost in the Commons. The Prime Minister selects his colleagues from among the ablest men of his party and its allies in both Houses, a significant feature of the scheme being the fact that the Ministers are actually members of Parliament, are present at its sessions, and play a most important part in its deliberations. The Cabinet so constituted is, therefore, a committee of the majority. But it is more than this. It is a committee "with power," charged with the duty of acting in momentous affairs, and often without previous consultation with Parliament. Upon it devolves, furthermore, nearly the whole initiative in legislation, — the duty of planning, introducing, and bringing to decision almost all measures discussed in Parliament. The promptness and completeness with which this body of men is vested with imperial power, in every realm save that of the Judiciary, is startling indeed to American ideas. The Ministry becomes at once both heart and brain of the government, and during its tenure of office wields a power far transcending that of our Presidential Administration. A sufficient safeguard against abuse of this power is found in the immediate responsibility of the Ministry to the Commons; that is, in the swiftness and certainty of its downfall if it fails to carry the majority with it. Out of the feeling that the Ministry is the vital centre of government, Englishmen have come to call it "Her Majesty's Government," "the Government," or simply "Government." In these expressions there is often an implied reference to that other equally important and equally recognized part of the system, "the Opposition;" that is, the organized minority, in its character of critic and advocate for the other side, charged with the duty of allowing nothing to pass without challenge and efficient scrutiny.

PARLIAMENT.

The Parliament of England consists of two bodies, or "Houses," the Lords and the Commons. The House of Lords stands for the conservatism of ancient privilege; the Commons, for the final sovereignty of the people. The one is for the most part hereditary, and often continues without radical change during long periods of time; the other is the direct representative of the people, and is kept such by frequent general elections. Parliament assembles at the summons of the Crown; that is, of the Ministry in the name of the Queen. It is opened by a Speech from the Throne read in the House of Lords. Its annual session is usually from February to August, at the close of which it is "prorogued" by the Crown; and in the end it is dissolved by the same authority. The term of a Parliament is really the term of the Lower House, since that alone is affected by elections. Its utmost possible term is fixed by statute at seven years; but no Parliament of modern times has survived so long. Dissolution of Parliament comes about at no stated time, but rather as an exigency of government. When the Ministers find themselves confronted by an adverse majority in the Commons, if issue is clearly joined and the majority decisive, they are expected to resign their power at once into the hands of the majority. But if there is doubt as to whether this majority really represents the will of the people, the Ministry may dissolve Parliament and "go to the country" — that is, appeal to the people upon the issue raised.

THE HOUSE OF LORDS.

The House of Lords has a membership of over five hundred, consisting of the following groups: (1) The Lords Temporal; i.e., the hereditary peerage of England with a small representation chosen from the peerage of Scotland and of Ireland. (2) The Lords Spiritual; i.e., the higher clergy of the Established Church, in the persons of the archbishops and bishops. (3) The higher judiciary, in the persons of the Lord Chancellor and three distinguished lawyers or judges designated by the Crown, and called Lords of Appeal in Ordinary, or, more popularly, "Law Lords."

These three groups are separately addressed in Chatham's speech, p. 87. The Lord Chancellor presides, and is a member of the regnant ministry; the Law Lords are advisers of the Lords upon legal matters. These persons, however, are not by virtue of their offices "lords of Parliament"—members entitled to speak and to vote in the ordinary business of the Upper House. Even the Chancellor's seat, the famous "woolsack," is theoretically outside the precincts of the Lords, although it is, in fact, almost in the centre of their chamber. But in recent practice the Chancellor is regularly made an hereditary peer, if he is not one already, and the Law Lords are made peers for life. Only a mere fraction of the membership is ordinarily found in attendance upon business. Three members, it is said, constitute a quorum; and, until recently, members might vote by proxy without being present or hearing discussion. In legislation, the House of Lords is theoretically of equal weight with the House of Commons, since the consent of both is requisite to the passage of any Act. But, in reality, the power of the former has greatly dwindled, partly because of what is felt to be the narrowness of its sympathy and interest outside of its own class; still more because of its exclusion from the great field of finance and taxation; and, most of all, because in the end it can always be forced to assent to the will of the Commons by the simple expedient of having new peers created by the Ministry in the name of the Crown, and thus overwhelming the adverse majority. The fear that such action would be taken was sufficient to secure the assent of the Lords to the Reform Bill of 1832;—a sufficient number of the majority, though bitterly opposed to the bill, deliberately absented themselves to avoid precipitating the crisis. The influence of the peerage upon legislation is still great in many ways; but the actual power of their House in a contested case is limited to a power of cautious revision and a veto to stay proceedings until the people shall have spoken again, and with decisive emphasis, upon the point in question.

It should be noted in passing, that the House of Lords has judicial functions in which its action is quite independent of the Commons. It sits as a Court of Impeachment in cases like that of Warren Hastings, and as a court for the trial of members of its own order charged with treason or felony. Furthermore, it sits, — or, as we should say, a committee consisting only of its legal members sits, — as a Supreme Court of Appeals for the kingdom.

THE HOUSE OF COMMONS.

As the result of successive changes in the representation of the realm, the House of Commons now numbers six hundred and seventy members. The constituencies which "return" these members are either rural — counties and subdivisions of counties; urban — boroughs and wards; or universities. On receipt of the writ, or order for an election, the "returning officer" of each constituency arranges the preliminaries and fixes a date before which all candidates must announce themselves. When that date is reached, if no more candidates appear than there are seats to be filled, the candidates are "returned" by the officer — are reported as duly elected — without further formality of balloting. If, however, a seat is "contested" by two or more candidates, the officer appoints a day for "taking the poll." In general elections, therefore, it comes about that the polls are not taken in all the constituencies on the same day, but are scattered over a considerable interval of time. Thus, in a hotly contested campaign it not infrequently happens that some distinguished party champion attempts in the first instance to carry some stronghold of the enemy, is defeated there, and yet saves his place in Parliament by offering himself at the eleventh hour as a candidate in one of these later elections. Any fully qualified citizen not a member of the House of Lords, an officer of government, nor a clergyman either of the Established or Roman Church, may "stand;" i.e., is eligible to Parliament. Residence outside of the district is no bar, as we have seen above. The candidate not only pays all the expenses of his canvass, but must render a sworn statement of every item of it. If successful, he is free thereafter to serve the public in Parliament at his own expense, for the government allows him no compensation whatever. Only in very rare cases does a constituency volunteer to maintain in Parliament a member too poor to maintain himself. If the member becomes distinguished enough to be sought for high political office, such as a place in the Cabinet, he must, by submitting to a second election, obtain from his constituency permission to serve them in the double capacity of member and minister.

The old Houses of Parliament, in which Burke, Chatham, and Macaulay spoke, were destroyed by fire in 1834. Their essential features, arrangements, and usages, however, have all been repeated in the new Houses; and these will require some brief notice in view of the frequent reference made to them in the speeches. The "House" in which the Commons sit, and in which is transacted the business of the British Empire, is an oblong chamber surrounded by lobbies. At one end, on an elevated platform, is the Speaker's Chair. At a table below and in front of him sit the Clerks; beyond them lies the Mace, emblem of the Speaker's authority. Parallel with the sides and with the further end of the room are arranged the members' seats, tier above tier, filling the whole space with the exception of a narrow, oblong portion of open floor in the centre. From this open space the main aisle runs down the centre of the chamber; while an aisle at right angles to this, and known as the "gangway," intersects the side benches. There are three well-known groups of sittings: The front row of seats on the Speaker's right is called the Treasury Bench, and is occupied by the Ministers. Behind these are ranged the supporters of the Government — the members of the dominant party. The seats on the Speaker's left, and directly facing these last, are the Opposition Benches, occupied by the leaders and body of "Her Majesty's Opposition." The "cross-benches" at the end of the room, directly facing the Speaker, are the place for members who do not affiliate with either of the great parties. One's location in the House is thus an indication of his political relationships. No member, however, can claim exclusive right to any particular seat, since the sittings are far fewer than the membership. There are regularly five sessions a week; four of these run from 4 o'clock P.M. till late at night — sometimes till after day-break — and one, on Wednesday, from midday till 6 o'clock P.M. Members sit with their hats on, but remove them when they rise to speak.

The "House" of the Lords is in the same building with that

of the Commons, but at the further end of the corridor. Its general arrangements are not unlike those of the other chamber, save that the Speaker's seat — the woolsack — is moved forward toward the centre to make place for a raised platform and the royal throne at the end of the room.

FORMS OF PROCEDURE.

At the opening of Parliament the Commons, headed by their Speaker, attend at the bar[1] of the Lords to listen to the Speech from the Throne, a paper prepared, of course, by the Ministry, and resembling somewhat, in its general scope, our President's Message. At the close of the Speech they retire to their chamber, and, first of all, go through the form of reading some unimportant bill, in order to assert once more their right to deliberate freely about whatever they will, even though matters urged upon them by the Crown have to wait. Some member previously designated for this duty then moves the "Address" — the formal reply to the royal Speech, couched in subservient language, and strictly echoing the tone and the suggestions of that paper. In the debate which follows, there is a general airing of views of all sorts, and not infrequently amendments are proposed sharply criticising the acts or the policy of Government.[2] These matters disposed of, the regular business of the session begins. Of this there is inevitably an enormous amount, since many matters which in our country never come before Congress, but belong either to State, or to county, or to municipal government, are in England directly under the control of Parliament. But there is no such deluge of proposed legislation as that which greets us Americans at the opening of Congress. The House of Lords, as we have seen, does very little in initiating measures; while individual members of the Commons may introduce bills but sparingly, not as of right, but only by consent of the House. Furthermore, only the Wednesday afternoon

[1] A movable barrier or rail in the main aisle of each House, beyond which none but officers and members are allowed to pass.

[2] A debate upon a similar Address in the House of Lords was the occasion of Chatham's speech printed in this volume, and of an amendment proposed by him.

session of each week is available for the consideration of business so introduced. The Ministry is held responsible for the introduction of all necessary legislation; while the duty of the House is primarily to scrutinize, discuss, amend, accept, or reject the measures the Ministry proposes. Government measures have, therefore, large right of way; three full sessions each week are devoted to them exclusively. Questions propounded to the Ministry form a noteworthy feature of the Parliamentary scheme, affording, as they do, to the House an admirable means of informing itself on matters it needs to know, and to the Ministers an opportunity of directly stating their case and explaining their action. But neither measures nor questions may be sprung upon the House unawares. Full notice and precise statement of each must in all cases be previously given.

The regular course through which a Bill must pass to become a a law is as follows: The Bill, having been drafted, printed, and properly endorsed, comes to its "first reading," after due notice given and motion passed "for leave to bring in the Bill." Its title then is read aloud by the Clerk, and a motion is made that the Bill be read a second time on a future day named. When the day arrives, the proposer moves its second reading, and enters into a full explanation and defence of its provisions. Debate follows; and if the House consents to the second reading, it is understood as accepting the general principle of the measure, though not committing itself to the details. If the House refuses, the Bill is of course defeated. This second reading is therefore the most critical stage of a Bill in its course in the Commons, and calls for the most strenuous efforts of its defenders. After its second reading, the House votes to consider it in detail in a Committee on some future day named. In this Committee changes and amendments are agreed upon, and the Committee rises and reports to the House the Bill, usually in its final shape. The House orders its third reading, again in the future; and when this is reached, the motion is put "that the Bill be passed." Votes in the House are taken first *viva voce;* but if the result is doubted, a "division" is taken in this way: Those voting "Ay" pass out of the chamber into the lobby on the Speaker's right, while those voting "No" pass into the lobby on the left, until the Speaker remains alone. The members are counted as they file back into the chamber, and the result is announced. A Bill that successfully passes this stage is sent up to the Lords. If the Lords accept it, it receives, as a matter of course, the royal assent,[1] and becomes a law. If the Lords amend it, it must return to the Commons for their concurrence in the amendments. If the Lords "throw it out," or if the Commons refuse to accept the amendments of the Lords, the Bill, of course, is lost.

FINANCE AND TAXATION.

The principle that a free people must be free to tax itself and to spend its money as it will, is a principle which our fathers brought with them from the old country. The difference between a tax "given and granted" to the Crown by the people themselves, and a tax imposed by the Crown upon the people, was in the last century, to Englishmen on both sides of the Atlantic, a very vital difference — the difference between freedom and subjugation. Burke speaks of this point on p. 49, l. 13–21; and the whole subject is eloquently set forth by him in a speech upon American Taxation, not included in this volume. Out of this very matter grew our Revolutionary War. Since that war, however, there has been for us neither Crown nor subject, nor any participant in our government other than the people itself; and the old distinction is lost. Our governments of all degrees regularly levy, or impose, taxes; and the form of expression no longer awakes our wrath. But in England the old distinction and the old usage still hold. There the vast framework of government — outside of the Commons — has absolutely no vital or sustaining power within itself; it can levy no tax, can raise no revenue for its own support, has no income at all save what the people from year to year through their representatives, the Commons, actually "give and grant." The Queen, in her Speech from the Throne, must each year ask anew that "her faithful Commons" vote her the

[1] There was once a veto power resident in the Sovereign, but it is now practically lost. The Queen *must* assent to whatever passes the two Houses. The last veto in English history was by Queen Anne.

supplies without which every wheel in the system must come to a standstill. The Commons hold the purse. One of the chief matters, therefore, in the annual business of the House, is the consideration of the "Budget." The minister in charge of the finances of the realm is termed the Chancellor of the Exchequer. His most arduous duty is the preparation of estimates of expenditure for the coming year, and plans for taxation whereby the necessary amount may be raised. When this Budget is ready, the House receives and considers it in a "Committee of Supply." This is a Committee of the whole House, formed for the purpose of securing the utmost freedom of question and discussion, which would otherwise be hampered by strict parliamentary rules. The Speaker leaves his seat, the Mace is carried away, some member is made Chairman, and discussion runs on with little heed to the formality of rules. In this Committee is settled the amount Commons will grant the Crown, and the ends to which it is to be applied. This done, the same body resolves itself into a Committee of Ways and Means, to determine in like manner how the money shall be raised. When this Committee has closed its deliberations, it rises, the Speaker resumes his place, and the Chairman of the Committees reports to the House the conclusions reached, which are then embodied in a motion and passed by the House in its formal capacity. When a "Money Bill" has duly passed all its stages in the Commons, it is sent to the Lords, who have no power to alter or amend it, though they may reject it — if they dare. Furthermore, such a bill does not go up to the Queen along with others through the hands of the Lords, but is returned to the Commons, and at the end of the session is presented to her by the Speaker in person, as the gift of the people alone. And on such an occasion the Queen never fails to thank the Commons for their generosity.

In the preparation of the foregoing sketch the author has consulted among others the following works, and would recommend them to the student for further study or reference:

A Primer of the English Constitution and Government, by Sheldon Amos (Longmans, Green & Co., N.Y.) — a compact topical statement, with good Index and Appendices.

The English Constitution, by Walter Bagehot (Chapman, Hall & Co., London) — a brilliant and popular discussion of its excellences and defects.

The State, by Woodrow Wilson (D. C. Heath & Co., Boston) — specially valuable as a topical digest and manual of the structure and organization of all the great constitutional governments of the modern world.

The Law of the Constitution, a series of lectures by A. V. Dicey (Macmillan & Co.) — giving with utmost logical clearness the lawyer's view of the English Constitution, and explaining some of its principal maxims.

EDMUND BURKE.

EDMUND BURKE was born in Dublin, Ireland, in January, 1729. His father was an attorney with a fair practice, and looked forward to the same profession for his son. The boy received his education first in a private school; then in Trinity College, Dublin, — where he took the bachelor's degree in his nineteenth year; and last of all, in the Middle Temple, London. His studies gained him at the time no special academic honors, and never brought him to the actual practice of the law; yet in them, and especially in the wide and profound reading which accompanied them, was laid the foundation of his future greatness.

Burke's first public venture was in literature. In 1756 appeared his *Vindication of Natural Society* — a clever bit of irony — and his *Inquiry into the Origin of Our Ideas of the Sublime and the Beautiful*, an essay which at once attracted attention both in England and upon the Continent. Meantime, however, he had discovered the true bent of his genius, and was diligently studying the governmental problems of England. The first fruit of this study appeared in 1757, in his *Account of English Settlements in America*. From about this time also dates his long friendship with Dr. Johnson and the members of his famous Literary Club.

His political career began in 1765, when he became private secretary to Lord Rockingham, the head of the new Whig Ministry. A little later he was returned to Parliament as member for Wendover, taking his seat in time to distinguish himself in the debates which preceded the repeal of the Stamp Act in 1766. His career in Parliament lasted without break from this time until 1794, when, broken in health and spirits, he withdrew from public life. His death occurred not long after, in 1797.

A passion for order and a passion for justice, some one has said, were the master-motives of Burke's thought and life. Both these passions led him directly into that field of human activity where they find their noblest play, the field of practical government. During his lifetime three mighty questions successively confronted the government of England: (1) How shall a great nation deal with colonies of its own proud blood and free traditions? (2) How shall such a nation treat subject provinces of alien race and temper? (3) How shall it meet the fierce spirit of change and revolution at its very doors? They were the questions of America, of India, and of France. Into their discussion Burke threw himself with all the ardor and force of his great nature. In his utterance upon the first of these questions Burke was undoubtedly at his best. It is not merely that this topic is one which naturally attracts American readers. It is not merely that his arguments have still a living interest in their application to great questions which confront England in our own day. Burke brought to it a fresher, truer insight, a judgment more sane, a temper more serene and genial, than he was able to command later, after years spent in unavailing struggle and bitter conflict. Furthermore, this question raised no schism within himself. His passion for the established order and his passion for justice both led him to the same conclusion.

When the American Colonies were forever lost, Burke turned his attention to the government of England's East Indian possessions. A series of brilliant speeches in Parliament led up to his crowning effort upon this subject, the speech at the trial of Warren Hastings, in 1787. Burke's grasp of facts is now more masterful, and his oratory more splendid than ever; but the noble effect is somewhat marred by a shrillness of tone, an excitement of personal feeling, and a fierceness of invective from which his earlier utterances were free.

In 1789 came the crash of the French Revolution. Burke's horror at the overthrow of long-established order was so great as to leave no room for calm consideration of justice as between oppressor and oppressed. With fiercer and fiercer outcry from this time onward he urged England to espouse the cause of the old tyranny, and to put down the Revolution.

SPEECH ON CONCILIATION WITH THE COLONIES.

At the opening of the year 1775 the harsh treatment which the Colonies were receiving from England had forced them to combine for mutual support against further aggression. The Continental Congress had already assembled. Lexington and Bunker Hill were not far off. It was becoming a matter of grave importance to the English government to break up this formidable union, and to bring the Colonies once more to deal separately and singly with England. At this juncture Lord North, the Prime Minister, unexpectedly announced what he was pleased to term a measure for "conciliating the differences with America." He proposed to exempt from further taxation any Colony which, after providing for the maintenance of its own government, should guarantee to the mother-country an amount satisfactory to her as being, "according to the condition, circumstances, and situation of such Colony," its proportionate contribution toward the common defence. This transparent scheme deceived no one, — it was really a plan to divide and conquer. To the friends of the Colonies, however, it was no small thing that the Ministry, after a long policy of coercion, should not merely accept, but of its own accord announce, the principle of conciliation. Burke seized the opportunity to propose conciliation which might really be effective.

TEXTUAL NOTES.

PAGE **1**, 1. **the austerity of the Chair** means, of course, 'the dignity and seriousness of this assembly.' The parliamentary fiction which regards not merely the dignity, but the personality, of the House as embodied in its Speaker, is an old-time device to banish from public deliberations the fierceness and the confusion of personal encounters. To it we owe our common rule of debate that all remarks must be addressed to the Chair, and that no mention be made by name of any person in the assembly. This rule was, no doubt, more rigidly observed in Burke's day than it is at present. But the literalness with which Burke at times carries out the fiction, though meant as pleasantry, has a strong dash of the grotesque; as it has here in his ascription to the Chair of the actual moods and temper of the members, and again on p. 9, l. 3, 4, where with doubtful compliment he speaks of "a blunter discernment than yours." In a like vein is his disparagement here of his own perfectly natural and worthy feeling as 'frailty' and 'superstition.' Burke's weighty genius is not always at its best in toying with trifles.

8. **the grand penal bill** was a measure of Lord North's, cutting off the New England colonies from all trade except with the mother country and her dependencies, and, worst of all, putting a stop to the fisheries, one of their most successful and important industries. See pp. 14–16. The Lords returned the bill with a savage amendment making it apply to *all* the American Colonies. The amendment was afterwards withdrawn.

PAGE **2**, 6, 7. This was at the beginning of 1766. Long before this date, however, Burke had discerned the gravity of the Colonial question, and had with characteristic energy set himself to master it; as is shown by his *Account of European Settlements in America*, published in 1757.

25, 26. The occasion was a memorable one — the repeal of the Stamp Act under Lord Rockingham's Ministry, March 18, 1766. The strength and sharpness of the impression made upon Burke are attested by a striking passage in his speech upon American Taxation, wherein, after sketching the situation within the House on that night, and the bearing of the great leaders there, he goes on to tell how, outside the walls of the chamber, "the whole trading interest of this Empire, crammed into your lobbies, with a trembling and anxious expectation waited, almost to a winter's return of light, their fate from your resolutions;" and how, when the result was announced, "from the whole of that grave multitude there arose an involuntary burst of gratitude and transport."

PAGE **3**, 15–17. This was a Mr. Rose Fuller, now in the Opposition along with Burke. During the previous session it was his proposition to repeal the Tea Tax which furnished the occasion of Burke's famous speech upon American Taxation, referred to in the last note.

PAGE 4, 12–19. Upon the Ministry and its supporters, Burke means to say, rests the responsibility for devising schemes for carrying on government. Schemes proposed by the Opposition are not merely sure to receive no fair consideration from the triumphant majority, but are apt thereby to be discredited in advance, and ruined for future usefulness. The scruple is thoroughly characteristic of Burke, as are also the considerations which induced him to set it aside.

PAGE 6, 9–14. **the project** has been outlined above in the Introductory Note to this speech. The impossibility of assigning any definite values to the factors which were to determine the proportionate share of each Colony, as well as the cool irony of talking about proportion at all, when the real object was in each case to extort the largest sum possible, strongly roused Burke. His imagination at once pictures the scenes Parliament is likely to witness in attempting to carry out such a scheme, and he sarcastically figures these as the splendors and sensations of a new entertainment provided by the Ministry. **The noble lord** was Frederick North, Prime Minister from 1770 till 1782, and largely responsible for the separation of the Colonies from England. He was at this time 'lord' only by courtesy of speech. He did not come into his earldom until his father's death in 1790. Sons and younger brothers of peers, though commonly styled lords, are only commoners in fact, and as such are eligible to the lower house, where they often seek a career. A notable example in our own day is Lord Randolph Churchill. The **blue ribbon** is the badge of the famous Order of the Garter, a decoration rarely conferred upon commoners, and therefore often mentioned by Burke in his parliamentary designation of this Prime Minister to whom he was so long opposed.

Colony agents. In default of any regular channel through which a colony could make its condition and its needs known to Parliament, the practice was to secure the services of some member of Parliament to act as agent for the colony, and to look after its interests in the general legislation. Burke himself was such an agent for New York. A fuller recognition is now accorded the colonies of England, in the addition to the Ministry of a special Secretary of State for the Colonies. But the Agents-General are still maintained. **the interposition of your mace.** When the ordinary call for order is ineffective to quell disturbance in the House, the Sergeant-at-Arms, at the Speaker's direction, takes up the mace from the table where it lies, and with it confronts the disorderly members. Before this symbol of the majesty of the House, they are expected to quail and sink into their seats. There is in the Speaker's power but one last resource more dreaded than this, and that is to "name" the disorderly member.

25, 26. For **the Address** see Note on the English Constitution, page 322. Its **menacing front** in this case was the declaration of a state of rebellion in Massachusetts, and a call for immediate action to suppress it. One of the **heavy bills of pains and penalities** was that referred to in the opening sentences of this speech as "the grand penal bill." See note, p. 1, l. 8.

PAGE **9**, 5–12. An **occasional system** here means a policy which lacks the guidance of far-reaching principles, and so contents itself with makeshifts to meet new occasions or emergencies as they arise — a policy of shifts. The **object** referred to in l. 6 and 12, and repeatedly throughout this discussion, is the Colonies themselves.

22. That is, 'the subject of their commerce has been treated,' etc. The gentleman was a Mr. Glover, who presented a petition from the West India planters praying that peace might be made with the American Colonies. His literary reputation, complimented here, is now quite forgotten. The **bar** is a movable barrier or rail in the main aisle, beyond which none but officers and members are allowed to pass. All other persons, if permitted to address the House, must do so standing outside this barrier.

PAGE **10**, 9. **state**, where we should say **statement.** See also p. 56, l. 4.

21–23. The exports from England to Africa consisted almost wholly of articles used in barter for slaves, who were shipped thence to the Colonies. The exchange on the coast of Africa was but an incident in a larger transaction beginning in England and ending in America. The amount of these exports is, therefore, rightly added by Burke to the total of direct exports to the Colonies.

PAGE **12**, 10 ff. To secure a more vivid sense of the unexampled vigor and growth of the Colonies than mere statistics could give, Burke pauses here to turn upon the subject the gorgeous illumination of this paragraph. The attempt is a daring one, and is carried out with characteristic opulence and splendor. The good taste of portions of it has been questioned; particularly the academic and conventional fulsomeness of lines 24–35; but that would hardly have counted as a fault in a century which admired such displays.

22, 23. 'Already old enough to read the deeds of his fathers, and able to know what virtue is;' — adapted from Virgil, Ecl. iv. 26.

27–35. **the fourth generation**, since George III., was, not the son, but the grandson of George II. **made Great Britain** by the union with Scotland in 1707. The **higher rank of peerage** was that of Earl, to which Lord Bathurst had been advanced from that of Baron, the lowest hereditary degree. The new title added to the honors of the family was that of Baron Apsley, conferred upon Lord Bathurst's son when the latter became Lord Chancellor.

PAGE **14**, 10. **deceive**, i.e., *beguile, lighten,* — an echo of Latin usage in the case of the parallel word, *fallere.*

27–29. Alluding to the famous story of a Roman father condemned to die of starvation, but secretly nourished by his daughter from her own breasts, until the discovery of her devotion and the admiration it aroused brought about his release.

PAGE **15**, 11. The **Serpent,** — a constellation within the Antartic circle.

17. **run the longitude.** This expression seems not to be current with nautical men; although they naturally interpret it as spoken of a course sailed due east or west, so that the ship's progress is reckoned in longitude alone. On the other hand, the context seems to call for a course due south, or nearly so — following a great circle of longitude, or meridian. It may be that Burke has used the phrase here strictly, as the sailors understand it; meaning that some of the American whalers, after their

African cruise, sailed westward to Brazil, as perhaps they might do on their homeward cruise. Or it may be that without strict question of nautical interpretation he used the sonorous phrase in the other sense, which seemed obvious enough to him.

PAGE **16**, 10. **complexion**, in its original signification of *temperament*, the way in which a person is 'put together;' and so generally in Burke. Passages like that which follows here (pp. 16, 17) justify Matthew Arnold's high praise of Burke, "because almost alone in England he brings thought to bear upon politics; he saturates politics with thought."

PAGE **18**, 9, 10. During the great struggle against the tyranny of the Stuarts.

21–24. Notably in Rome, an example always present to Burke's mind. PAYNE.

PAGE **19**, 27–29. **popular**, — democratic, 'of the people and by the people.' **merely** popular, — wholly so. **the popular representative** — the portion which represents the people. Cf. Burke's more explicit statement, p. 52, l. 34 ff.

31. **aversion** is now followed by *to*, after the manner of its synonyms, *dislike*, *repugnance*, etc. But in Burke's time the force of a Latin etymology or of Latin usage was still strongly felt, and often determined both idiom and meaning of English words. Hence the *from* in this case. The young student, whose sense for idiom and usage needs to grow more sure and more intelligent, should not fail to notice these cases as they arise. Even though unacquainted with Latin, he should lose no time in acquiring the habit of consulting directly the Latin Lexicon. With a little resolution and a little help at first, the difficulties will speedily vanish; while the gain in conscious power and in grasp of language is invaluable. For examples at hand try *piety*, p. 14, l. 27, *communion*, p. 20, l. 27, and *constitution*, p. 22, l. 21.

PAGE **21**, 29–31. This high and jealous spirit of the free-born in Rome in the midst of a servile class may be illustrated from almost any page of Shakespeare's *Julius Cæsar*. Our Teutonic and Scandinavian ancestry was habitually, though incorrectly, called Gothic by writers of the last century. **such were the Poles**, for at this time they had ceased to be an independent nation.

PAGE **22**, 6, 7. The lead seems still to be held by the lawyers. The law is still considered to be the most natural avenue to a political career.

12. **Plantations** — colonies, the *plantings* of a new society or race. The term is regularly so used in acts and charters, and has no reference whatever to cultivation of the soil.

18–21. In the hope of paralyzing all concerted action on the part of the colonists, an order was issued forbidding the calling of town-meetings after Aug. 1, 1774. But a way was soon found, and within the limit of the law, to *hold* such meetings without calling them. The last called meeting before that date was simply *adjourned* to whatever time was thought desirable, and its legal existence was thus prolonged indefinitely.

25, 26. This was Thurlow, a famous lawyer, and afterwards Lord Chancellor. At this time he was Attorney-General, and a conspicuous figure among the Ministers on the Treasury Bench. Directly in front of him was the narrow space of open floor; hence, the designation of his position as "on the floor." To guard its freedom of speech, the House of Commons in earlier times used its utmost powers to prevent any attempt at reporting its debates. It thus became, and still is, a grave breach of decorum for a member to use pencil and paper in the House at all, unless it were to make a brief note of a point to which he would reply. Burke thus understands Thurlow's note-book and pencil, and avails himself of the unusual action to identify, without naming him, the person he means.

32. "Studies pass over into character," or "What we pursue takes shape again in our life;" a famous aphorism from Ovid, Heroid. Ep. xv. 83, quoted also by Bacon in his essay *Of Studies*.

PAGE **23**, 15–17. A splendid figure developed out of Horace's fine phrase in the opening of one of his Odes (Bk. iv. 4), comparing Drusus in his victorious career to Jove's eagle, "the thunder's winged minister," *ministrum fulminis alitem*.

PAGE **24**, 26, 27. **with all its imperfections on its head.** Adapted from the words of the ghost in *Hamlet*, Act I., Scene v. 79.

PAGE **30**, 8. "To the despoiled are still left arms."—JUVENAL, *Sat.* viii. 124.

26. Cf. Acts xix. 19.

33. **more chargeable**, involving heavier charge, more expensive.

PAGE **31**, 35, 36. Quoted from that treasury of bathos, *The Art of Sinking in Poetry*, ch. xi. The remote source of the lines in "one of Dryden's plays," though affirmed by various editors, seems to lack verification.

PAGE **32**, 26, 27. **Sir Edward Coke**, a famous lawyer under Elizabeth and James; Attorney-General in 1603, when Raleigh was tried for treason. "While the prisoner defended himself with the calmest dignity and self-possession, Coke burst into the bitterest invective, brutally addressing the great courtier, as if he were a servant, in the phrase long remembered for its insolence and injustice, 'Thou hast an English face, but a Spanish heart!'" —*Encyc. Brit.*

PAGE **33**, 14, 15. *ex vi termini*—by the very nature of the expression.

PAGE **34**, 29. **addressed**—petitioned the Crown in an Address. Cf. Note on Forms of Procedure, p. 322.

PAGE **36**, 7. **startle**, intransitive, meaning *start*. Cf. Dictionary.

27–29. From *Paradise Lost*, II., 592–594.

PAGE **38**, 12, 13. **American financiers**—financiers who would hope to raise a revenue by taxing America.

24. Mr. Rice.

34. **shall** tell you—'is bound to,' 'is sure to;' with fuller recognition than is now common of the original meaning of this auxiliary.

PAGE **39**, 3. **Acts of Navigation**, passed first in 1651, re-enacted later, and repealed only within our own century. They were designed to secure to England a practical monopoly of the carrying trade by sea. According to them, no vessel of another realm might bring either to England or to her colonies anything except the actual products of that realm. Cf. Encyclopedia, s. v. Navigation Laws.

22, 23. **the pamphlet**, by Dean Tucker, somewhat famous in the discussions of this time, and noticed by Johnson, as well as by Burke in his previous speech on American Taxation.

PAGE **41**, 30. For a clear understanding of the various matters referred to in this paragraph, the student should consult some succinct sketch of the history of Ireland, such, for example, as may be found in Chambers's Encyclopedia; or, better still, with the help of the Index, the subject may be followed up in Green's *Short History of the English People*, a work which ought always to be within reach of the student of English Literature.

PAGE **42**, 17. **Sir John Davis**, or rather, Davies, "Speaker of the First Irish House of Commons in 1612." — PAYNE.

33–35. The two great crises which have occurred in the course of English constitutional history are the revolt of the Parliament against Charles I., and the revolution which brought in William and Mary and established the principle of ministerial responsibility to Parliament. The first is habitually called by Englishmen the Great Rebellion, and the other the Revolution. Their application of these terms must not be confounded with other applications more familiar to us.

PAGE **43**, 3, 4. Burke here goes much further than the facts with regard to Ireland warrant. Ireland has never been "a principal part of England's strength and name."

21. Cf. Green's *Short History*. The parallel between Ireland and Wales is close and cogent so far as concerns the era of repression and savage coercion in each. On the other hand, the difference in the remedial measures applied to the two, and the difference in the results, have furnished a powerful argument in the discussion of the Irish question since Burke's time. Many parts of this speech gather fresh significance when read in the light of recent English history.

33. **as secondary** — as deputy. The word is a noun here.

PAGE **45**, 25–30. From Horace, Odes, Book I. xii. 27, comparing the advent of Augustus upon the distracted world to the rising of Castor and Pollux (the constellation of Gemini), upon the stormy sea. "As soon as the bright star has flashed on the view of the sailors, the raging sea retires from the rocks, winds sink and clouds disperse, and on the open main — so they [the deities] have willed it — the threatening swell is laid."

Page **46,** 6. **shewen,** the older spelling of *show* with the old English plural ending, identical with that of modern German.

Page **48,** 19. "Nature has planted [a barrier] in the way."— Juvenal, *Sat.* x. 152. The Latin poets and the English Bible fortunately were both familiar to Burke's audience, and one of the notable features of his oratory is the telling effect with which he marks his climaxes of thought by some pregnant text from these sources or from the English poets.

Page **49,** 4, 5. From *Comus*, l. 634, 635, inexactly quoted.

28. **temple of British concord,** with obvious allusion to the Temple of Concord in Rome, in which the Senate met during the troublous times of Catiline's conspiracy. The richness and frequency of allusion in Burke far transcend the possibility of annotation, but they should not be overlooked by any one who would feel the force and charm of his writing. See, for example, the whole of the first paragraph on p. 51.

Page **50,** 34, 35. "Not mine is this language, but what Ofellus taught me; rustic, but of wisdom not learned in schools." — Horace, *Sat.* II. ii. 2, 3.

Page **55,** 27, 28. **misguided people,** *sc.* of England. **engaged in,** enlisted in favor of.

Page **62,** 33, 34. **the immediate jewel of his soul,** *Othello*, III. iii. 156. A **great house,** etc. — even slaves feel a pride in the glory of a princely establishment to which they belong, and are willing to sacrifice something for the distinction it confers upon them. A reminiscence from Juvenal, *Sat.* v. 66.

Page **64,** 10, 11. Burke lived to see this state of things reversed, and to approve the abolition of a separate Irish legislature. — Payne.

Page **65,** 5, 6. "Experiments should be tried on objects of no value."

Page **68,** 4. **a Treasury Extent,** — a summary process of compelling the payment of debts due the Crown by seizure of persons, lands, and goods.

13. **empire of Germany,** — the so-called Holy Roman Empire,

already little more than a name in Burke's time, and formally brought to an end in 1806. Cf. Bryce's *Holy Roman Empire.*

PAGE **69**, 31. "The treasure-chest is staked on the game" — the utmost resources of the Colonies will thus be pledged to secure England's success. See p. 70, l. 21 ff.

PAGE **70**, 34, 35. *Paradise Lost*, iv., 96, 97, inexactly quoted.

PAGE **74**, 3, 4. **warning** in the old sense of summons or call. *Sursum corda*, "Lift up your hearts!" — the exhortation which, in all the old liturgies, as well as in the Prayer Book, prefaces the sacrament of the Communion.

15, 16. "Happy and auspicious may it prove!" — the old Roman invocation prefacing all high and solemn acts.

Burke's propositions, it will be noticed, are strictly resolutions, as he calls them. If passed, they would have been mere expressions of the views and opinions of the assembly, and not legislation proper in the form of an Act of Parliament. After the recital of circumstances (Resolutions 1–6), instead of an "enacting clause" to make that which follows law, we have in each section the words, "That it may be proper to." — In this way it was possible to bring these matters to discussion and to a vote; whereas legislation would at best have incurred many delays, and in this case, with the Ministry to oppose it at every step, it could hardly have been brought to the consideration of the House at all. (See Note on Forms of Procedure, p. 323.) Still, could these resolutions have passed, the Ministers would, in effect, have been instructed to introduce and forward the legislation indicated, or else to vacate their places.

This speech shared the fate which attended most of Burke's efforts. Its force and eloquence commanded universal admiration, but were powerless to bring about what he desired. The resolutions were lost by an overwhelming majority. What actually took place is stated in Hansard's *Parliamentary History* as follows:[1]

[1] The statement appended to the first edition of this speech, and copied by almost every editor since, that "upon this [first] Resolution the previous question was put *and carried*," is manifestly in error and absurd.

"Mr. Jenkinson moved the previous question upon the first Resolution. Upon this the House divided. . . . Yeas . . . 78, Noes, . . . 270. So it passed in the negative. The second, third, fourth and thirteenth Resolutions had also the previous question put on them. The others were negatived."

In American practice the motion "that the previous question be *now* put," is a well-known device to stop debate, and to force a vote on the main question pending before the assembly. It is made and seconded by persons who hope to carry first it, and then the main question immediately afterwards. If it fails, things are only as they were before. In England, on the contrary, the motion "that the previous question be put," is a device for killing the main question altogether, without coming to any direct vote upon it; is, in fact, a back-handed way of "tabling" it. The motion is made and seconded by persons who mean to vote against it; for, according to English theory, the assembly is not at liberty to consider further any question upon which it has decided that a vote shall not be taken. Thus, in the present instance, the Ministerial party used the "previous question" to get rid of Burke's troublesome array of facts without either admitting or denying them, and then voted down the policy he based upon those facts.

LORD CHATHAM.

William Pitt, the "Great Commoner," afterwards Earl of Chatham, was born in 1708, was educated at Eton and Oxford, and entered Parliament in 1735. His remarkable powers of oratory and his fiery spirit soon made him one of the foremost men of the Commons, and the most formidable antagonist of Walpole's administration. His uncompromising and successful hostility during these years earned for him the King's lasting resentment. When Walpole was overthrown, and the Opposition came into power, Pitt's mastery in the House should have been recognized, and a seat should have been given him in the Ministry. But it was long before the King could be brought to offer him even a subordinate position. It was not until 1746 that he became Paymaster of the Forces; ten more years passed, and every other experiment was tried, before he was asked to become Prime Minister. At this time he was confessedly the only man capable of saving England from the desperate straits into which the weakness and wickedness of his predecessors had brought her. He soon won for her far more than all that had been lost. He made the name of England to be known and respected in every quarter of the globe. The five years of his administration are accounted the most glorious in all her history. For five years after that Pitt was out of office. After his return in 1766 with the title of Earl of Chatham, ill-health prevented him from taking an active part in the administration of which he was nominally the head; and he retired finally from office two years later. But his interest in public affairs, and especially in whatever concerned the greatness of England, remained undiminished to the end. His most memorable speeches were those in which he denounced that pride and folly which was driving the American Colonies into war; yet he could not endure to think that England should ever lose these jewels from her crown. In 1778, on learning that a motion was to be made to grant to the Colonies their independence, he struggled up from his sick-bed to make a passionate and successful protest against a policy that would dismember England, and let her "fall prostrate before the House of Bourbon." He was already a dying man. At the close of the speech he fell in convulsions, was carried out, and, after lingering a few days, breathed his last, May 11, 1778.

SPEECH ON AMERICAN AFFAIRS.

Reporters of the last century rarely attempted to do more than to give the general drift of thought and argument; at their hands a fiery eloquence like that of Chatham was sure to lose most of its vital quality. Barely five of his speeches seem to have been written out by competent listeners from notes taken on the spot; and in these alone have we any clear approximation to what was actually said. The one we have chosen for this volume claims to have had Chatham's revision; but of this there is no certainty. By many critics it is accounted his master effort. The occasion was this: The assembling of Parliament in November, 1777, had called forth the usual Address to the Throne, congratulating the King on the birth of a princess, indorsing the measures adopted by the Ministry, and promising to support the Crown to the uttermost in its struggle with the Colonies. Chatham seized the occasion to move an Amendment to the Address, and to protest once more against the injustice and folly of the war.

TEXTUAL NOTES.

PAGE **76**, 5–7. The Minister was Lord North. See note to page 6.

30, 31. Adapted from Shakespeare, *Julius Cæsar*, III. ii. 123–125.

PAGE **78**, 21. Lord Amherst, in the campaign of 1758–1759, ending in the capture of Quebec.

28. The force under General Burgoyne, which surrendered at Saratoga, Oct. 13, 1777. "The news of this terrible calamity gave force to the words with which Chatham, at the very time of the surrender, was pressing for peace." — *Green's History.*

33, 34. **in any event,** because British success would only serve to make reconciliation impossible. See p. 79, l. 7–14.

PAGE **79**, 18. Lord Percy.

PAGE **80**, 8, 9. Shakespeare, *Othello*, III. iii. 349 ff.

PAGE **82**, 18. Note how carefully the speaker avoids recognizing the validity of Washington's military title.

PAGE **83**, 20. **but you can address.** A special use of the verb *address* growing out of the special use of the noun explained in the Note on Forms of Procedure, p. 322. The thought is expanded below, l. 24, 25.

PAGE **87**, 13–23. For the classes separately appealed to here, see Note on the House of Lords, p. 318.

27. The walls of the old House of Lords were hung with tapestry representing striking scenes in English history. Among these was the fight with the Spanish Armada, in August, 1588. Lord Howard, Admiral of the English fleet on that occasion, and presumably conspicuous on the tapestry, was the ancestor of Lord Suffolk referred to.

PAGE **88**, 29. **enormous,** in the sense of *atrocious*, a sense which survives in the kindred noun *enormity*.

Chatham's eloquence, like that of Burke, was all in vain upon this question. The amendment was rejected by a vote of 97 to 24.

EDMUND BURKE.

SPEECH AT BRISTOL.

During his first and second Parliaments, Burke sat as member for Wendover. At the dissolution of 1774 he lost his seat because the friend who owned the borough, and who had given him the election, was now in need of money, and must sell the seat to some one who could pay for it. Burke was proposed for a little borough in Yorkshire, and his election was actually secured, when there appeared on the scene a deputation from Bristol, the second city in the kingdom, urging him to "stand" for them. The honor and the opportunity were too great to be neglected. Burke waived his election at Malton, hurried to Bristol, and after an exciting canvass was elected as one of the two representatives of that city. In thanking his constituents after the election, Burke's colleague promised strictly to obey their wishes in all his parliamentary action. With characteristic independence, Burke took a different view of the relation between a representative and his constituents. "Their wishes," said he, "ought to have great weight with him; their opinions, high respect; their business, unremitted attention. It is his duty to sacrifice his repose, his pleasure, his satisfactions to theirs; and, above all, ever and in all cases to prefer their interest to his own. But his unbiassed opinion, his mature judgment, his enlightened conscience, he ought not to sacrifice to you, to any man, or to any set of men living. Your representative owes you, not his industry only, but his judgment; and he betrays, instead of serving you, if he sacrifices it to your opinion. . . . Government and legislation are matters of reason and judgment, and not of inclination; and what sort of reason is that in which the determination precedes the discussion, in which one set of men deliberate and another decide, and where those who form the conclusion are perhaps three hundred miles distant from those who hear the arguments?"

For six years the proud merchants of Bristol were content to be served by a man of this sort. But upon the sudden dissolution of Parliament in 1780, Burke came down to Bristol to find an active canvass against him already in progress. Calling a meeting of the Mayor and prominent citizens, he rendered an account of his stewardship in the speech we are now considering. Its simplicity, its directness, and the calm dignity of its tone, are finely suited to the audience and the occasion, and are in marked contrast with the splendid rhetoric and the magnificent movement of the speech on Conciliation with America. But in devotion to principle, in lofty patriotism, in manly courage, in all that makes the difference between the statesman and the adroit politician, Burke is the same in both. As a noble defence of his own conduct on the part of a public servant, this speech is unsurpassed.

Burke's arguments presuppose a somewhat broad acquaintance with the history of that eventful time, and especially with England's part in it, whether at home or in America, Ireland, France, and the East Indies. The materials for such a synoptic view may be found in Green's *Short History of the English People*, chapter X., sections ii., iii., iv., supplemented by topical readings from other standard works, especially Lecky's *England in the Eighteenth Century*.

TEXTUAL NOTES.

PAGE **89**, 13, 14. **the means of honorable service** — his election to a seat in Parliament.

19. For the general conduct of elections, see note on the House of Commons, p. 320. In the United States all elections are "contested;" i.e., are brought to the test of actual voting. In England such is not always the case. Where there is no hope of carrying the election, or of gain from agitation, the weaker party often saves itself trouble and expense either by putting forward no candidates at all, or by withdrawing them after the canvass has progressed far enough to demonstrate its futility. In such

cases, if there are no more candidates than there are seats to fill, the proper officer "returns" those candidates — certifies that they are duly elected — without actually calling for the votes. Such would seem to have been the case in this election — see note upon the conclusion of this speech. For vivid portrayals of the excitements and strain of a contested election in England, the student should consult George Eliot's *Middlemarch* and Charles Reade's *Put Yourself in His Place.*

PAGE **91,** 20–30. The student can hardly fail to note the striking application which Burke's utterances often have to present conditions in our own politics and public life. Cf. pp. 92–93, 103, *et passim.* This is due to his habit of fixing his attention upon the principles involved, rather than upon the passing forms of life and thought.

PAGE **92,** 24 ff. The most shameless intrigues and bribery were resorted to under George III., to enable him to control the legislation and policy of the realm, that he might rule as well as reign. See Green's *Short History,* X. ii., the House of Commons and the Crown. Burke himself has left a startling picture of this state of affairs in his *Thoughts on the Present Discontents.* A court party in English politics seems happily now no longer possible. The initial step towards reform Burke had already been urging with characteristic energy in the session just ended (see p. 96, l. 2 ff). It was — not unlike our own Civil Service Reform — an attempt to cut short the means for bribery by greatly curtailing the lucrative offices within the gift of the Crown. (Cf. Burke's speech on Economical Reform, delivered Feb. 11, 1780.) The final steps in this same reform were the redistricting of the realm and the extension of the franchise in such a way as to make the House of Commons a body really representing the people. See Macaulay's speech on the Reform Bill, p. 252 ff. of this volume.

35. **violate their consciences**; e.g., by pledging absolute subserviency to the dictates of their constituents. This is the "infallible receipt" spoken of below.

PAGE **96,** 31. This was in August, 1776, when Washington was obliged to abandon New York. The victory seemed so decisive that further resistance on the part of the Colonies was thought to be impossible.

PAGE **98**, 3. **wounds . . . yet green**; i.e., fresh — a Shakespearian touch.

9. **state** = statement; a frequent use in Burke's time.

20 ff. For a full account of Irish affairs as touched upon in this section, consult Lecky's *England in the Eighteenth Century.* chapter xvii. The following sketch, adapted from Professor Goodrich, will serve to supplement and explain what is said in the speech: —

Ireland at this time had a parliament of her own, but not Home Rule, since all legislation was really dictated by the British Ministry. Under the Navigation Laws almost no foreign trade was allowed her, save with England, and that was greatly restricted in order to protect English industries. At last the country was reduced to such distress that in 1778, and again in 1779, it was proposed to remove the restrictions, and allow her a considerable participation in the commerce of the world. Though this was vehemently opposed by Bristol, in common with other great commercial towns, Burke felt himself bound to support the measure. The ministry, however, became alarmed at the general outcry, and no effectual relief was secured in either session. The Irish, indignant at this treatment, copied the example of the Americans, and formed associations pledged to abstain from the use of all English manufactures. In August, 1779, the French and Spanish fleets swept the Channel without resistance, and threatened a descent upon Ireland. England, with her own coasts in danger, and her armies engaged in America and India, could spare no more troops. The Irish people flew to arms. With no commission or authority whatever, save that of the necessity of national defence, the celebrated corps of Irish Volunteers, consisting of over forty thousand men, was organized, armed, and officered within a few weeks. The Irish Parliament, meeting shortly after, approved the conduct of the Volunteers by a unanimous vote of thanks. With these troops at their command, they sent a significant Address to the King, declaring that "it was not by temporary expedients, but by a *free trade* that the nation was to be saved from impending ruin." To enforce this Address, they limited the "supply" they granted the Crown to the period of six months instead of the customary two years. It was now clear that Ireland would follow the American Colonies in rebellion, unless the Ministry yielded at once. Hence the instantaneous concessions so graphically described on page 100. Even the woollen trade,—the "sacred fleece,"—which the English had guarded with such jealous care, was thrown open to the Irish.

PAGE **100**, 1. It was the Irish House of Commons which refused to make any new grant to the English Crown.

27, ff. After their experiences during the seventeenth century, Englishmen came to regard a standing army in the hands of the King as a standing menace to their liberties. By the Bill of Rights (1679) it was declared illegal to raise and maintain such an army except by consent of Parliament. Ever since that time the maintenance and discipline of the English army has been authorized each year anew—and for a single year—by a special Act of Parliament called, somewhat oddly, the Mutiny Act. In the flush of success and of national enthusiasm at this time, the Irish denied the validity in Ireland of all Acts of the English Parliament, though they did not abate in the least their loyalty to the King of England, who was also their King. English Acts being thus inoperative, and the civil law alone being in force, it became impossible to maintain military discipline—not among the Volunteers, for their conduct was a matter of national pride—but among the royal troops in Ireland. The Irish Parliament with great spirit seized the opportunity to prepare a Mutiny Act for Ireland, backed it by an overwhelming vote, and, in accordance with the regular procedure, sent it to the English Ministry for approval—a challenge to acknowledge their independence. The Bill came back with no other change save the loss of those words which limited its action to a single year. At this counter-challenge a panic seized Parliament. It could not be rallied to restore the expunged words, and the Act passed in that form. The maintenance of royal troops in Ireland was thus to be made perpetual, and independent of control by either Parliament; a state of affairs fraught with danger to the liberties of both countries.

PAGE **101**, 14–16. Burke withstood English pride by urging measures for the relief of Ireland in spite of the selfish opposition of his constituents. The **humiliation of Great Britain**, — in being terrified into making concessions, and in the passage of the Perpetual Mutiny Act.

21, ff. The special point of this reference to American affairs comes out on page 103. The news of the loss of Burgoyne's army reached England at the end of the session, December, 1777. After the holiday recess Lord North amazed all parties alike by taking this "well-chosen hour of defeat" to offer to the Americans in effect the very measures of conciliation which Burke had urged, and which Lord North had refused, three years before. At the same time was sent out the Commission described below.

PAGE **103**, 27. **Beauchamp** — pronounced *Beecham*. The student should make sure of the pronunciation of unfamiliar names encountered in his study.

PAGE **104**, 27. For the **frantic tumult about Popery**, see the next section of this speech (p. 108 ff.) and the notes.

PAGE **106**, 2, 3. The Act of 1780 merely allowed an insolvent debtor to establish the fact of his insolvency before a proper court, and left the court to decide whether he should or should not be imprisoned. Moreover, release from imprisonment was not release from the debt, for the payment of which his future earnings were liable. Imprisonment for debt was not finally abolished in England until 1869.

12. **mistaken**, in its original and natural meaning of *taken wrongly, misunderstood*. By a singular shift this word, strictly a passive participle, has come at last to be practically active in meaning, as though it were *mistaking*. It has, in fact, displaced this last in all attributive uses.

PAGE **108**, 14, 15. News of the tragic end of Captain Cook's famous voyage had but lately reached England, and the general interest awakened in the matter gave point to Burke's expression.

22. This section of the speech is worthy of the closest study, whether we regard its theme, its broad statesmanship and humanity, its clear and cogent argument, or the courage and skill displayed in defending an unpopular cause.

For a long time the legal position of Roman Catholics in England had been exceedingly precarious. Outrageous laws against them had been enacted in the passion and intolerance of a previous age. Although these laws had, in large part, been allowed to drop out of actual use, with characteristic English conservatism they were allowed to stand on the Statute Book. They thus became ready weapons in the hands of private avarice or revenge, as is shown in the speech (pp. 111–115). In 1778 the injustice and disgrace of this state of things became intolerable to fair-minded men; and a Relief Bill, annulling the worst of the penal acts, was passed without even a call for a division in either House, so unanimous was the conviction concerning it (p. 118). But the old-time fanaticism of the masses had only been slumbering. At the passage of the Relief Bill it suddenly flashed again into flame. The "Protestant Association" was formed, an organization pledged to bring about the re-enactment of the annulled law and to prevent any further measures of relief. Under such stimulus madness spread far and fast. Rioting soon began in Edinburgh and Glasgow, where furious mobs destroyed the houses and property of Catholics and of those suspected of sympathizing with them. After months of fitful disorder in various parts of the realm, matters culminated in June, 1780, in an attempt which recalls a very recent chapter in our own history — but with results more immediately tragic than in our case. A monster petition, calling for immediate repeal of the Relief Bill, was prepared; and Lord George Gordon, a leader in the agitation, undertook to lay it before Parliament in person, and at the head of an army of his followers. On the afternoon of June 2, three great bodies of men, wearing blue cockades and marching by different roads, met in front of the Parliament building just as the Houses were assembling. The petition was presented as planned. The roaring mob surged in, filled all the courts, stairways, and lobbies, insulted and outraged members, and for many hours held the Houses in a state of siege. At nightfall it dispersed to begin its work of pillage and destruction elsewhere. The five days and nights that followed were a veritable reign of terror. All authority was paralyzed. The city was completely at the mercy of the mob. For an admirable picture of the scenes in London, the student is referred to Dickens's *Barnaby Rudge*. The history of the whole matter may be read in Lecky's *England in the Eighteenth Century*, chapter xiii.

PAGE **109**. Bristol had sympathized with the "No Popery" movement, and had had its share of disorder as well. There is grave irony, therefore, in Burke's remarks here and on page 116.

PAGE **111**, 16. **pious**, in the old Roman sense of reverent attitude toward *all* natural claims, whether from above, or around, or beneath us; — here used with special reference to the claims of humanity and justice. Students of Latin should look up in this connection the various connotations of Virgil's *pius Æneas*.

20, 21. **the saying mass**. The student will notice the change in this idiom since Burke's time. Wherever the gerund has become so nearly like a common noun as to take an adjective modifier, the noun-construction is now commonly extended to its object as well — "saying mass," or else "*the* saying *of* mass."

PAGE **112**, 18. **Revolution**. See note to p. 42, l. 33–35.

PAGE **113**, 27–30. The children of Catholic families were commonly educated in France, under circumstances not at all calculated to inspire in them patriotism and a love for free government.

PAGE **114**, 9. For the Talbots, consult an Encyclopædia or Biographical Dictionary.

PAGE **116**, 21 ff. Writers and speakers of the last century had a notable fashion of diversifying their compositions with what they called "characters," — elaborate and rhetorical descriptions of persons, — an example of which we have already encountered in this speech. An academic flavor and fulsomeness almost always characterize these passages, and in this instance these qualities are the more conspicuous because of the general simplicity and directness of the context.

PAGE **117**, 4. *peculium* — "a special fund for private and personal uses." The student will be interested to trace the origin of this word from the Latin *pecus*, and the development of meaning in its English cognates and derivatives, *peculiar*, *pecuniary*, *peculate*, and *fee*. Consult the Latin Lexicon and the Etymological Dictionary.

13, 14. The "Nullum Tempus Act." See Lecky, Index, s.v.

PAGE **121**, 6. The **most Protestant part of this Protestant Empire** was, of course, the American Colonies. Compare what Burke says of them in his Speech on Conciliation, p. 20 of this volume.

PAGE **125**, 10–14. The **persecutions** under Philip of Spain, carried out by the bloody Alva. See Motley's *Rise of the Dutch Republic.* Many craftsmen of the Low Countries found refuge in England, and planted their trades there.

33. Austria, as the successor of the "Holy Roman Empire," was *the* imperial court of Europe. Russia was not yet accorded that rank; the French and German Empires were yet to be.

PAGE **126**, 11. The minister was Necker, the famous banker and financier of France.

PAGE **127**, 8–12. This was Thurlow. See note to p. 22, l. 25, 26.

PAGE **132**, 29. **our resolves** — the resolution refusing to repeal the Relief Bill. See p. 131, l. 7 ff.

PAGE **133**, 5, 6. **read three times**, passed the three formal readings which mark the regular stages in the progress of an Act through the House. See Note on Forms of Procedure, p. 323.

9. **offences of presumption** — presumed offences.

PAGE **134**, 5. **lean more to the Crown**, support the kingly power and prerogative. See note to p. 113, l. 27–30.

25. "No man ever touched with such force that proud and cruel spirit which actuates a people who hold others in subjection. It was just the spirit of the Athenian mob toward their colonies, and of every Roman toward the provinces of the empire, and it was, no doubt, one principal cause of the American war." — PROFESSOR GOODRICH.

PAGE **135**, 31 ff. An expansion of his own famous utterance in the Speech on Conciliation (p. 32): "I do not know the method of drawing up an indictment against a whole people."

PAGE **136**, 30. **help it**, *not* in the sense now common, of *prevent it.* It is worth while to notice how the scathing flash of irony, with which the paragraph opens, furnishes the heat and convincing force with which the orator resumes and welds together as one the various topics with which he has separately dealt. He had *said* the same before (p. 108), but now the underlying unity is felt.

35. In these concluding paragraphs Burke addresses himself to those *practical* arguments — alas, too familiar to us all! — which may generally be counted on to bring to terms a politician somewhat too high-minded. If such words as these could be read and taken to heart by all in our country who are to exercise the public trusts of citizenship, we should have a very different condition of things from that which we see all about us.

Upon the conclusion of this speech resolutions were adopted by the meeting, warmly commending Mr. Burke's conduct in Parliament, and asking him to present himself as a candidate for the coming election. Having received this indorsement, Mr. Burke announced his candidacy in the usual manner, and began his canvass. Two days later one of his three competitors fell dead, overcome with the excitement and strain of the contest. Next morning — the very morning of the election — Mr. Burke, satisfied that his election was hopeless, publicly withdrew — "declined the poll" — in a little speech which is a fit pendant to the one just read. It may be found in any complete edition of his works.

Through the influence of Lord Rockingham, Burke was at once returned from Malton, and sat for that borough till the close of his political life.

LORD ERSKINE.

Thomas, Lord Erskine, was born in Edinburgh, in 1750, of a family famous in Scottish history, but at this time sadly reduced in circumstances. He grew to be a lad of much brightness and promise, and his ambition was to enter a learned profession; but the expense of an education could not be met. At fourteen years of age he was sent to sea as a midshipman; and he spent eleven years of service in the navy and the army before he found it possible to prepare himself for the calling in which he afterwards attained distinction as an advocate and orator. Meantime he had married at twenty, and was struggling to maintain his growing family. At the age of twenty-eight he was admitted to the bar. His first case, coming fortunately not long afterwards, revealed such surprising courage, eloquence, and forensic skill, that his fame and fortune were instantly made. His talents were engaged in the most celebrated trials of those times. In 1793 he entered Parliament. His brilliant career culminated in 1806, when the dream of his life was realized, and he became Lord Chancellor of England. This honor, however, was not long to be his; for he had to vacate the woolsack in the next year, on the downfall of the Grenville Ministry. His later life again was clouded by poverty and by that idleness to which English etiquette condemns distinguished lawyers who have once reached the highest position open to the profession. He died in 1823, in Scotland, on the only visit he ever made to the native land he had left fifty years before.

The effect of his oratory upon those who heard him was surprising. Into the dull, heavy style of the courts he infused a warmth, a daring, an imaginative play, unknown before his time. His most memorable speeches were delivered before the Court of the King's

Bench, and from this series the one in behalf of Stockdale has been chosen as an example of argument and eloquence specially addressed to a jury. The circumstances were these: During the slow progress of the trial of Warren Hastings, a Scotch clergyman had written, and a Mr. John Stockdale of London had published, a pamphlet defending Mr. Hastings, and criticizing severely the conduct of the prosecution. The managers brought the matter before the House, and secured an order directing the Attorney-General to prosecute Mr. Stockdale for libel. The liberty of the press was a question which had already been before the public in two separate aspects. Though direct censorship had ceased shortly after the downfall of the Stuarts, there long remained two formidable engines of coercion which the political party in power could use — and did use unmercifully — to prevent the publication of matters distasteful to it. One was the power of Parliament to punish by summary imprisonment anything which it deemed a breach of its ancient privileges; and such it considered the publication of any report of its proceedings, save such as itself had authorized (see note to page 22). But the battle upon this point had recently been fought out; the Commons, after a fierce struggle, had yielded; and since that time reporters have regularly had admission to the gallery of the House. Prosecution for "seditious libel" was the other agency employed; and it was at that time rendered far more effective for mischief than it could be now, by the following means: Instead of submitting to the jury the whole question of the guilt or innocence of the defendant in view of *all* the facts and motives shown, as was done in the case of every other crime and misdemeanor, the practice in libel suits was to allow the jury to consider nothing beyond the question whether the defendant had or had not published the matter as alleged. The vital question of the guilt or innocence of the publication was reserved for the decision of the judge alone; and in these political suits he was often an interested party. "Writers, prosecuted by an officer of the crown, without the investigation of a grand jury, and denied even a trial by their peers, were placed beyond the pale of the law." This vicious principle had been clearly revealed by the persecutions which Wilkes endured, and in the

Letters of Junius. Mr. Erskine had attacked it with splendid force and skill in his defence of the Dean of St. Asaph's, claiming for the person accused of libel the same right which was accorded to one accused of any other crime or misdemeanor known to the law of England — the right to be tried by the jury on the *whole* issue raised. Mr. Erskine's argument on that occasion was before judges alone, and, naturally enough, he was unceremoniously overruled. But the matter was not to be thus summarily disposed of. The public was aroused. The trial of Stockdale soon afforded an opportunity of bringing the question before the jury itself. Their answer was the verdict "Not Guilty," rendered in defiance of all precedent, and in spite of the fact that the publication was admitted. It was the last case of libel tried under the old *régime.* In 1792 Parliament was constrained to register this triumph of freedom by establishing in the Libel Act the very principle for which Mr. Erskine had contended.

Among the champions of liberty Erskine stands thus linked with Milton, whose eloquent appeal "for the liberty of unlicensed printing," — his *Areopagitica* — was the trumpet-call which opened the attack on this stronghold of tyranny. The history of this interesting subject may be found in May's *Constitutional History of England*, chapter ix.

TEXTUAL NOTES.

PAGE **141**, 5–7. The reference is to Erskine's political friends, Fox and the Whigs, and especially Burke, whom he greatly admired. See repeated references to them farther on in this speech.

PAGE **142**, 10. **information**. The precise meaning of technical terms should be ascertained upon the student's first encounter with them. See also, *innuendoes*, *fine*, *farm*, *rent*, and others farther on.

PAGE **152**, 18 ff. Compare with this Macaulay's description of the famous trial in his Essay on Warren Hastings.

PAGE **153**, 8. **without prospect of conclusion**. The trial dragged on for seven years. One hundred and forty-eight days were actually spent in its sessions.

PAGE **155**, 24. **This great hall** was Westminster Hall, built by William Rufus. It still stands, and forms part of the new Houses of Parliament. The Court of the King's Bench, before which Erskine was speaking, sat under the same roof, and in a chamber directly adjoining it. See also p. 178.

PAGE **156**, 27. **brought home to** — intrusted to, undertaken by.

PAGE **159**, 22. **government**, in the parliamentary sense explained in the next sentence.

27. **I wish he would.** To admit that the Tory party then in power was a faction would be to give up the political battle.

34. **my friends** — Burke, Fox, and the Whigs now in opposition.

PAGE **160**, 18. A committee which was appointed in 1781 to inquire into East Indian affairs, and which reported in 1782. The charges made by it are not to be confounded with the Articles of Impeachment presented by the House. See below, p. 161, l. 3.

PAGE **162**, 20–27. A striking proof of the dangers at that time attending free speech is found in the extreme pains Erskine thinks it necessary to take in order to guard what he says from the charge of interfering with, or anticipating, the regular process of judicial investigation — the very same charge under which his client was suffering.

PAGE **163**, 11. **Verres.** Consult the Classical Dictionary, s.v.

PAGE **166**, 31. **Gothic**, a term formerly used with utmost looseness of signification, to designate confusedly anything Teutonic, mediæval, or barbaric. Such was its meaning as at first applied to a style of architecture. In no other sense were our ancestors Gothic.

PAGE **170**, 6. **amenable to no law**, with reference to the privileges of members of Parliament, and particularly to their exemption from action or indictment for any freedom of speech they may use.

PAGE **170**, 28 ff. The keen edge which lurks under these innocent-looking remarks will be appreciated when we recall the notorious fact that Pitt carried the very same majority with him on *both* sides of the impeachment question — first against, and then for it. The interval of ten days between the two votes sufficed for the Minister's change of front; but the rank and file were so well trained that, without the least warning of what was intended, they executed their manœuvre in perfect form, at the word of command given on the very evening the vote was taken.

PAGE **171**, 12. **assumed** — exercised, brought into requisition.

21. **the saving judgment** — the judgment which forbears to punish as crimes mere errors of the understanding.

PAGE **172**, 8. **extraordinary**, since the trial is based upon "information" only, and not upon regular indictment by a grand jury, as explained below.

30. **the law**, i. e., the common law, working through its ordinary instruments.

PAGE **174**, 24. **commentaries**, where we should say *comments*. There is not a little adroitness in the suggestion which follows, that the Attorney-General is, after all, only discharging perfunctorily his official duty.

PAGE **180**, 1. The position of the word *only* in a sentence is a matter which used to be determined almost wholly by considerations of euphony and rhythm. The claims of clearness and of precision are now more generally recognized, and we are apt to insist that the word be placed next to that which it qualifies. The difference is sharply brought out in this particular case. Odd as the sentence now sounds, it would be difficult, unless we recast the whole, to find another place for *only* without destroying either sense or rhythm, or both.

DANIEL WEBSTER.

Daniel Webster, statesman and orator, was born in Salisbury, N. H., Jan. 18, 1782. His father, a sturdy frontiersman, soldier, farmer, member of the legislature, and county judge, was, after the manner of his kind, always struggling with poverty, and handicapped with a sense of the deficiencies of his early education. He purposed that Daniel, his youngest son, a delicate lad and little fitted for the heavy tasks of a farmer's life, should not be so handicapped. Through struggles and self-denial by no means rare in such cases, a way was made to send him to college. After an exceedingly brief and fragmentary preparation, he entered Dartmouth College in 1797, and was graduated in 1801, at the age of nineteen. He turned at once to the study of law, supporting himself meanwhile, and assisting his elder brother in college, by copying, teaching, and other miscellaneous labors. Admitted to the bar in 1805, his remarkable abilities soon gained him recognition, and the field of political life opened before him. In 1813 he took his seat in Congress. From this time on his life is writ so large on the pages of his country's history as to need little further notice here. The greatest service he rendered his country was doubtless as champion of the national idea, and the speech before us is probably his most memorable utterance upon that subject. Honors and fame came thick upon him — all save the honor he had come to covet most, the Presidency. After thirty-nine years of public life he died Oct. 24, 1852.

SPEECH IN REPLY TO HAYNE.

The circumstances which called forth this speech may be thus summarized: For a long time before 1830 there had been a grave divergence of conviction among American statesmen as to the real nature of the union between the various States, and as to the limitations thereby imposed upon the powers of the separate States, as well as the limitations exercised by them upon the powers of the general government. One side held that the United States was *one* nation; that the general government was charged with the conduct of all matters which concern the nation as a whole; that laws made by the representatives of all in the general government are binding upon all alike; and that such laws may be peacefully set aside in one of two ways only, either by having them declared unconstitutional by the Supreme Court, or by having them repealed by the power which made them. The other side held the several States to be sovereign powers, very much as if they were separate nations, united, it is true, for certain common purposes, and delegating certain limited powers to a common organization; but reserving each to itself alone the decision as to whether measures enacted by the general government should be operative within its territory. This was the doctrine of State-Rights; and its application in nullifying laws passed by Congress was at this time much talked about, and was soon to be tried by South Carolina with this very Robert Y. Hayne as Governor. These views were not confined to separate sections of country; but the National idea found its strongest support in New England, while the State-Rights idea — with its corollary, nullification — was warmly espoused in the South.

At the end of December, 1829, Mr. Foote of Connecticut introduced into the Senate the innocent resolution, printed on page 185 of this volume, calling for an inquiry into the sales and surveys of the public lands. Nothing special was elicited by the fitful discussion which ensued until, on January 19, Mr. Robert Y. Hayne of South Carolina made a speech, "accusing the New England States of a selfish design to retard the growth of the Western States — a design originating the tariff;" and appealing to a natural sympathy, which, as he affirmed, existed between the Western and the Southern States, and which should unite them against the policy and the assumption of New England. Engaged as Mr. Webster was at this time in the Supreme Court, he had not followed the discussion, and had no thought of taking part in it at all until by chance he heard this speech of Mr. Hayne. Its tone and spirit were so unusual that he felt it must be answered. He rose to speak as soon as Mr. Hayne sat down, but an adjournment of the Senate postponed his reply. Next day he delivered his first speech in this debate, defending New England against the charges brought against her, and upholding the doctrine of a national union and a national policy, as opposed to the divisive tendencies and sectional jealousies to which appeal had been made. The discussion took on at once a range and an importance far transcending the scope of the simple resolution which started it. The champions of State-Rights and Nullification, together with those who insisted that slavery should be provided for in the settlement of new territories, rallied to the charge. "There seemed to be," said an observer, "a preconcerted action on the part of Southern members to break down the Northern men, and to destroy their influence by a premeditated assault." John C. Calhoun, the foremost of them all, was presiding officer of the Senate, and could take no part in the debate; but his place in the lists was made good by Thomas H. Benton and Robert Y. Hayne. The speech of the latter, in particular, by its eloquence and acuteness, as well as by the relentlessness of its personal attack, produced a profound impression. By many persons it was felt to be unanswerable. At its close the Senate adjourned.

This second speech of Mr. Hayne was the one to which Mr. Webster was next morning to reply. The previous strokes in this battle-royal had roused public interest to the highest pitch. For two or three days strangers had been pouring into Washington to witness the outcome. When the Senate met, all the usual restrictions had proved of no avail against the mighty throng that gathered there. "Its chamber — galleries, floor, and even lobbies — was filled to its utmost capacity. The very stairways were dark with men who clung to one another like bees in a swarm." The ordinary ceremonial of opening the session of the Senate was impatiently set aside. In the presence of this vast and anxious audience, without the least sign of tremor or perturbation, Mr. Webster rose and began his second speech upon the resolution of Mr. Foote.

TEXTUAL NOTES.

PAGE **186**, 15. **elsewhere** — in the Supreme Court, where Mr. Webster had a very important suit pending.

PAGE **188**, 9. The friend was the famous Thomas H. Benton, who had twice taken an important part in the debate. His first speech — referred to in the next paragraph — Mr. Webster did not hear.

19 ff. The notes used by Mr. Webster on these two occasions have been preserved. They are of the briefest possible nature, covering in the one case only three, and in the other case only five loosely written letter-sheets. But the great questions involved had been thought out by him many months before, as he himself has told us.

PAGE **192**, 8. **the Missouri question**, referring to the bitter strife which arose over the admission of Missouri as a slave-state. Cf. any good History of the United States s.v. The Missouri Compromise. The same question in its later aspects is discussed by Mr. Calhoun in his speech printed in this volume.

PAGE **194**, 9. In determining the number of Representatives in Congress to which any State was entitled, the number of free persons in it was increased by three-fifths of the whole number of slaves it contained. Thus, in proportion to the number of voters, the slave-states had a much larger representation than the free-states. Cf. the Constitution, Article I., section 2.

PAGE **202**, 15, 16. Because the terms "neutral" and "belligerent" are applicable only to a state of war, and lose all their significance in peace.

PAGE **204**, 12. *Teucro duce* — "with Teucer as my leader" — from a famous line in Horace. The "Teucer" thus referred to was none other than Calhoun himself, the "Mr. President" whom he here addresses, now the leader of the extreme Southern wing, presumably even in its opposition to the national policy of internal improvements which Mr. Webster learned from him in 1816. Few things in the speech are more adroit than the manner in which Mr. Webster here parries and returns with a home-thrust the double charge of personal inconsistency and of sectional greed and selfishness. By the pleasantry of this sally upon Mr. Calhoun he withdraws the attention of the audience from his immediate antagonist, and fixes it upon the real leader and champion of these extreme views. With unfailing good humor he piles up opinions and votes of "leading and distinguished gentlemen from South Carolina" in maintenance of the very policy his opponent has condemned. He recalls how gladly he followed the star of South Carolina — until it changed its position. The Vice-President at last winces. He interrupts the speech with a question (p. 209) which may be taken either as an indignant denial of any change in his views, or as a "bluff." Nothing could have better served Mr. Webster's purpose. Having "drawn" Mr. Calhoun, he graciously accepts his remark in the *former* sense, and then recalls that there are other gentlemen, too, from South Carolina who are not implacably opposed to internal improvements at the general cost — if only they are to be carried out in South Carolina.

PAGE **205**, 21. *causa causans* — the *causing* cause, — the schoolmen's phrase to distinguish the essential or efficient cause from various co-operating or conditioning causes.

PAGE **207**, 4. *et noscitur a sociis* — "and he is [was] recognized by his companions." But Mr. Webster seems to give it a punning turn not borne out by the Latin — "and he was known by the company he kept."

PAGE **207**, 13. For the party designations of those days, see note to page 298.

PAGE **212**, 21. **had proved a legal settlement** in South Carolina — was found to be regularly domiciled there.

PAGE **218**, 11. The **Hartford Convention** of 1814, a convention of New England delegates opposed to the policy of the government, and especially to the war with England. It sat with closed doors, and was at the time strongly suspected of treasonable designs. No proof, however, of this charge has ever been produced, and it is now generally discredited. Cf. U. S. History.

PAGE **220**, 12–15. The peculiar turn of expression here is a reminiscence of the closing lines of Dryden's *Alexander's Feast.*

The student who has his English classics in mind cannot fail to notice the frequent occurrence of such echoes in this speech, and the striking originality of their application.

PAGE **221**, 29. With this eloquent passage Mr. Webster leaves the personal and sectional matters that had been forced upon him, for what was much more congenial to his nature — the discussion of principles. All through this defence, in fact, has been apparent his strong feeling that personalities have no claim whatever upon public attention, save as they stand for ideas and principles. Mr. Webster's manly dignity and his unruffled temper in repelling a caustic attack have made this section a classic of its kind. It may be profitably compared with Burke's defence of himself in his Speech at Bristol.

PAGE **223**, 29. The citation is from the famous resolutions of the Virginia Legislature, passed December, 1798, to express its opposition to the Alien and Sedition Laws recently enacted by Congress. The language was understood to be Mr. Madison's.

PAGE **227**, 5, 6. One finds here, and farther on (p. 239), the first drafts of Lincoln's immortal phrase — "government of the people, by the people, and for the people." See p. 312.

PAGE **234**, 21. The *not* does not appear in any edition consulted, but seems imperatively demanded by the sense. Its omission was doubtless due to a slip of the printer and the proof-reader.

PAGE **246**, 7. **John Fries** was a turbulent fellow who, in 1799, headed some Pennsylvanians in riotous resistance to the laws of the United States and in the rescue of prisoners. He was twice tried for treason, twice convicted and sentenced to be hanged, but was finally pardoned by the President.

"At the conclusion of Mr. Webster's argument, General Hayne rose to reply. Although one of his friends proposed an adjournment, he declined to avail himself of it, and addressed the Senate for a short time on the constitutional question. Mr. Webster then rose again, restated both sides of the controversy with great force, giving General Hayne the benefit of that clear setting forth of the position of an adversary, which none could do better than Mr. Webster, and which none could doubt was the strongest method of stating it; and then following it, step by step, with the appropriate answer. This was the reduction of the whole controversy to the severest forms of logic." — *Life of Daniel Webster*, by GEORGE T. CURTIS, vol. i. p. 359.

Two years passed, and again Mr. Webster faced this same question in the Senate, but this time with an antagonist more formidable than Mr. Hayne. Mr. Calhoun's speech on that occasion has been considered as perhaps the ablest effort of his life. It became the scripture from which almost a whole generation of the young men of the South learned those lessons which afterward carried them into the War of Secession. Mr. Webster's reply was this time more closely reasoned, more compact and powerful as an intellectual effort than the earlier speech, though less interesting, it may be, to the general reader. But the great debate of 1830 seems to have exhausted the arguments upon this subject. Whatever was said later upon either side seemed to be but restatement or re-arrangement of what was there laid down. One thing only remained, and that was to bring the opposing views to the arbitrament of actual conflict. That crisis seemed actually to have come, even while this second debate was going on. South Carolina, with Mr. Hayne as Governor, undertook to put her views in practice, and armed herself to stop the collection of United States duties in her ports. President Jackson sternly prepared to enforce the laws with all the powers the goverment could wield. But the storm that threatened did not break then after all. The matter was compromised, and South Carolina took back her Act of Nullification. The final issue came a generation later, and on those battle-fields where brave men freely gave their lives "that government of the people, by the people, and for the people should not perish from the earth."

LORD MACAULAY.

Thomas Babington Macaulay was born Oct. 25, 1800, the eldest son of Zachary Macaulay, a prominent reformer and abolitionist, a follower and friend of Wilberforce. His boyhood was passed at his father's home in London, and afterwards at a private school, until at eighteen years of age he entered Cambridge. Here he took his degree in 1822, and was elected Fellow two years later. While yet a mere child he had become interested in the great public questions discussed at his father's table. At the university he won academic honors for composition, oratory, and political debate. Thus were already outlined the two fields of his future achievement. His literary career opened first with the publication in 1825 of his famous essay on Milton, the first of a long and brilliant series of papers which ended only with his death. In 1842 appeared his *Lays of Ancient Rome*, inspired in part by a visit to Italy. Of his *History of England* two volumes were published in 1848, two in 1855, and one after his death.

His political career began with his entrance into Parliament in 1830. It continued unbroken for seventeen years, and was even resumed for a time at a later period. His voice was heard with no uncertain sound on all the great questions of that stirring time, but he is specially remembered for the ardor with which he threw himself into the great Reform Movement of 1832. Twice he held cabinet offices in Whig Ministries; and once he was sent to India as legal adviser to the Supreme Council and president of an important Commission. In 1857 he was made Baron Macaulay of Rothley — "the first literary man to receive such a distinction."

Into each of these careers he put energy and talent enough to have made him famous without aid from the other. Between them both his life was crowded with effort and excitement beyond the lot of most famous men, and beyond the powers of his own abounding vitality to sustain. A weakness of the heart ended in his death on December 28, 1859.

SPEECH ON THE REFORM BILL.

The House of Commons was formally established in England when Edward I. in 1295 summoned to his Great Council two burgesses to be elected "from every city, borough, and leading town" of his realm, and two knights from every shire. A body so constituted must have been fairly representative of the nation. There was, however, no definite settlement of the details of representation; it still remained with the Crown to determine what boroughs should be invited to participate. In the sixteenth century the Tudor sovereigns had learned the art of managing their Commons by managing the election of members. Elections, of course, could most easily be controlled in small and unimportant places; hence such from time to time were added to the list. Thus began one form of the "rotten borough." In the seventeenth century representation in Parliament crystallized permanently almost in the form in which the Tudors left it. As time went on, places once important and populous often dwindled or stood still, while the mighty towns of modern England were growing up about them, and wholly without representation. These boroughs thus accidentally decayed were quite as ready means for corrupt uses — were quite as "rotten" — as were those of the other sort. By this time Parliament had ceased to be in any true sense the representative of the nation. The pressure of the "new wine in old bottles" was already alarming in the eighteenth century, when it attracted the attention of such men as Chatham and Burke. But consideration of it was impossible amid the tumults of the French Revolution and of the Napoleonic wars. It had to wait till 1820, when Lord John Russell proposed his bill for Parliamentary Reform. The demand was nothing less than that a corrupt Parliament, intrenched within these "rotten boroughs," should reform itself, and abolish these instruments of corruption. This, of course, it would not do without external pressure. The bill was therefore promptly rejected, as were others brought forward in later sessions. In 1830 the popular demand grew so formidable that Wellington and the Tory Ministry, who held out stiffly against it, were forced to resign, while the Whigs under Earl Grey came into power, pledged to the reform. On the 1st of March, 1831, their scheme was laid before Parliament by Lord John Russell, who, though not a Cabinet Minister, was chosen for this important duty on account of his ability and of his long and honorable service in the cause. It was proposed to disfranchise fifty-six "rotten" boroughs, and to distribute their one hundred and forty-three seats among the great cities and the towns hitherto not represented. The battle thus joined continued with but little interruption for fifteen months. In it was engaged every man of ability on either side, while the whole nation waited for the issue with ever-growing excitement. The bill came to its second reading with a majority of one vote. In the discussions which followed, the Ministry was defeated on a point of detail, and promptly dissolved Parliament and appealed to the people in a new election. Intrenched as corruption was in the existing order of things, the reformers were nevertheless returned in overwhelming majority. At the assembling of the new Parliament in June, Lord John Russell introduced his bill again, in the form known as the Second Reform Bill. All that its opponents in the House could now do was to delay its progress. It finally passed the Commons by a majority of over a hundred votes, but was rejected by the Lords. Parliament was then prorogued. After the recess the bill was introduced for the third time, and at the end of March had passed the House by a majority more decisive than ever. Popular excitement was now at fever heat, and repeatedly broke out into rioting. The Lords seemed as obstinately bent on defeating the measure as ever before; but the gravity of the crisis, and the knowledge that the king's consent had been given to the creation of enough new peers to overcome their majority, at last sobered them. Wellington and his followers decided to withdraw from the final deliberations and voting, and to allow the bill to pass in their absence, rather than face an issue so hazardous to their order. The bill became law on June 7, 1832.

During this long debate Macaulay spoke many times. Of the five speeches on the Reform Bill, which he himself corrected for the press, we have chosen the first as the most comprehensive and the best suited for our purpose. In it his characteristic brilliancy of expression and of argument are abundantly exemplified. Those who are interested in looking further into the points of his style will find the matter fully treated in Minto's *Manual of English Prose Literature*, pp. 76–130.

TEXTUAL NOTES.

PAGE **252**, 20. **Paymaster of the Forces** — Lord John Russell, mentioned in the Introductory Note above. He was afterwards Earl Russell, and a conspicuous figure in European politics as late as the close of the Crimean War. For the "courtesy-title" borne by him at this time, see note to page 6, l. 9–14.

It is not thought necessary to burden the student with the names of all the persons referred to in this speech. Many of them are unknown to general fame. The exceptions will be noted as they occur.

PAGE **253**, 28. **those cheers** — the cries of "Hear, hear," with which the Commons punctuate, or rather annotate, the utterances of their speakers. An astonishing variety of meaning can be put into them. Macaulay understands the contemptuous irony of these cheers from the Opposition. So, too, on the next page, l. 12.

PAGE **258**, 33, 34. **Benevolences** and **Shipmoney** were exactions of money made by the earlier English kings without authorization of Parliament, and consequently illegal.

PAGE **259**, 24. **liverymen** — members of the great guilds of London, entitled to wear their livery, and to vote as burgesses.

PAGE **265**, 5–7. The list brought forward in this debate contained such names as North, Burke, Pitt, Fox, Grenville, Wellington, Brougham, and Grey. Macaulay himself might have been added — member for Calne, "one of the most degraded of the rotten boroughs," as one of the speakers took pains to remind him.

PAGE **267**, 5. The famous agitator and "uncrowned king of Ireland," Daniel O'Connell. Note the striking reference to him again, p. 269, l. 24–26. The circumstances here concerned are these: The franchise in Ireland had been limited to persons who owned freehold property of forty shillings' yearly value or rental. On the basis of this representation, in 1828 O'Connell was elected to Parliament as member for Clare, in spite of the fact that he was a Catholic, and that Catholics were ineligible to sit in Parliament. Ireland was aflame with enthusiasm over this victory. The English Ministry under Wellington, fearing lest civil war should break out, consented in 1829 to measures of relief which allowed Catholics to sit in Parliament, but at the same time raised the property qualification of voters. O'Connell now came forward to claim his seat; but the Commons insisted that, having been elected on the old basis of representation, he must take the oaths formerly required, and renounce Catholicism, which he refused to do. The seat was then declared vacant, and a new election was ordered. O'Connell was triumphantly returned, and took his seat in 1830. The supposed "crime" of the electors of Clare was their defiance of the established order in electing a representative who could not legally sit in Parliament. The supposed "punishment" was the disfranchising of the poorer electors, Protestant as well as Catholic.

PAGE **268**, 2. Sir Robert Peel, member of the last Tory cabinet, and a distinguished statesman, in spite of the humiliating position in which he here appears.

The **Test and Corporation Acts** mentioned below were parts of the machinery for disqualifying Catholics for positions of public trust.

PAGE **269**, 24. The **Rent** was O'Connell's campaign fund, raised by the Catholic Association through voluntary contributions from all classes in Ireland. It amounted at times to $2,500 per month.

28. **that . . . cruel test of military fidelity**—in the case of

soldiers ordered to charge upon mobs of their countrymen, with whose cause they could not but sympathize.

PAGE **270**, 5–9. The reference is to the memorable Revolution of July, and the downfall and exile from France of the last of her Bourbon kings.

22. **property divided against itself.** The newer wealth of England — her manufactures and trade — obstinately opposed in its claims for representation by the older wealth of landed estates in the hands of the old aristocracy.

JOHN C. CALHOUN.

John C. Calhoun was of Irish Presbyterian descent, born in the Abbeville District, South Carolina, March 18, 1782. His father died while he was yet young. His boyhood and youth were spent with his mother on the plantation, and without any regular schooling until he was eighteen years old. It is a striking proof of the intensity and power of his mind, that after only two years of study under private instruction he was able to enter the Junior class in Yale College. Two years later he was graduated with honors. Three years more he devoted to the study of law. Not long after this he was elected to the legislature of his State, and in 1811 he was sent to Congress, taking at once a prominent place as a supporter of the measures which brought on the war with England. He was of the same age as Daniel Webster, and but little younger than Henry Clay — men with whom he was so incessantly brought in contact in public life, that, in spite of the fact of their almost constant antagonism, the three are often spoken of as "the great triumvirate" of American statesmen. Mr. Calhoun had the qualities of a born leader of men — high intellectual force, albeit somewhat narrow, unflinching determination, fiery earnestness, and splendid oratorical powers. During the early part of his career he was broadly and generously national in the policies he supported, as is seen in Mr. Webster's sketch (pp. 204–207 of this volume). He filled successively many high positions, becoming Vice-President under John Quincy Adams, and again under Jackson in 1829. About this time his attitude seemed to change. His view was more and more concentrated upon the institutions and interests of the South. Henceforward he stood as the champion of State-Rights, and of whatever that doctrine finally involved — nullification and the extension of the slave-holding power. As such he was frequently opposed to Mr. Webster and Mr. Clay (see concluding note to Mr. Webster's speech, p. 365). As time went on, and troubles gathered about the nation, Mr. Calhoun set himself with unflinching determination against all compromise, and used his utmost endeavor to make the whole South a unit for what he believed to be its right and its duty. He did not live to see the direful harvest which sprang up from the dragon's teeth he had sown. He died March 31, 1850.

SPEECH ON THE SLAVERY QUESTION.

At the conclusion of the Mexican War the country was thrown into a ferment over the question whether slavery should be admitted into the newly acquired territory, which under Mexican rule had been free. Southern men felt that their social and economic system would not be secure, even in its own home, unless it could maintain its equality of power in the general government, and particularly in the Senate. To accomplish this, a new slave State must be organized to match every new free State admitted into the Union. Now, the ordinance of 1787 and the Missouri Compromise had left very little territory out of which slave States could in future be formed. The Mexican War, therefore, had been supported by the South, mainly with a view to provide such territory. But before the war was over this design came very near being thwarted by the Wilmot Proviso (for which see below, note to page 293); and though the proviso failed at that time, there was every indication that it would be revived later, and that it might eventually succeed. At this juncture the inhabitants of California, without waiting for an "enabling act," met in convention, drafted for themselves a State Constitution prohibiting slavery, ratified it by an overwhelming popular vote, and applied to Congress to be received into the Union. It seemed that the territorial acquisition which the slave-holding interest had counted on so confidently as its own was already slipping out of its grasp. The South was greatly roused. Its more fiery spirits denounced in unmeasured terms this violation of what they thought their rights, and threatened more fiercely than ever to break up the Union. More thoughtful men regarded the crisis with profound distress and alarm. Among these, Henry Clay, then seventy-three years old, and retired from public life, felt called upon to come forward once more to avert, if possible, the impending ruin. His scheme for restoring harmony was presented to the Senate, Jan. 29, 1850, in a series of resolutions, and was supported by him in a great speech on Feb. 5 and 6. The debate which followed brought out, we are told, every man of note in the Senate, not merely its great leaders of the past,—Webster, Calhoun, and Clay,—whose race was almost run, but those who were to shape the future of the country—Seward, Chase, and Jefferson Davis.

The speech we have chosen from this great debate is specially memorable as being the last great utterance of Mr. Calhoun on the subject to which he had given the strength and force of his life. Of the purity of his purpose and of his profound sincerity there could be no question. His intellect was as bright and keen as ever, though the hand of death was visibly upon him. The speech, which he had carefully prepared, he was unable to deliver; it was read for him by a friend while he sat by. "Every senator listened with profound attention and unfeigned emotion; the galleries were hushed into the deepest silence by the extraordinary scene, which had something of the impressive solemnity of a funereal ceremony." But apart from the interest arising out of the occasion, the speech has a profounder interest of its own, as being one of the frankest, clearest, and calmest statements ever made of the fundamental question at issue, as viewed from the Southern side,—a statement in which all subsidiary matters are brushed aside, and the central and naked issue is confronted with an unerring aim and an unflinching logic which is Calhoun's own.

TEXTUAL NOTES.

Page **274**, 13. **federal numbers**—that count of population upon which representation in Congress is apportioned.

Page **277**, 14. **Louisiana**—not the limited area now embraced by the State of that name, but the immense territory between the Mississippi and the Rocky Mountains purchased from France in 1803.

25 ff. By some inadvertence "the portion lying south of 36° 30′" is enumerated twice in this statement. The sense will be clear if we omit the first mention altogether, and read, "To the South was left . . . the portion of Louisiana lying north of 36° 30′ included in the state of Missouri, with" etc.

PAGE **284**, 25. **I then so expressed myself**, notably in the debates of 1836–1837.

PAGE **288**, 7 ff. The rupture between the Northern and Southern wings of the Methodist and Baptist Churches occurred in 1845. That in the Presbyterian Church, which the speaker foresaw, occurred shortly after the outbreak of the war, in 1862. The schism in all these cases still exists.

PAGE **289**, 31. The reader will recall in point such utterances as the peroration of Mr. Webster's speech of twenty years before.

PAGE **292**, 25. The **distinguished senator** was Henry Clay. His plan, the Compromise of 1850, was this: "The admission of California was to be made acceptable to the South by giving slavery a chance in Utah and New Mexico, and by the enactment of a more efficient fugitive slave law. The Northern people were to be reconciled to the abandonment of the Wilmot Proviso [for which see just below], as to Utah and New Mexico, and to a more efficient fugitive slave law by the admission of California as a free State and by the abolition of the slave-trade in the District of Columbia." — CARL SCHURZ, in his *Henry Clay*, ii., p. 332.

PAGE **293**, 9. The **Wilmot Proviso** was a rider attached to a bill providing for the settlement of difficulties with Mexico by a purchase of territory. It stipulated "that neither slavery nor involuntary servitude shall ever exist in any part of said territory." This proviso passed the House, but was defeated in the Senate. Its principle, however, was affirmed by nearly all the Northern legislatures, and was taken as the foundation of the Free Soil party.

PAGE **297**, 7 ff. "These were the last words of the last speech of the great and honest nullifier. He could no more support himself.

Two friends had to lead him out of the Senate chamber. Slowly and heavily the curtain rolled down to shut from the public gaze the last scene of the grand tragedy of this brilliant life. For nearly twenty years the suspicion, and even the direct accusation, had weighed on his shoulders that he was systematically working at the destruction of the Union. By doing more than any other single man towards raising the slavocracy to the pinnacle of power, he had actually done more than any other man to hasten the catastrophe and to determine its character; and yet he labored to the last with the intense anxiety of a true patriot to avert the fearful calamity. But the last efforts of his powerful mind were a most overwhelming refutation of all the doctrines whose foremost champion he had been ever since the days of nullification. It would have been impossible to pass a more annihilating judgment on them than he himself did in his speech of March 4, 1850." — Von Holst in his *John C. Calhoun*, page 348.

WILLIAM H. SEWARD.

William H. Seward was born in Orange County, New York, in 1801. At nineteen years of age he was graduated from Union College. At twenty-three he began the practice of law. After filling the positions of Senator and Governor of his own State, in 1849 he entered the United States Senate. There he found Webster, Calhoun, and Clay, those giants of the elder time, whose sands of life were nearly run. The dawn of the newer time was indeed already discerned, though its troubled light was destined to fade out in darkness and tempest before the day could be fully ushered in. For twelve years, while the forces were mustering for the deadly conflict, he kept his post, alert and watchful, in the Senate. For four years, while the conflict lasted, he stood by Lincoln's side as his faithful Secretary of State. Stricken almost unto death at the same time with Lincoln, he nevertheless recovered, and stood by Lincoln's successor to the end of his term. Three years of rest from the burdens of public service — of enjoyment of well-earned honors — were left to round out his life. He died Oct. 10, 1872.

The speech on the Irrepressible Conflict was a political address delivered at Rochester, New York, in Mr. Seward's canvass of that State in behalf of the newly formed Republican party. It made a profound impression. Though separated by a considerable interval from Calhoun's stern arraignment of the spirit of the North as the spirit of disunion, this is, perhaps, the most direct answer to that speech in its counter-arraignment of the spirit of the South. In simplicity, in directness, and in determined concentration upon the one point at issue, the two speeches are strikingly alike. As compared with the genial largeness and range of Webster's view, these qualities mark a much later stage of the struggle between the opposing ideas — a stage in which all accessories and complications are impatiently brushed aside, and the naked issue is confronted. One feels, as he hears such challenge and defiance, that the sword-strokes are not long to wait.

PAGE **298**, 7. The young student, of course, will not make the mistake of supposing that what is said in this speech is to be understood of political parties now calling themselves Democratic and Republican. Names often outlast the ideas they once stood for. As a matter of fact, Democrat and Republican in early American politics were synonymous terms, applied alike to the party opposed to the Federal Union, — the party originally made up, as Mr. Hayne put it, of "those who wanted no union of the States, and [those] who disliked the proposed form of union." Their opponents were the Federalists. After 1808 the name Republican was gradually dropped, and was not heard of again until, in 1856, it was taken up by the new party formed to oppose the Democrats. See pages 207 and 310, l. 4 ff.

PAGE **303**, 24. For the **ordinance of 1787**, see Webster's Speech, p. 191, and consult U. S. History s. v.

PAGE **305**, 15. **Dred Scott** was a negro who brought suit for his freedom on the ground that his master had taken him to a State where slavery was prohibited, and that he had thereby become free. The case was taken up to the Supreme Court, which rendered in 1857 the famous decision declaring not only that free colored persons whose ancestors were imported into this country and sold as slaves, "had no rights which the white man is bound to respect," but furthermore that Congress had no power to prohibit slavery in the Territories, and that the Missouri Compromise Act was null and void.

PAGE **310**, 6 ff. The party was organized for the first time in February, 1856. Its first convention met in June of the same year, and nominated Colonel Frémont for the presidency. In the election which followed, Colonel Frémont secured one hundred and fourteen electoral votes, as against Mr. Buchanan's one hundred and seventy-four. In thirteen of the sixteen free States the Republicans elected their State tickets, and gave Frémont a majority over Buchanan, all told, of two hundred thousand votes. See Seward's Works, iv., p. 43.

ABRAHAM LINCOLN.

ABRAHAM LINCOLN — Born February 12, 1809; died April 15, 1865. The story of his early life, the discipline in which his powers were trained, the part he played in the tremendous drama of our Civil War, — his steadfastness, his gentleness, the greatness of his heart, and the pathos of his death in the very hour of victory, — are known unto all men.

After the battle of Gettysburg, in July, 1863, it was proposed to set apart a portion of the battle-ground as a perpetual memorial of those who had there laid down their lives at their country's need. The suggestion was carried out; and on November 19 of that year the National Cemetery was solemnly consecrated.

The words spoken by President Lincoln on that day have been chosen as a fitting conclusion to this collection of speeches. A fac-simile of the original manuscript may be seen in *The Century Magazine* for February, 1894.

THE END.

Conciliation with Colonies - Burke
Topical Outline.

The Introduction

I. Renewed opportunity to consider the question
II. The Awfulness of the subject.
III. The " for a fixed policy.
IV. Burke's proposition is Peace.
V. Parliament has already granted that conciliation is admissable.

The Developement.

A. Whether Parliament ought to concede.
B. What Parliament's concession ought to be.
The argument is that Parliament ought to concede because of.
I. Population of the colonies.
II. The Industries.
1. Commerce.
2. Agriculture
3. Fisheries
4. Objections to the employment of force in overcoming the opposition of the colonies.
a. It is temporary.
b. It is uncertain.
c. Parliament has had no experience.
III. The temper & character of the People.
Determined by. –
1. Descent.
2. Their form of gov.
3. Form of religion in north.
4. The haughty spirit in South.
5. Education of the people.
6. Their remoteness.
Here Burke changes the form of his argument giving details of its first & from these draws a conclusion.

I. The three ways of dealing with this spirit are -

a. to change it by removing cause.
b. to prosecute it as criminal.
c. to comply with it as a necessity.

II. But to change it is impossible, to prosecute it is as a criminal is unexpedient and impossible.
Burke concludes therefore that nothing is left to Parliament to do but to comply with their demands for a concession - namely.

A. Compliance with the demand for concession is a necessity.
B. What Parliament's concession should be.

I. The nature of the concession demanded

1. The colonies are taxed without representation
2. Burke's idea is that the people should be admitted to an interest in a constitution
3. Precedents for Conciliation

(a). Ireland (b). Wales (c). Chester (d) Durham.

II. The actual concession proposed to pass a resolution acknowledging that

1. The colonies have no rep. in Parliament
2. They have been troubled & grieved by taxation
3. The method has not yet been devised for giving them Rep.
4. They have legal assemblies for taxation
5. These assemblies in past granted aid to his Majesty.

1. Experience shows that these aids have been more profited than the measures for taxing the colonies